ON TOBACCO ROAD
Basketball in North Carolina

A publication of
Leisure Press.
597 Fifth Avenue; New York, N.Y. 10017

Library of Congress Catalog Card Number: 83-80734

ISBN: 0-88011-175-5
Book design: Rick Binger
Book production: John Jett

Text photographs courtesy of:
Hugh Morton, Grandfather Mountain, North Carolina
Burnie Batchelor, Raleigh, North Carolina
Greensboro Daily News
Albuquerque Journal
Naismith Basketball Hall of Fame
College Sports Information Directors of North Carolina, N.C. State,
Duke, Wake Forest, Davidson, Western Carolina, Guilford College.

ON TOBACCO ROAD
Basketball in North Carolina

BY SMITH BARRIER

LEISURE PRESS

NEW YORK

Dedication

To Sis, and the millions of basketball fans in the great state of North Carolina, of which she is the greatest.

Contents

State Of North Carolina
From The Office Of The Governor

I've done a lot of traveling around the country and around the world to recruit business and industry to North Carolina. Everywhere I've been, especially during the past two years, conversations with business and government leaders inevitably turn to basketball. The subject is a great ice-breaker, given the state's reputation for college basketball and the sport's growing international stature. I can't prove it, but I really believe those consecutive national championships have helped us bring a few more jobs to North Carolina. I've been Governor for almost seven years now, and I'm often asked in interviews what I'm most proud of in terms of accomplishments. I am always tempted to respond by saying I am the only Governor in North Carolina history to "preside over" two NCAA titles, let alone two in a row.

James B. Hunt, Jr.
Governor

1
On Tobacco Road

Crops long ago grew to their fullest leaves, the tobacco farms covering the state of North Carolina from the bright leaf of the sandy, flat coastal plains to the burley of the beautiful Blue Ridge Mountains. Long before Erskine Caldwell discovered it, there was tobacco road, with production plants that rolled the leaves to the world's satisfaction.

And long before Caldwell put his characters into play time, there was Tobacco Road for college basketball visitors who wanted a nice little trip into the sunshine of the South, felt nobody around the plants or the machines had ever heard of a basketball.

It was tough then, as it is now, to win on Tobacco Road, but in recent calendars, such as the very last two, North Carolina has tossed the full challenge on top of the table, and it wouldn't take a tobacco auctioneer, with his own version of the king's English, to obtain top prices.

Back to back, two straight years, 1982 and 1983, and counting, North Carolina has captured national championships — the Tar Heels over Georgetown in New Orleans when Michael Jordan made a good shot, and then the Wolfpack in Albuquerque when Lorenzo Charles found something and stuffed it. Two titles, together, by two different schools in the state. It had been accomplished only once before in NCAA annals, Ohio State 1960 and Cincinnati 1961.

Not Kentucky, where Adolph Rupp was the South's first monarch and refused to duel Everett Case. Not Indiana, where Case got his first North Carolina State players and Bobby Knight currently reigns. The coach—the young one, Knight—carries a good needle, and it was Philadelphia's Spectrum on the nation's bicentennial, 1976, with two Big Ten teams in the Final Four, Bobby's and Michigan. It had never happened before, two from one league.

Telecasting the finals was the NBC-TV team of Dick Enberg, Billy Packer and Al McGuire, which was the best the networks ever put together. Knight slyly sauntered over to the TV announcers' table and inquired of Packer, bred in the ACC and outspoken to the subject at times: "Say, where's the ACC?"

7

When Everett Case came to North Carolina State in 1946, he brought an old Indiana victory custom with him. He and the Wolfpack clipped nets, this on one of his many conference championships.

It was a point well taken, but back in Philadelphia in 1981 there were North Carolina and Virginia, but, of course, Bobby's Hoosiers won. So, the needle moves to the back-to-back nationals on the current fire, and it's North Carolina and North Carolina State celebrating.

ACC basketball has become synonymous with North Carolina, a touchy matter which the other four conference members abhor. Maryland, Virginia, Clemson and Georgia Tech—and South Carolina when it was an honored member of the family, which it still should be—never recognized any such conglomerate as the "Big Four." But it is there, the four schools in the state of North Carolina. They win basketball championships, but there's more. Hanes Hosiery won the National

AAU women's nationals in 1951. Winston-Salem State the NCAA College Division 1967, Guilford College the NAIA 1973, and High Point College the AIAW Division II 1978.

Many things have contributed to this phenomenon, and it is said in many circles, including the fans' where the matter comes to rest, that Everett Case is the father of basketball as the state currently enjoys. There were good teams before World War II, but it is true that Case's "Hoosier Hotshots," these kids had played high school in Indiana and gone to war, ran up and down the court with such abandon that they adopted fans instantly. They built Reynolds Coliseum, which would make Raleigh the college basketball capital of the nation.

And Everett must be credited with erecting all those basketball goals which appear in every other driveway, from a lodge at Grandfather Mountain to the boarded side of a seafood eatery in Southport. His teams clipped the nets in victory, and it spread all over the South, to the point that finally the state high school athletic association banned it, for whatever reason yet to be understood. John Belk, then the mayor of the city of Charlotte, made this statement of truth: "This building, the Charlotte Coliseum, and yours, the Greensboro Coliseum, are here because of Everett Case, and only Everett Case."

But there are others in his coaching profession who have a hand in the proceedings, and there are two other ingredients which have contributed to the modern day spectacle. One, there is the black athlete, the young man born and bred in North Carolina who used to go elsewhere, like Walt Bellamy and Lou Hudson, because they couldn't stay at home. The mid-60s broke that barrier, and basketball improved. It was played on a new level, much nearer the basket rim, or above. Two, there is television, direct from arenas coast to coast, plus Hawaii and Alaska, to your den or living room, in color, loaded with excitement like the 1:40 a.m. conclusions of the Wolfpack winning the West in the spring of 1983. TV has brought the games live every night and twice on weekends, in recent years, and it has taken basketball to all the state as a selling commodity. Jim Valvano has never settled down from the N.C. State title in Albuquerque, but he realized: "Incredible. We figured that in our run to the championship over 250 million people saw us play on television. I never realized we had touched so many lives."

His athletic director, Willis Casey, who came to the West Raleigh campus the same year as Everett Case, 1946, added this comment to what has just transpired—not just happened, but transpired: "The fantastic thing has been the reaction of fans all over the United States. We were very lucky, the fact we won in the sensational comeback against Pepperdine, CBS-TV elected to do a promo with us. The promo for all the playoffs. And we fulfilled their dream. They opened all their sports news centers with film from that Pepperdine game, then the win over Vegas, then Virginia. I'm sure they just said, we'll ride N.C. State as long as it's doing this, and we kept doing it. I think the whole country, literally, picked us up as the underdog, and if there's one thing the American public loves, it's the underdog."

Live television coverage of college basketball began in the state with the 1957 Carolina team, which captured triple overtime triumphs in Kansas City, the finale over Wilt Chamberlain, whose Kansas team wasn't supposed to lose. About this time also the summer basketball camps or schools opened, 1955 at Campbell College, where 1,500 boys and girls attended this summer. Big Four coaches now more than double their university salary with their camps.

Tobacco Road has been no picnic for teams that bring their nationally rated clubs for the trip South, then become disturbed when Southern hospitality never extends to the basketball floor.

Even the four non-North Carolina teams in the Atlantic Coast Conference express open fear when they come to Greensboro, for example, to play the ACC tournament. Wake Forest now plays its home conference games there, but before such scheduling days, Maryland athletic director Jim Kehoe made absolutely no bones about his strong feelings on the site: "The North Carolina teams play here in the regular season and they get adjusted to the building and the lighting and the floor. It's the climate here. It's no neutral site for Maryland. Anybody who argues against this is a bit naive, I think. I cannot view Greensboro as neutral. If so, then I am ill-advised and misinformed." The conference tournament has been conducted outside North Carolina on only three occasions since it moved to Raleigh (1933).

John Wooden, the venerable wizard of Westwood, where UCLA is located, played two games in the state in December 1965, losing to Duke 82-66 on campus there, 94-75 in Charlotte. Not very close affairs. Coach Wooden was asked to recall the experience: "Oh, the Duke students were a bit boisterous. Some places are worse than others, no question about it. That particular time, which I don't think happens any more, we had one black player that the people sitting behind us said some things which they really shouldn't have. It disturbed us somewhat, but that's past and gone, we shouldn't even dwell on it. Duke beat us twice, they had a fine team, but I think it was good we came down here and played. I think it was good for basketball in North Carolina, it was good for basketball throughout the country."

The Dixie Classic, which Case orchestrated, quickly became the nation's leading holiday tournament, and was copied in many places. It did pay good guarantees, expenses and $4,000 in 1949, when Reynolds Coliseum was completed. It grew to $10,000 in a dozen years, good money for a college trip in those days, when there was no TV and live radio was just formulating. But the visiting teams, who played the Big Four, did not win often. They never won the biggest trophies, and only seven of them ever got to play the championship bracket finale.

Greatest of the holiday fields came December 1958, and the

guests were Cincinnati, No. 1 UPI, and Michigan State, No. 2 UPI. Carolina was No. 5, State No. 6. The AP had them 2-3-6-9. Cincinnati gave up its own holiday tournament to play in Raleigh, and it had Oscar Robertson to show off. Cincinnati lost two games, the Wolfpack beat Michigan State. The following week the national polls had State and Carolina 1-3. Slats Gill of Oregon State came in 1953, ranked No. 4, played for seventh spot the last day. He told Coach Case: "I certainly don't envy you having to play Wake Forest, Duke and North Carolina twice this season."

Frank McGuire won his national title at Chapel Hill (1957), left for the pros, got back to college ball at South Carolina. He bristled on question: "Fans in the state were really nice, I got standing ovations when I came back (with South Carolina), but we were getting beat then. When we started winning, they went after my tail good. They really got to John Roche, great player, but they got on him individually. Last time I remember, I see his eyes popping out. I said, 'John, we got one minute to go. Easy.' We were playing Penn in the regional (in Raleigh) and N.C. State fans rooting against us, students and all, and they're after John. He's looking in the stands."

Home courts were tough, and the Big Four players knew just what their advantage was. Jack Marin, Duke all-American who finished at Duke Law School, recalled: "As for playing ball, it was a real experience to play in Duke Indoor Stadium. Almost indescribable. One night I heard the loudest noise I've ever heard in my life. We were playing Michigan and we were behind and started catching up. The fans got behind us and began roaring, and the noise was incredible. It was like a jet engine." And Duke won, and won, and won there.

Eddie Biedenbach, who came to N.C. State from the Pittsburgh area in the mid-60s, has never forgotten: "To this day, when I walk up the steps at Reynolds (Coliseum), with a packed house, I get goose bumps. I remember the ACC tournament in Raleigh that year, we beat Duke in the finals and went on to play Bill Bradley's Princeton team. The feeling in Reynolds, there's never been anything like it in any basketball arena I've ever been in. Reynolds is the loudest, the most enthusiastic, the toughest place to play if you're the visitor, and the best if you're the home team. The years I played it was loud, the years David Thompson played it was ridiculous. You walked in the gym, the Maryland games, the Carolina games, they were just tremendous. Tom McMillen at Maryland, Bobby Jones over at Carolina, those two guys were unbelievably great players, and they were kind of neutralized in those games."

Charlie Davis was one of the first blacks in the Big Four, became the first to be selected ACC player of the year while at Wake Forest. The experiences of a New York street guy were a bit different, but memorable: "My transition from a basketball player to normal life, into

Greatest basketball event in the state's history was the 1974 NCAA finals in the Greensboro Coliseum. Here is N.C. State's David Thompson going high over UCLA's Bill Walton. The two were back-to-back national players of the year.

business later, was made easier by some friends like Billy Packer. As for my college days, I always thought New York fans were very knowledgeable, but I found that when I came down here, basketball fans in North Carolina know their basketball, appreciate their basketball. That's one of the things that really helped me, they appreciated me when I played well, whether I was black or white."

The ACC tournament has been "the in thing" for several decades now, and with the new 23,000-seat arena at Chapel Hill, more fans will be able to see when the ACC moves there, probably 1986.

It has changed, from a one-shot, go-home deal, when only the champion advanced to the NCAAs, to the modern day spectacle which still declares the conference champion but means little more in the now-more-important NCAA selection. Coaches get fired if they don't make the NCAAs, with its rich pot and glamorous TV.

Dean Smith of Carolina has been through the full cycle, and he talked about the metamorphosis: "Our goals change. When I started at Carolina (1962), we always said the No. 1 goal was the Atlantic Coast Conference tournament. It had to be, because it determined the ACC champion and only the champion went to the NCAA playoffs. Then it began to change. We brought in the NIT (1967), then with the 32-team bracket (1975) two conference teams could go to the NCAA. Now it's wide open, five teams in 1980. I still think the best team is the regular season winner, after a 14-game schedule home and home in so many different surroundings. And the new NCAA formula recognizes that, you don't have to win the ACC tournament to make it. Today, we can always be a national contender, even if we finish last in the ACC."

Popularity of the tournament has not diminished, not in the slightest. Tournament tickets go for $70 list, but that's just the teaser in the market. It may cost a thousand to get your name on a school list to make the purchase, and both room and food are upped at the site. Bill Foster, when he came to Duke from Utah, made this observation: "In Utah we had tremendous interest. I really felt Utah had great college basketball interest, great arenas, great crowds, and then they get into the recreational thing, skiing, the mountains. But in North Carolina you have a 12-month interest in basketball, every day of the year, and it has been generated for some time."

The Greensboro Coliseum managing director, Jim Oshust, looked to the tournament as a social event, much like Willis Casey of N.C. State. Oshust remarked between seasons, scheduling seasons that is: "There are so many women in the basketball crowds. They like what they see. They're supporters of their husbands, their husbands go to the symphony because the wife makes him go. Lot of women find basketball is a good healthy outlet, good physical outlet, maybe they don't play golf, they don't play tennis or jog. Basketball fandom is a very athletic and very exuberant way of getting their emotions out."

13

Norman Sloan, with a national title (1974), has been in several good conferences, has watched basketball all over the Eastern seaboard. The former N.C. State coach said: "The biggest difference in basketball in North Carolina or the ACC — as opposed to the Big Ten or the SEC, where the play, the calibre of the players is the same — is the maniacal interest of the fans. The media is also special. I have found that out since I've left, the media interest. I didn't always agree with it when I was there, because you always wanted it to be 100 percent for you, against the other guy, but as I look back on it, the media is very much into the game in North Carolina, more knowledgeable in the ACC than anywhere I have ever been in the coaching business, or even traveling around to clinics. And the fan interest, the fact you've got the four schools right there, that's what makes it unique. That's what generates all the things you want to talk about in the ACC. That's the ACC. I know Maryland doesn't want to hear that, Virginia doesn't, neither does Clemson or Georgia Tech, or South Carolina when they were in it, but the ACC is the Big Four. That's where all of it stems from."

The tournament fever began in Atlanta decades ago, 1921 to be exact, on a court built over the front seats and orchestra pit to a level with the stage. North Carolina became heroes in Atlanta, won four tournaments — and a national championship (1924). Some of these Chapel Hill teams did not have coaches, per se. Certainly not to be called chaperons. Jimmy Poole, a reserve guard in the Roarin' Twenties, summarized the coach's approach to his duty: "One year, 1923, Bill Fetzer went with us as coach. He always told us, 'Boys, I'm not a basketball coach. Only thing I can tell you, if you're nearer the goal, you got a better chance to make it.'" It hasn't changed an iota, either.

There have been stars like Earl Monroe, who did everything, plus one, in an NCAA College Basketball Division title — part of Clarence (Bighouse) Gaines' 698 victories, which is tops among active coaches. And Billy Cunningham, who just guided the Philadelphia 76ers to NBA kingdom, having been the "Kangaroo Kid" when he played at Carolina. And John McLendon, coach and ambassador, who finagled the NBA into signing his boy as the first black in pro basketball (Harold Hunter).

When Everett Case came to Raleigh, he began a personal war with Adolph Rupp of Kentucky, which was never settled eye-to-eye. On the evening Rupp brought his Wildcats to the 1951 NCAA regional opening round, which was in Raleigh, N.C. State alumni gave Case a brand new Cadillac, with the Baron watching during his team warm-ups. The NCAA regional always had something of interest going on. The Charlotte Coliseum served as a welcomed off-campus host for years in the late 50s. In the 60s, the regional was dominated by North Carolina teams.

And then the biggest basketball event in state history, the 1974

NCAA finals, were in the Greensboro Coliseum, and the Wolfpack of David Thompson, Tom Burleson and all took UCLA and Marquette and the No. 1 position.

Research has uncovered that the most points ever scored in a single game by a North Carolinian, meaning a member of a state team, was 69, and it was done by Clarence Burks of St. Augustine's in Raleigh. He did it one night at St. Paul's (Virginia) in January 1953. Earl Monroe got 68 against Fayetteville State in December 1966. Modern day basketball does not permit that opportunity.

For years it was historical concession that the first college basketball game played in the state was March 2, 1906, when Wake Forest made a short trip to Trinity (now Duke) and beat Trinity 24-10. But that bit of history has been rewritten on research of Guilford College files. Not only did the Quakers have the first college team (1905), but they played Wake Forest on the Guilford College campus February 6, 1906, in the very first intercollegiate game of basketball played in North Carolina. The Quakers won 26-19. Such matters of information should be duly recorded, and commemorated.

Eight decades have been covered in college basketball in the state, but nothing can compare with the past two years and back-to-back national championships.

Participating in the Campbell University summer camp for 12 years, several springs ago being awarded an honorary degree at the university, John Wooden of UCLA has been able to follow the blood lines of North Carolina basketball fans.

"No question about it," he said when he attended the ACC tournament in Atlanta last March, on hand to award to Ralph Sampson, who did play 20 games within the state of North Carolina, the established Wooden Award as the nation's player of the year.

"Interest in college basketball in North Carolina is unsurpassed. I won't say it's the best, but there's none better. It's hard to say that any particular state is better, and often it runs in cycles. Visiting Buies Creek in the summer, people talk basketball all the time, but maybe that's because my life has been connected with the game, and I'm there on a basketball purpose. But I have a feeling they would be talking basketball most of the year round."

They did, they do. On Tobacco Road there's no better show.

When Coach Wooden got home, he wrote Coach Valvano a letter: "I have said a number of times and sincerely feel that your effort in the tournament this year and that of Don Haskins (Texas Western) in 1966 are the two finest NCAA tournament coaching jobs I have ever seen. You are great for the profession, Jimmy. Please do not change. Sincerely, John."

It is the subject of conversation in the Governor's Mansion.

When the conference tournament came to Raleigh, back there in

Two champions at the 1983 ACC tournament in the Atlanta Omni, Jim Valvano, left, of winning N.C. State and John Wooden of many, many UCLA triumphs.

1933, the governor began practicing to toss the first ball. Gov. J. C. B. Ehringhaus had the initial honor, and his family became so enthused, daughter Matilda was one of the tournament team hosts the next year.

Gov. Luther Hodges was there when the Atlanta Coast Conference was brought into being (1954), and he did the opening tipoff. When Carolina went to Kansas City for the 1957 finals, Governor Hodges even sat on the Tar Heel team bench the first half, but he couldn't yell there so he moved.

For State College's 1974 championship in the Greensboro Coliseum, Gov. James Holshouser not only did the tipoff but he also wrote a daily tournament column in the *Greensboro Daily News*. And it was his work, too.

Maybe Gov. Jim Hunt has the bragging rights. First he was in Carolina's ardent fan section when the Tar Heels won everything at New Orleans. Rushing to his seat for the final game, he scooted by the press table, saying "Got to win one tonight, and we are." The calendar flipped once, and Governor Hunt was back in the NCAA Final Four. It was Albuquerque, with thousands of others he was waving his red-and-white shaker. When the task was done, Governor Hunt sighed: "Can you beat this for excitement?" He had two on his record.

2
On the First Day

Professor Naismith had been directed a special assignment that winter of 1891.

He had just joined the staff at the International Young Men's Christian Association Training School in Springfield, Massachusetts, having decided, at 30 years of age, to make physical education his life's work after studying for the ministry for three years.

The training school was for future YMCA general secretaries and physical instructors, and on the class schedule there was a 60-minute period for daily physical activity. Football in the fall, yes, baseball in the spring, okay, but the class revolted against the winter's indoor challenge: marching and calisthenics. Thus the young Professor Naismith was instructed by the department head to devise a game for these headstrong young students. They had tried rugby indoors, but tackling on the hard gymnasium floor caused bruises. Soccer resulted in broken windows, and lacrosse found them beating each other with the sticks. A hardy bunch, to say the least.

His "new" game would have a ball, a large ball if you wish. The soccer ball was just right. No running with the ball, thus eliminating tackling. Elevated goal, novel idea, making accuracy more important than brute strength. The goals would be boxes, but the janitor at the school gymnasium didn't have the right kind, although he just happened to have two old peach baskets. And the gym had a running balcony, the baskets could be nailed to the balcony, which just happened to be 10 feet above the floor. A peach basket was so attached at each end, and a ladder placed at each goal. You had to get the ball out of the basket when somebody made a goal, didn't you? A bright lad later cut the bottoms out of the peach baskets. Each team had nine players, because the class numbered 18 that particular day.

Dr. James Naismith had invented basketball, rather than boxball, and America's very own game had been founded by a Canadian who had come to Springfield University from McGill University.

That day, early December 1981, living in Springfield and taking part in the professor's experiment, was Raymond Kaighn, who in 1953 moved to Chapel Hill for his retirement days. He was the last surviving player from that inaugural game. Also playing in the game was a young student from Lynn, Massachusetts, Frank Mahan whose first job upon graduation was to be general secretary at the YMCA in Charlotte. He worked there from 1893 until 1899, when he returned home. He died in 1905.

There were also two visitors from North Carolina, each taking a training course for gym instructors at the Springfield YMCA College. George Stephens of Asheville was then a student at Oak Ridge Military Institute, and Charles S. Mangum was a gym instructor at the university in Chapel Hill. Stephens later went to the university where in 1895 he would throw what is claimed to be the first forward pass in college football. It was not legal at the time, but the officials allowed the short pass, with a 70-yard run for touchdown to beat Georgia 6-0. In the crowd was John W. Heisman who relayed the incident to Walter Camp.

Years later, in Chapel Hill, Stephens related his experiences in Springfield to *Chapel Hill Weekly* editor Louis Graves: "Nobody had ever thought of such rules as govern the game today. For one thing, there were many more persons on the team, nine or 10, as I remember it. It was all very informal. We just chose up sides and played. When the ball went in (the basket), one of us would climb up the ladder and get it out. Later somebody had the brilliant idea of taking the bottom out of the basket, and still later a net was substituted."

The game did not spread rapidly on the campuses of America, but it did move around, coming South shortly after the turn of the century. There is recorded basketball activity at Chapel Hill when on January 30, 1903, the "Professional Students" beat the "College Team" 30-8, and later an intramural league was formed. But there was no intercollegiate competition until the winter of 1911.

At Guilford College near Greensboro, where the first baseball team in the state is claimed (1889), students played baseball as early as 1867 at then-named New Garden Boarding School. The first "official" football game was Carolina and Wake Forest at the State Fairgrounds in Raleigh on a Thursday afternoon, October 18, 1888. Guilford played both the University and A&M (now N.C. State) in football. In October 1903 the student paper advocated at Guilford "the institution of intercollegiate basket ball (two words), a class in dumb bells and the construction of good tennis courts for the women."

In the February 1905 issue of *Guilford Collegian*, the student paper-magazine, there is this report signed W.G.L.: "We note with pleasure the interest our people are taking in athletics. During the present year we have entered two new intercollegiate games, one in tennis, in which we won our first and only tournament, and the other in

Basketball pioneers, Dr. James Naismith and those who played in the first game December 1891. With later North Carolina association, Raymond Kaign, second row third from right, who retired in Chapel Hill, and Frank Mahan, bottom row second left, whose first job was general secretary at Charlotte YMCA. (Naismith Basketball Hall of Fame photo)

The 1906 Trinity College, now Duke, team which played Wake Forest in the first "Big Four" game on record. Front row, left to right, B. S. Womble, C. R. Claywell, T. G. Stem, Garland Greever and L. G. White. Back row, C. R. Pugh, Coach W. W. (Cap) Card, T. M. Grant, and T. A. Holton. The first college game in the state was Wake Forest at Guilford College.

basketball, in which we won two very good and interesting games over the Winston-Salem YMCA. We believe that both tennis and basketball should be made more prominent in Southern intercollegiate athletics. They are played at such a season of the year as not to interfere very much with baseball and football. Especially is basketball preeminently suited for intercollegiate contests since it is a gymnasium game occupying the winter months from the close of football season until baseball begins."

Thus, the first report of a college basketball team playing a game in the state of North Carolina, Guilford College in 1905.

W.G.L. went on to describe what had happened, in his most inimitable style: "Excellent work was done by (Thomas) Hinkle and the maneuvers of (Carroll) Rabb, his comrade at that position, to advance the ball to his basket and to keep his opponent guessing what he would do next. (Cabell) Lindsay played his position at centre with interesting energy and made some beautiful throws into the basket from long distances. (John) Anderson was always at his post as forward and could be relied upon for reaching as high as anyone and also for keeping the ball in Guilford's possession. It was on account of our being able to keep the ball in our possession that we won."

You may note only four players mentioned, and research in the Friends Historical Collection at the college library developed that W.G.L. was William Gibbon Lindsay, who just happened to be the captain of the team. He was also in the college's graduating class of 11 that spring 1905.

Lindsay wrote on, of interest today perhaps: "The experience we have had in basketball this season impresses upon our mind the need of such a game between the colleges of the state. It is played during a time when no outdoor sports can be engaged in. It is the best all around game for the development of the physical man. It has the developing qualities of football, yet is not so dangerous. It makes the mind act quickly and in that respect, as good as baseball. To sum it up, basketball is an all-around good sport and the student body can do no better thing than to encourage it next season and to arrange intercollegiate contests."

Students, who formed the college athletic association, were in charge of athletic team management and scheduling. Lindsay became the Guilford College basketball manager in April 1905, the first time the association accorded basketball priority status. It was a short season, however, since the gym had to be taken over for the annual gym meet February 25, and basketball had to be content with the two Winston-Salem YMCA games.

By the winter of 1905-06 there were three colleges in the state playing basketball. Not full schedules, just games. Guilford again played Winston-Salem YMCA, but the student paper listed only the halftime score (Guilford 17-8), not the final.

It led directly to the first intercollegiate basketball played in the state of North Carolina, February 6, 1906.

Again to the *Guilford Collegian* for this live report: "For a number of years a friendly rivalry has been growing between the Baptists of Wake Forest and the Quakers of Guilford. A number of baseball games has been played and last term two tennis tournaments but never before have we had the pleasure of meeting them in an indoor game. The game was played in the afternoon of Feb. 6 in the presence of an enthusiastic crowd of supporters. According to a new interpretation of the rules, our team was not able to show their best ability in basketball. However, in the first half they succeeded in running the score up to 19 against Wake Forest's 11. In the second half the game started off with more speed, both teams using more team work. Wake Forest added eight points more and Guilford seven, which made the total score 26 to 19 in favor of Guilford. For Wake Forest Captain Couch at right forward and Beverly at guard played good ball although nothing could be said to the disparagement of the other players. For Guilford, Anderson continued his good work at right forward and succeeded in scoring 14 of Guilford's 26 points. Hobbs played an unusually good game at centre. Throughout the entire game Guilford showed superior team work."

The story, however, never said where the game was played.

Some years ago the late Dr. George W. Paschal did *A History of Wake Forest College*, and he turned to the new sport with this observation: "To Mr. J. Richard Crozier goes the credit of introducing intercollegiate basketball in North Carolina. He began to give serious attention to training in that sport in the fall of 1905 and had two games between student teams in November and December of that year. Later in the same year he had some class games. Making selection from those he had trained, he formed a team and arranged games with some other college teams for January, February and March 1906, when the team played its first games away from home. On the trip it lost to Guilford, Spartanburg YMCA and Wofford and won from the Charlotte YMCA."

Thus, to be established herein for the first time, Guilford College was the site of the first intercollegiate game of basketball in the state; its opponent was Wake Forest, the Quakers were victors.

Apparently, the Quaker season again consisted of two games, but Wake Forest continued its competition as Dr. Paschal noted: "The next two games, however, excited much more interest. They were with Trinity College (now Duke), the first at Durham which Wake Forest won by the score of 24 to 10, the second at Wake Forest which Wake Forest won by the score of 15 to 5. The Wake Forest team consisted of Capt. V.F. Cough and O.W. Ward forwards, Kyle Elliott center, T.H. Beverly and Earl Gore guards, with B.F. Keith and J.B. Turner substitutes. By putting a narrow gallery in the gymnasium and reserving the part of the main floor just under it for seats, Mr. Crozier provided for the accommodation of students and interest in the game soon made the seating capacity very inadequate. As director of the gymnasium, Mr. Crozier, in making playing basketball a regular part of the work, had opportunity to find and train players, and so long as he was at the college, until June 1917, he never failed to have a good team which won a creditable number of the intercollegiate games which it played."

Until this time, it had been generally credited that the first game in the state was played at Trinity against Wake Forest. It was the first among the Big Four, being played March 2, 1906 in Angier Duke Gymnasium, a building known to present-day Duke students as "The Ark," the East Campus social center. Add Penfield, writing in the program for the formal opening of Duke Indoor Stadium, now Cameron Indoor Stadium, on January 6, 1940, reported: "There were 16 candidates for that first Duke basketball team. Mr. W. W. (Cap) Card, the grand old gentleman of the Duke Campus, was the coach of the squad. Coach Card used six of his players in that opener against Wake Forest. Gardland Greever and C. R. Claywell were the forwards, T. G. Stem played the entire game at center, C. R. Pugh and L. G. White handled the assignments at guard, with T. M. Grant. Trinity lost that first game. Captain Stem and Claywell divided scoring honors with four points each and Greever tossed in the other bucket for Trinity."

In Raleigh, home of North Carolina A&M (now N.C. State), basketball became an intramural activity in the winter of 1908, and the students managed to obtain a varsity team in 1911, and it was called the A&M Farmers. Their initial intercollegiate contest was at Wake Forest February 16, 1911. The Deacons won 33-6, but in the return meeting on the West Raleigh campus A&M scored its first basketball triumph, beating the Deacons 19-18. There are no records as to A&M team personnel or coach.

Dr. Roy McKnight, Sr. recalled the beginning of the game at Carolina, having been a member of its first team in 1911. On approval of the administration, team members set up poles in front of Bynum Gymnasium and mounted backboards and baskets. Dr. R. B. Lawson didn't want players of this new sport scuffling the floor of the nice new Bynum Gymnasium, built in 1904. The university president, Francis P. Venable, intervened and got the gym opened for the new varsity team. There was a coach, Nat Cartmell, former Olympic runner, but the team was actually coached by Philly Ritch, who had learned about the game at his home in Charlotte. Five of the eight team members came from Charlotte: Marvin L. (Philly) Ritch, Cy Long, Junior Smith, Will Tillett, Roy McKnight and manager Spurgeon Cook. McKnight wrote years later: "Big sports on campus were football, baseball and track.

Basketball was put in the category of gymnastics and tennis and added as a minor sport. The biggest honor on campus was to be named manager of the baseball team." Early games in Bynum Gym brought crowds of "a dozen or two." Carolina's first game was with Virginia Christian College, and McKnight wrote: "No regular schedule, we just picked up games as the season went along. The game started with a scramble at center court. I've been thrown halfway across the gym floor on that opening scramble."

Elon College built a gym as an annex to West Dorm in 1906, another one in 1912. Coach Bob Doak attended a meeting in Raleigh (at the Yarborough House) for the formation of a North Carolina State Intercollegiate Basketball League in 1912, but the Elon board of trustees were faced with a more searching question. In his 1982 masters thesis, Jerry Tolley in his "History of Intercollegiate Athletics for Men at Elon College" wrote of this 1912 dilemma: "The trustees faced this. Will the regular basketball suit, which leaves about four inches of the lower limb bare at the knee, between the pants and the top of the stocking, and which also leaves the arms bare from the shoulder, be allowed? The coach recommended, our men will be absolutely handicapped in intercollegiate contests if not allowed to wear the regular suits, movements which cannot be made with trousers coming below the knee and the jersey coming to the elbow."

3

Then the Real Beginning, Hotlanta

Even though the days of spacious, cushioned and bright-hued coliseums were yet to come in the South, it's still somewhat difficult to comprehend, honestly, that the college basketball game was focused in an old city auditorium where music, before Lawrence Welk but probably of the same tempo, and drama, of the Shakespeare ilk, were the curtain calls of the day.

That was the old Atlanta Auditorium where each winter, like late February, a piecemeal basketball court was built over the best seats and the orchestra pit, on a level with the stage. It left seats, therefore, on three sides, plus the balcony, maybe 3,500. It costs about $2,000 annually to construct and place the court.

Al Doonan was a member of the Atlanta Athletic Club who came up with the idea of a tournament to settle a Southern collegiate basketball champion, right after World War I. It came about simultaneously, or almost, with a move to reorganize the old Southern Intercollegiate Athletic Association (SIAA), formed for football in 1894, the fourth oldest in the nation. First plans for withdrawal of the major universities, or the forming of the Southern Conference, came at the annual SIAA meeting in Gainesville, Florida, December 12-13, 1920. Second meeting came February 25-26, 1921 in Atlanta during Doonan's first Southern Invitational tournament to which he invited major teams. Fifteen accepted, including Millsaps and Mercer, and Kentucky won, even in pre-Adolph Rupp days. Neither North Carolina or N.C. State, charter members of the newly-formed Southern Conference, played in the first one.

Doonan, quite an entrepreneur, obviously persuaded North Carolina to enter the tournament in 1922, and Carolina won the championship and became Atlanta favorites, but then they won so often (four of the first six tournaments) that Doonan feared the domination would hurt the crowds by the mid-20s. That was important even then; the tournament didn't meet expenses in 1925.

Dean C. P. (Sally) Miles of Virginia Tech, who attended the Southern Conference organizational meeting, remembered years ago: "There was a great need for a working collegiate conference, the basketball tournament just came along. The Southern Conference made this invitational tournament its own championship event. I remember going to the first game in the old Atlanta Auditorium with its high roof and the fans hanging off the girders. Georgia Tech and Georgia did not play each other in any sport then, but the first tournament they met in the semifinals. People actually fell out of the girders that night. I also remember Wallace Wade quit coaching basketball at the tournament. He came with his Vanderbilt team (1923) and we beat him (26-23). It was the first time he had ever seen a basketball shot with one hand, and he said that was it."

The Tar Heels, later to be nicknamed White Phantoms by Atlantans (before they got Tar Heels again about 1940), won their first in 1923, a monstrosity of a tournament with 25 teams. They played all day and night Friday and Saturday, finals on Wednesday. North Carolina was captained by Cartwright Carmichael, coached by the two Carmichael boys from Durham, Cart and Billy. They beat Mercer in the finals. It must have been impressive. The esteemed Morgan Blake of the *Atlanta Journal* expounded: "Never since the great NYU team performed on an Atlanta floor has a team made such an impression on the local fans as North Carolina. The way it manipulated the ball was bewildering to all opposition faced. Cool and phlegmatic they went about their business, showing super generalship at all times, and an uncanny faculty for knowing just where everybody on the team was located at all stages of the game."

That initial Atlanta trip began an amazing string of championship basketball for North Carolina — over five tournaments, 19 victories, one defeat, four titles. The defeat came in 1923 to Mississippi in the second round. The Tar Heels had gone to Atlanta undefeated (14-0).

Big year was 1924, bringing the Southern championship and a 26-0 record which would later gain Helms Foundation nomination as the national champions.

Jimmy Poole, a reserve guard, now a retired banker in Greensboro, went to his scrapbook and vivid memory for some of 1924: "It was a great ball club, and you must remember, tournament rules allowed only eight players, and you got only four personal fouls. We took the train to Atlanta, changing in Greensboro, and we had a coach about the same age we were, Norman Shepard, who had returned to Carolina from Davidson. Our forwards were Cart Carmichael and Jack Cobb, both about six feet tall, and Cart could play today. He was the finest all-round athlete I had ever seen, for many years. I will never

The 1924 national champions from Carolina. First row, left to right: Jack Cobb, Bill Dodderer, Capt. Winton Green, Cartwright Carmichael and Monk McDonald. Second row, Manager Bretney Smith, Jimmy Poole, Ed Koonce, Billy Devlin and Henry Lineberger.

Reunion of the Carolina teams which won four Southern championships in Atlanta 1922-24-25-26 was held in Chapel Hill in 1952. Front row, left to right, Tom Graham, Bretney Smith, Arthur Newcombe, W. D. Carmichael Jr., Lloyd Williams, John Purser and Sam Mc Donald, Harold Lineberger, and Howard Barber. Back row, Abie Neiman, Curtis (Sis) Perry, Jack London, Jack Cobb, Bill Dodderer, Cartwright Carmichael, Henry Lineberger and Bill Devin.

forget one play. In the Alabama game (tournament finals) I saw him intercept a ball off a guy shooting, back of the foul line on one side. Cart just jumped up and intercepted the ball, then dribbled all the way down to make a Carolina goal. Jack Cobb just stayed down there near the basket, he did the scoring.

"Our center was Bill Dodderer, about 6 foot-1 and just as soon as he jumped center, he moved back to the defensive foul line and stayed there. We had a four-man offense, and Dodderer just stayed back there except maybe to come down and take one shot a game. We played a man-to-man defense except for Dodderer, who stayed in the foul lane. He was so big, so spread out that two guys coming down, he'd give them trouble.

"The guards were Monk McDonald and Billy Devlin, real good players though small. Whoever got the ball, dribbled down; there was lot of dribbling going on. Cobb got sick 4-5 games late in the season, and I filled in then. Winton Green was probably the strongest player we had, he was captain, but at Maryland he got hit on the leg, charley horse, and he missed the rest of the season."

They played home games at the Tin Can, which had replaced Bynum Gym. And on Wednesday, before the tournament which began Thursday, they had a home game with Washington & Lee, whose starters included Eddie Cameron, later coach at Duke. In Atlanta they beat Kentucky 41-20, Vanderbilt 37-20, Mississippi State 33-23 and Alabama 26-18. Scores were a bit higher than normal for the day, and Jimmy Poole explained: "There was really no clock, no time-out for shooting fouls or jumping center. It just ran, so the actual games were shorter. Too, if anybody shot outside the foul line, the rest of the team would razz him, say he's playing to the crowd. Rarely ever was a shot taken out there, we worked the ball inside. Two-hand shots, even in close, only layups were taken with one hand." Five men played the title game. The reserves on that Atlanta trip were Poole, Donald Koonce and Henry Lineberger.

Monk McDonald was to coach the 1925 team, which he did while enrolled in medical school, but his classwork piled up so much that he couldn't make the tournament trip to Atlanta. It was also N.C. State's first tournament with a new coach, Gus Tebell. The Red Terrors, as the State College teams were called then, included Capt. F. P. Pickens, Gordon Gresham, Harry Brown and Jack McDowall. North Carolina beat Tulane 36-28 in the championship game, Sam McDonald moving in at forward, Bunn Hackney at guard.

They had a new coach, Harlan Sanborn, and the same old crowd in 1926. Bill Dodderer moved up to forward, teaming with Capt. Jack Cobb, who was named Helms Foundation player of the year for the nation. Tall Artie Newcomb was center, Billy Devlin and Bunn Hackney again guards. For the first time the conference tournament was limited to an even bracket, 16 teams, and in the finals Carolina rallied to beat Mississippi State. Cobb with 19 and Newcomb with 11 did most of the scoring. It must have been warm that February night in Atlanta, because the AP story made this notation: "Both teams swabbed energetically with towels when the Aggies took their first timeout." When Carolina got the lead, it held the ball and won 38-23.

The tournament developed problems; only 14 teams showed up in 1927. Virginia decided not to participate due to exams. It was worse in 1928. Maryland passed it because it had other games scheduled. Alabama claimed it had mailed in its entry by deadline, but it wasn't received. It was allowed to play in a "bye spot."

Duke University became a conference member by the 1929 season, and N.C. State had an experienced team to take to Atlanta. Although North Carolina were pre-tournament favorites, it was N.C. State and Duke in the finals. Coach Gus Tebells' State team had Capt. Henry Young and Larry Haar forwards, Frank Goodwin center, Maurice Johnson and Bob Warren guards. The new Duke coach was Eddie Cameron, and moving by North Carolina and Georgia, the Dukes started Coke Candler and George Rogers forwards, Joe Croson center, Bill Werber and Bo Farley guards. In the tournament championship Goodwin scored 14 points, and Duke lost Werber on fouls with four remaining, and N.C. State earned the title 44-35. However, the Atlanta crowd, with two North Carolina teams, was only 1,800 for the final night.

Capt. Bo Farley paced the Blue Devils the following year, 1930, once again to the finals while neither North Carolina or N.C. State got beyond the first round. The Raleigh team lost forward Jimmy Brown just before the tournament on academic ineligibility. In the finals with Alabama, Duke rallied with Farley and Werber scoring before losing 31-24. The Tide had a 10-0 conference season to match its tournament win.

The Tar Heels, now called the White Phantoms, reached the finals again in 1932, rallying to beat Tennessee, upsetting favored Kentucky and Auburn. Bo Shepard was in his first year as coach, the team including Wilmer Hines, Tom Alexander, Virgil Weathers and Dave McCachren. The finals with Georgia came to the final four minutes all tied, but the Bulldogs won 26-24.

It would be the last tournament in Atlanta for the North Carolina teams. For several years there had developed an undercurrent of dissatisfaction in the conference which now numbered 23 members from College Park, Maryland to New Orleans and Baton Rouge, Louisiana. Reasons for the dissension were "geography and wide difference in athletic eligibility requirements." At first the 11 state universities talked about withdrawing and forming their own group, then the schools in more Southern states, which would leave Georgia

28

Reynolds Coliseum on the N.C. State campus became the mecca of college basketball in the 1950's, setting national attendance records for a decade. Wolfpack championship banners wave on high.

and Tennessee colleges in the Southern Conference. Meanwhile, there were petitions from six schools to join: Wake Forest, Davidson, Furman, William & Mary, Richmond and Loyola New Orleans. At the annual conference meeting in Knoxville December 8-10, 1932, the 13 more Southern schools presented their resignation and formed the Southeastern Conference. It was not a particularly happy divorce. One report stated a reason being "the Southeastern emphasis on football in contrast to trends in other sections."

Among the first acts of business for the 10 members remaining in the Southern Conference was awarding the basketball tournament to Raleigh, North Carolina, where a new city auditorium awaited.

4

Coming Home/
Eddie Cameron

Edmund McCullough Cameron could not stay out of coaching. When he graduated at Washington & Lee, he spent a year at the university as economics professor, then joined his father in the banking business, but athletics was in his blood. He began coaching at Greenbrier Military Academy, joined Duke's freshman football staff in 1926.

Becoming Duke's head basketball coach coincided with the university's entrance into the Southern Conference, 1929, and he remembered it well: "That was a great big 23-team tournament which had been narrowed to 16 by the time Duke entered the conference. They built a basketball court in an old auditorium, and I remember the press guys sat along the sides with their heads sticking just above the floor."

Coach Cameron's first two teams reached the tournament finals, quite an achievement. Coach Cameron said recently: "Werber, Councilor, Rogers, Farley and Croson, that's all we played, five of them. We beat Alabama by five points, but we didn't beat anybody much more than that. You didn't shoot until you brought your feet together, a two-hand set shot. Such a thing as a running one-hand or hook shot, you didn't do that in those days. We got to the finals that first trip, but of all things we lost to State by nine points and we had beaten them twice in the season." The Blue Devils came right back in 1930, losing to Alabama in the finals 31-24.

That was a practical introduction to tournament basketball as the Southern Conference began in 1921 and as the Atlantic Coast Conference continues to this date.

Coach Cameron was involved in the inaugural tournaments at Raleigh, with the Southern Conference split, but just as important in that day and time was the state championship. Duke had captured three consecutive state titles when the Southern Conference moved to Raleigh in 1933. He was the only coach in the state to schedule December games, that season having taken a three-night train trip to Baltimore, Georgetown and George Washington. The team then went home for Christmas, returned for a January 6 game with Furman. Coach Doc Sermon's N.C. State team opened January 4-5 at George Washington and Catholic University, while Carolina and Davidson started against each other in Charlotte January 7. At Wake Forest, Coach Fred Emmerson took a 14-day Christmas holiday, opened the season January 7 at Catawba.

The "new" Southern Conference, minus the 13 who withdrew to form the Southeastern Conference in December 1932, met again January 14, 1933 in Richmond. They had some weighty matters, like flagrant recruiting and subsidization of athletes, plus low scholastic standards. They did invite Raleigh to stage the basketball tournament again in 1934, voting to advance the dates a week to avoid conflict with the conference boxing tournament. First things first.

Doc Sermon was chairman of the conference basketball committee in the transition, aided by Gus Tebell of Virginia, Burton Shipley of Maryland and Rock Norman of South Carolina. The Raleigh Auditorium was a new facility, seating about 3,500 with an additional 500 chairs on the stage if needed. Several of the state's teams rearranged regular season games to play in the auditorium. First game was Carolina beating Wake Forest January 20 when the Deacons failed to get a field goal the first half. N.C. State on February 4 also played the Deacons there, and Wake won this time. But the big game of regular season came January 31 at Card Gymnasium at Duke, both teams unbeaten in the Big Five (state championship), some 5,000 fans making it the largest crowd ever to see a game in the state. Jim Thompson's 14 points led to Duke's 36-32 win, under Coach Eddie Cameron, who invited the 1929-30 players for reunion in the final home game against Carolina.

The committee decided to have an eight-team tournament, three days, based on season standings, and the conference approved. It was an innovation. The tournament schedule had the first round Friday (February 24), semifinals Saturday night, finals Monday night at 8 p.m. Chairman Sermon told the AP:"It will be difficult to pick the eight best teams if all continue their present type of play. Not one of the 10 teams has shown any complete superiority over the others, but instead all seem to be almost equal strength." South Carolina only played four conference games (4-0), so Duke got top seed (7-3). The committee then chose W&L (1-8) over VMI (2-8) because the Generals had one less overall season loss. Raleigh was ready. The Jaycees and other civic clubs hosted the eight teams, and there was a dance to honor the players after the championship game Monday night. Paul Menton of Baltimore, Gummy Proctor of Richmond and Gerry Gerard of Durham were the officials, and in the tournament the conference used three officials per game. One slight difference in modern day methods — all three officials worked every game, four the first day. North Carolina Gov. J. C. B. Ehringhaus started a custom, throwing out the first ball.

North Carolina registered the first win in the first Raleigh tournament, 32-27 over Virginia Tech, as Virgil Weathers scored 14, and then W&L, which barely got in, remember, upset N.C. State 35-34 on free throws. It was the first upset. In the evening South Carolina, off to an 18-0 start, downed Maryland 65-28 and Duke eliminated Virginia 38-24. Saturday's semifinals had a sellout, some 400 turned away, thus assuring financial success as the committee spent all day Sunday counting the money. On O. W. Horne's 13 points Duke beat W&L 41-32, then South Carolina downed North Carolina 34-32 in double N.C. State was the top conference scorer with 158 points in 13 league games. In the semifinals the White Phantoms (Carolina) beat the Red cocks, with four sophomores off the Athens, Texas team that won two national high school championships, beat Duke 33-21.

The city of Raleigh had put together a winning program for the tournament. By 1935, there was a big parade in downtown Raleigh Thursday preceding the first round games, with proper decorations, and each team had a young lady as sponsor. Southern Conference bylaws book has Eddie Cameron as chairman of the basketball committee by 1935, and Coach Cameron had his Blue Devils in the finals once again in 1934. The team consisted of Connie Mack Jr., Phil Weaver, Herb Thompson, Jim Thompson and Sam Bell. W&L beat Duke 30-29, stealing the ball with 90 seconds left and dribbling in to score. For three straight years Coach Cy Young's W&L was to play North Carolina in the final game, the Tar Heels winning 1935 and 1936. The Tar Heels used a "rhythmic passing attack" starring 5'-7" Capt. Snooks Aiken and guard Jim McCachren. Under a new coach, Walter Skidmore, Carolina repeated in 1936 although they lost forward Ramsay Potts February 11 to an appendectomy. Connie Mac Berry of N.C. State was the top conference scorer with 158 points in 13 league games. In the semifinals the White Phantoms (Carolina) beat the Red Terrors (State), their nicknames not yet changed to the modern Tar Heels and Wolfpack. Andy Bershak led Carolina to the title, while Earl Ruth got the final goal, reported by the AP as "pitching the ball 44 feet from near center line."

The auditorium had purchased 1,800 new seats by 1938, the actual seat count now 3,941, and for the first time the Thursday afternoon session sold out. The conference had gone to a Saturday finals after 1933. Pairings were determined by four seeds and draw for opponents, and this matched W&L and North Carolina in the first round. The Generals won. Coach Cameron's Blue Devils had been tagged by publi-

Two neighborhood rivals, just eight miles apart in early 40s, Eddie
Cameron of Duke, right, and Bill Lange of Carolina.

When Cameron assumed athletic directorship and football coach at Duke,
Gerry Gerard took over basketball and won championships. Shown to his
right, All-American Dick Groat.

cist Ted Mann as the "Never A Dull Moment Boys," a lineup including Fred Edwards and Ed Swindell forwards, Bob O'Mara center, Russ Bergman and John Hoffman guards. They beat Clemson 40-30, and it was Eddie Cameron's first conference championship, the fifth time in the finals during his first decade.

His Duke teams were running. Coach Cameron, now retired, reminisced recently: "Indiana had the best high school basketball in the mid-30s and I was out there looking at a center. I also went to Anderson, Indiana, to attend a clinic Everett Case was holding. I wanted to hear him talk about the fast break. He had something there the others didn't have."

But 1939 sent both Duke and North Carolina out the first day, first time that had happened since the move to Raleigh, and Banks McFadden, with his two-hand over-the-head shot, led Clemson to its only basketball title. It was also the year five teams tied for the last spot, so the committee paired those with sixth–seeded N.C. State in Wednesday preliminary games. Ned Irish of Madison Square Garden was on hand, not only to present the tournament trophies but also to extend a possible invitation to the new National Invitation Tournament, which began the previous year. Instead, Wake Forest, loser to Clemson, was later invited to the inaugural NCAA playoffs where it lost to Ohio State in the East.

North Carolina presented tall hook-artist George Glamack in 1940, with Paul Severin and Bob Rose feeding the ball under Coach Bill Lange. As the Tar Heels won the title, Glamack had a simply-unheard-of 62 points in three tournament games. By 1941 the Blue Devils were champions again, and Coach Lange took Carolina to the NCAA playoffs after a first round loss to Duke 38-37. Coach Cameron's defense called for two men to stay with Glamack, one of them his center, Chuck Holley. Duke took the title over South Carolina 53-30, Holley getting 16 points, other regulars being Ray Spuhler and Bill Mock forward, Cy Valasek and Eddie Stokes guards.

Coach Cameron had a repeat titlist in 1942, beating W&L, Wake Forest and N.C. State. Both finalists had outstanding young teams, but Coach Cameron started his veteran lineup, then moved the sophomores in after 10 minutes. They included the Durham boys, the Loftis brothers, Bob Gantt and Gordon Carver. State had Bones McKinney as a sophomore under Coach Bob Warren.

World War II had been activated. Wallace Wade, Duke athletic and football coach, went to the Army and Eddie Cameron took both positions and relinquished basketball to Gerry Gerard. As such, he had to turn down NIT bids because the players were naval and army reserves, subject to call at any moment. Coach Gerard won conference titles in 1944 and 1946, then Everett Case came to N.C. State and basketball in the state hasn't been the same since. Coach Cameron agreed recently: "Case was so well organized. I always like to pay tribute to him for having a lot to do with basketball finesse that later developed in this part of the country, in the state of North Carolina. Of course, we had basketball before he came here, but I think he brought something into it which was very worthwhile."

Cameron remained active as basketball committee chairman, also with the conference television committee, and by the spring conference meeting in May 1953, there was the movement to again split the Southern Conference.

For years the "haves" had been displeased with the "have nots" in setting conference regulations. College presidents had been meeting the day prior to the annual spring session 1953, and this was again done Thursday, May 7. Only six attended, however. Pointed discussion centered over the bowl penalties enacted against Maryland and Clemson for playing in the Sugar and Gator Bowls, respectively, following the 1951 season. Both schools were not allowed to schedule any conference football teams in 1952. Maryland had prepared a motion to extend the football season to post-season games, but it would take a two-thirds majority of 17 members. Virginia Tech proposed an end to all competition for freshmen — repeat, all competition. Seven schools, which had met informally before, gathered in a second-floor suite at Sedgefield Inn near Greensboro, and shortly after midnight had decided to resign from the Southern Conference. That was done at the 10 a.m. conference meeting on Friday, May 8, 1953. The eighth member became Virginia (December 1953), while both Miami and Florida State expressed unofficial interest. Both West Virginia and Virginia Tech, which later withdrew from the Southern, desired to go with the new organization, but were not invited.

The conference (now ACC) basketball committee remained almost intact: Roy Clogston of N.C. State, Chuck Erickson of North Carolina, Rex Enright of South Carolina, the current president of the coaches association . . . and Eddie Cameron as chairman. He retired in 1972.

George Glamack, who averaged over 20 points in 1941, led Carolina to NCAA, twice selected Helms Foundation player of the year.

5
National Focus/
Ben Carnevale

The Deacons of Wake Forest went to the inaugural NCAA playoffs in 1939, but the 40s proved to be even more affiliated with national prominence in the game of college basketball.

There was a tall Pennsylvanian known as "The Blind Bomber" at Carolina. George Glamack, 6-foot-6, wore glasses except when he played basketball, and he did that so well that as a junior and again as a senior he was acclaimed by the Helms Foundation as the player of the year in the nation. His poor eyesight made it vitally important for Glamack to know his exact position on the floor, right at the foul line, where his feet were. He could see them. From that position he hooked the ball, as a senior (1941) averaging an amazing 20.6 points.

Glamack was the catalyst for Coach Bill Lange's first team at Chapel Hill. Glamack, getting 62 points in three tournament games (16, 28 and 18), a record at the time, sparked the 39-23 triumph over Duke in 1940. Inserting sophomore Bob Rose, the Tar Heels were able to get the ball to Glamack.

In 1941 Carolina topped season standings at 14-1. Four teams got tournament seeds, their opponents then came by draw, and Duke, whose 8-4 missed No. 2 seed by a half-game, was pulled as the Tar Heels' first opponent. Coach Eddie Cameron contained Glamack with two, the Blue Devils won an exciting 38-37 game and went on to take the title.

Two weeks before the tournament, Coach Lange received a mailed invitation to the NCAA playoffs. Carolina accepted. All games would be at Madison, Wisconsin. The Tar Heels left by train Wednesday night, changed in Greensboro and arrived in Washington the next morning. There was a workout at College Park, then the team boarded the train again bound for Wisconsin. They worked out Friday on arrival and played the University of Pittsburgh that night. Glamack had a boil on his elbow and had to wear a rubber shield for it. He scored only nine points and the team lost 26-20. Carolina led 12-8 at halftime, then was almost completely shut down. Low scoring games were not common with Glamack. Dartmouth beat Carolina 60-59 for third place in the East. Glamack tallied 31 points for an NCAA tournament record.

World War II brought Ben Carnevale to Chapel Hill.

During the NCAA East early round recently, Carnevale, on the NCAA basketball committee, talked about the background which took him from New York to Chapel Hill and back to New York. He related: "I remember Snuffy Stirnweiss who played football and baseball at North Carolina, then came to the New York Yankees. I used to go to camp in the Catskills and Bobby Gersten went there, too, in the summer. He was at Chapel Hill. Then when I played at NYU, we came South and played at Richmond and Chapel Hill, in the old Tin Can, I remember. Carolina had Andy Bershak, Pete Mullis, Pete Boone. They came to the Garden the following year. I remember the Tin Can, completely filled but it was the middle of winter, very cold inside. In my four years at NYU, Coach Howard Cann lost only four games and our team qualified for the 1936 Olympics, but they took two AAU teams instead. They went to Berlin, and that was the first basketball game in the Olympics.

"After overseas duty in the Navy, I was up for reassignment, had the choice of upstate New York, Miami or Chapel Hill, and I chose Chapel Hill because it was too cold in New York and too hot in Miami. I got there in the summer (1944) and Bill Lange was coaching, and left just before the season. Coach Bob Fetzer (athletic director) didn't have a coach and nobody wanted to coach the team because all the players were gone. Coach Bob came to me — I was athletic director for the Navy V-12 program at Chapel Hill—and almost begged me.

"I asked him to give me a little time, let me go to Washington and several other places to look into the possibility of getting me some ball players. I did go to Washington, picked up a young man by the name of Jordan, then Paxton, then Ira Norfolk who I knew was about ready to get out of the service. And there was a great ballplayer down at Georgia Tech named Hook Dillon, who was unhappy, and in those two weeks I was able to assemble a pretty good group of boys. If you recall, those two years we lost only 11 games, won 52, and about the only teams that beat us were Greensboro ORD, Norfolk Training Station, Norfolk Air Station with all the pros. We had a great basketball club."

They did develop quickly, John Dillon, Jim Paxton and Jim Jordan in the frontcourt, Manny Alvarez and Don Anderson in the backcourt. There were wartime regulations, the Navy personnel on the team had a 48-hour travel rule. It was ruled Carolina could only play at night if it went to the conference tournament. South Carolina led the season 9-0, Richmond 8-0, but a mumps epidemic cancelled out Richmond's tournament play. Pairings for the tournament were changed after announced, service teams playing Thursday night, civilians Friday afternoon, then Friday night semifinals. It was Duke and Carolina in the finals, Ed Koffenberger and Dan Buckley leading the Blue Devils. Carolina called on Manny Alvarez for 40 minutes. He had spent the entire morning in the final review of Naval ROTC students at the university. Coach Carnevale said of his team star: "Manny has been the most underrated player in the state all season." Carolina had invitations from both NIT and NCAA but Navy requirements prevented it.

By the following year, 1946, the Carolina lineup had been reinforced by Bones McKinney, the former N.C. State sophomore star who was just out of Fort Bragg. He moved to the center spot, Dillon and Paxton forwards, Jordan and Jim White guards. Carolina and Duke came to the tournament with a single loss, to each other. They were to meet in the finals again, but something happened. Wake Forest beat Carolina in the semifinals 31-29, failing to pierce the Deacon defense which held Carolina without a field goal for 11 minutes at the start of the second half. Duke won the title again.

Another hassle arose over the NCAA selection method, which seemed to be in annual controversy in those days. Four teams were under consideration: North Carolina, Duke, Kentucky (SEC winner) and Navy. The Middies were marked off because they refused the year before. Kentucky accepted the NIT, and LSU, the SEC runnerup, got involved. The NCAA committee proposed a playoff between Duke and North Carolina, but the former vetoed that. Chairman Norman Shepard of Davidson pointed out that Carolina's better overall record (26-3) gave it the edge. Carolina went by train to New York, four players in double figures, Paxton just a shade under. Carolina beat NYU 57-49, for Lt. Carnevale quite an experience: "I once played for Coach Cann. He is like a dad to me." Dillon got 15 points, Paxton 13, McKinney 11 and Jordan 10. In the Eastern finals, playing Ohio State, Carolina tied regulation at 54 on Paxton's shot from his favorite position, side court. McKinney fouled out with 10 minutes left, but Anderson and Dillon got goals for a 60-57 victory.

That was Saturday night. The national finals were Tuesday. Oklahoma A&M (State), defending champion, had 7-foot Bob Kurland, the nation's No. 1 scorer who in NCAA play had made 30 vs Kansas, 20 vs Baylor and 29 vs California. Coach Henry Iba's Aggies had a 14-game win streak.

Coach Carnevale replayed the final game recently: "Oklahoma State had a good passing team, good control, but we emphasized that, too. We would freeze the ball for 2-3 minutes at a time. Dillon was exceptional with his hook shots, but Bones got in foul trouble. Yet, the whole key to the ball game came late, down to the last couple minutes. We had come back well, and we got a rebound and were breaking out

Coach Ben Carnevale receives NCAA award from chairman Harold Olsen, being national finalist to Oklahoma A&M in 1946.

Big Four Coaches' Records

(Coaches with more than a single year.)

Coach, School, Seasons	No. Years	Won	Lost	Pct.
Ben Carnevale, Carolina (1945-46)	2	52	11	82.5
Bo Shepard, Carolina (1932-35)	4	69	16	81.2
Chick Doak, Duke (1917-18)	2	30	9	76.9
Dean Smith, Carolina (1962-)	22	496	153	76.4
Vic Bubas, Duke (1960-69)	10	213	67	76.1
Press Maravich, N.C. State (1965-66)	2	38	13	74.5
Frank McGuire, Carolina (1953-61)	9	164	58	73.873
Everett Case, N. C. State (1947-64*)	19	377	134	73.776
Walter Skidmore, Carolina (1936-39)	4	65	25	72.2
J. S. Burbage, Duke (1923-24)	2	33	13	71.7
Hank Garrity, Wake Forest (1924-25)	2	33	14	70.2
Eddie Cameron, Duke (1929-42)	14	226	99	69.5
Harold Bradley, Duke (1951-59)	9	167	78	68.163
James Ashmore, Carolina (1927-31)	5	79	37	68.103
Norman Sloan, N.C. State (1967-80)	14	266	127	67.684
Richard Crozier, Wake Forest (1906-17)	12	95	46	67.375
Bill Holding, Wake Forest (1920, 1922)	2	20	10	66.7
Bill Foster, Duke (1975-80)	6	113	64	63.841
W.W. Card, Duke (1906-12)	7	30	17	63.827
Gerry Gerard, Duke (1943-50)	8	131	78	62.679

*retired after second game in 1965.

**MIKE KRZYZEWSKI Now In 4th
Season With Blue Devils**

**DEAN SMITH Now In 23rd Season
With Tar Heels**

CARL TRACY Now In 12th Season With Deacons

JIM VALVANO Now In 4th Season With Wolfpack

with just one point down. Kurland was running down the court with his back to the ball, he put his hand up and the ball hit his hand, fell at his feet. We kept going down the court in the right direction, obviously. Kurland picked it up and threw the ball back, and they scored an easy goal. It turned into a four-point play for them, and we only lost by three."

Kurland had his 23 points and a stack of rebounds, Dillon got 16 points but Don Anderson paced the others with eight. Kurland fouled out with 38 seconds remaining, then Dillon in the frantic five seconds.

For Coach Carnevale it had been an exciting trip home. Madison Square Garden was filled for three nights watching Carolina basketball. He recalled: "Riding back on the train with the university president, Dr. Frank Porter Graham, we talked about what it had meant to the university and to the state. We didn't have TV then but we had a national radio network, and Dr. Graham felt it gave the university a national image. He felt we had really done something for the state of North Carolina as well as the university's basketball program."

When he won the NCAA Eastern and played in the finals, a number of opportunities came up and Ben Carnevale went to the U.S. Naval Academy. He remained as coach there 20 years, then accepted the athletic directorship at his alma mater NYU. He chaired the USOC basketball committee 1964-68.

Several times as Navy coach, Carnevale returned to the state to play in the Dixie Classic and single games. In fact, they handed N.C. State its first Dixie Classic defeat ever in the 1953 event.

Ben Carnevale's two seasons at Chapel Hill posted a 52-11 mark. It remains the best percentage of any coach at a Big Four school, those who have coached more than one season. His winning figure comes out to 82.5 per cent.

6
Everett Case

Ev Case never played college basketball. He started coaching his high school team, as a volunteer, at age 18.

Everett Case became a college basketball coach at age 46. He accepted the position at North Carolina State without ever seeing the place.

Everett Norris Case was instant success in his new environs, and his legacy, now placed in the Basketball Hall of Fame, far surpasses any honors which are strictly Wolfpack. They are possessed by the state of North Carolina.

Maybe the thought of college coaching never crossed the man's always busy mind until World War II, when he learned, possibly, there was a grade of basketball a notch, at the most, above Indiana high school. It began one morning at Connersville, Indiana, high school when the principal discovered he had a boys basketball team but no boys basketball coach. Ev Case, age 18, high school senior, volunteered for the position. It was during World War I. He continued to coach the team in the winter to help pay his way through the University of Wisconsin in the summer, where he graduated in 1923. He also coached at Columbus, Indiana. He became coach at Frankfort in 1922 where in 10 seasons his teams played in every Indiana state tournament, a definite mark of achievement, winning the state title in 1925 and 1929. He moved over to Anderson for two years, then in 1933 went to Southern Cal to become Sam Barry's assistant and get his master's degree. Returning to Frankfort in 1934, he won two more state championships (1936, 1939). In 23 years his high school record was 726-75.

During World War II he became a Navy lieutenant, first at DePauw Naval Training Station where two teams were 29-3, then in 1946 at Ottumwa Air Station in Iowa, 27-2 that season. He drew his discharge in the spring of 1946.

In Raleigh, a bit distant from Ottumwa, there were some discussions taking place about athletics in the postwar period. Dick

Herbert, then *Raleigh News and Observer* sports editor, recalled recently: "The Consolidated University had ruled there could not be duplicate schools in the system. That left N.C. State with agriculture, engineering, textiles and forestry, UNC with liberal arts, physical education. State felt it was almost impossible to get enough good football players to succeed. They had money with the Delaware Loan Foundation and it didn't work. But they made the decision they could succeed in basketball. When the war was over, they would get a good coach and provide him with more scholarships than anybody around here. At the time there was little help at Carolina, practically none at Duke, Wake Forest more than others.

"A week before the Southern Conference tournament (1946) in Raleigh, I went out to the campus for a spring football practice. Sitting in the stands were Dr. H. A. Fisher, the faculty chairman of athletics, and John Von Glahn, business manager of athletics. I asked them if they had picked their coach yet, they said they hadn't. I asked, are you open for suggestions? They said, yes, so I got them with Chuck Taylor, who was with Converse, and Chuck told them the best in the United States was Everett Case who was just getting out of the Navy."

Contact was made, Case flew to Atlanta to meet with the State officials, he agreed to be coach. He arrived on the job July 1, 1946, along with Butter Anderson as assistant. Case did not sign a contract, saying later: "I told them, I don't know whether I will like State or whether you will like me. I want to be free to leave if things don't work out." Later, he only signed a contract when Frank McGuire got one at Chapel Hill, and Frank told him about it.

Case had work to do, he had to get ball players just getting out of the service. Dick Dickey became all-American. Jack McComas and Pete Negley became all-conference, along with Eddie Bartels of New York City. Leo Katkaveck, back in school from the 1942 Wolfpack, became captain. Case looked at old Frank Thompson Gym and knew the fans would soon pack that barn. He looked several hundred yards to the West and saw the steel girders where a coliseum had begun in 1941, with people like Dave Clark of Charlotte spearheading the money drive among alumni. World War II had stopped the structure, but now it had to be renewed, not for 8,000 either, but at least 4,000 more, Case said. With the steel already set, the most economical way to add seats would be making it longer, thus a lot of end zone seats. Case had to get a schedule, and he wanted to play before Christmas. No area colleges, except Coach Eddie Cameron's Duke team before the war, played basketball in December.

In comments of review, made with Frank Weedon for a special commemorative program at State later, Coach Case talked about the early years: "When I first came down here, we couldn't find anybody to play until after Christmas so we had to play military and industrial

Case huddles with the stars of his last conference champion in 1959. Players, left to right, Lou Pucillo, Bob MacGillivray, John Richter, George Stepanovich and Dan Englehart.

teams. My first team at State was mostly freshmen, and nobody heard of us until we took a trip to the Midwest and won all six games. Highlight of that trip was the only defeat Holy Cross, with Bob Cousy, suffered all year. They went on to win the national title. Then people began to notice us. New York University came here, thinking we were a setup, but we nipped them, and they had Dolph Schayes, too."

Tobacco Road was being paved, but for visitors it was already rough sledding.

Case continued: "We played our games in Frank Thompson Gym and had to cancel the Carolina game when the students broke down the doors and the fire marshal wouldn't let us play. The Southern Conference tournament was supposed to be in Raleigh's Memorial Auditorium, but was switched to Duke Indoor Stadium when they got 10,000 orders for tickets. They never had anything like it before. We won the tournament, beating Carolina again with the first real display of the full-court press. They had us 22-7 before we started to press. Nobody had used the press that long before. We then went to the NIT and beat St. John's and West Virginia, but lost to Kentucky."

Good review of the first one, coach, but it was more than that. They lost to Cherry Point Marines, then right after the six-win road trip to Indiana and Ohio, they were beaten by Hanes Hosiery, but the fans were ignited by Case's racehorse game. Conference tournament tickets went on sale in late January, and the first mail brought orders for three times as many seats as the Raleigh Auditorium could handle. The place could take 3,900, the orders were nearer 10,000. Von Glahn called Eddie Cameron at Duke, who was chairman of the conference basketball committee, and within the hour, they concluded the tournament had to be moved to Duke Indoor Stadium which could seat 8,000-plus. It was a virtual sellout for the four years it remained at Durham, and it was there, during the 1948 tournament, that the Southern Conference Sports Writers Association was formed.

On a Tuesday night, February 25, Carolina was supposed to visit Frank Thompson Gym. Two days before, two students had been killed at Purdue when bleachers collapsed. An hour before game time, Frank Thompson's 3,500 bleacher seats already filled, one of the front entrance doors was broken down by onrushing students and fans. Eight policemen and 10 firemen were rushed to the scene, and the game was cancelled. State's team was in the dressing room, Carolina never got in. Students chanted, "We want a ball game, we want a ball game." The fire marshal had police clear the place in 15 minutes. Reporters, unable to enter the front doors, crawled through toilet windows in the basement to get to the court. It was mutually agreed by the two coaches to cancel the game.

With that tempo, the first Everett Case conference tournament was held at Duke. The Hoosier Hotshots, as his young team of Indiana players was called, beat Maryland 55-43, George Washington 70-47 and North Carolina in the finals 50-48. Coach Tom Scott's Tar Heels built a 13-point lead midways the game, but Dickey sparked the Wolfpack comeback. Bartels got the 50th point, but at 50-48 with 20 seconds, John Dillon's Tar Heel hook bounced off the rim. It was the forerunner of more than a few Case thrillers with Carolina.

Coach Case's problems with the NCAA basketball committee began at once. The district committee, headed by Norman Shepard of Davidson and including Kentucky's Adolph Rupp, then the kingpin of the South, picked the NCAA team. Before the conference tournament, Case accepted the NIT bid, but with the conference title, Case was obviously miffed when the NCAA committee selected the U.S. Naval Academy with a 16-1 record, coached by Ben Carnevale, who just the year before had taken North Carolina to the NCAA finals. In the Garden's NIT, State beat St. John's, whose new coach was Frank McGuire, then lost to Kentucky in the semifinals, beat West Virginia for third spot. It climaxed an outstanding debut for the Indiana high school coach into college circles, 26-5 overall.

The second recruiting class brought in Sammy Ranzino, the pure-shooting forward who could hit on the run, and Vic Bubas, the guard who became a coach on the floor. They became the No. 1 scoring team in the nation, ranked nationally No. 2 in early February. Duke's appearance in Frank Thompson was called off by the fire marshal who was making as many plays as the Wolfpack players. It was rescheduled in Memorial Auditorium downtown. In the tournament the Pack beat William & Mary, North Carolina and Duke, but Friday at 10 a.m. the coaches learned that Dick Dickey had the mumps and could not play. Coach Case said postgame: "That meant we had a lot of work to do between our first and second games. Dickey was the center of our racehorse basketball, and without him we had to change to a slower, more deliberate style within a few hours." It worked in Durham but not in New York. Kentucky was selected by the NCAA committee, but Asa Bushnell of the sponsoring ECAC had mailed an NIT bid before the conference tournament. That's right, mailed. Without Dickey the Wolfpack lost in the NIT to DePaul with George Mikan 75-64.

Sammy Ranzino, now living in Raleigh, an all-American three seasons, told about his coming to the state recently: "I never knew where North Carolina was, really. When Coach Case came to talk to me, I asked where N.C. State was. He said it was where all the good Indiana players were going. I was going to Alabama, but there was a tryout at Pendleton High School with at least 300 boys. It was legit then. We worked out, and there were Butter Anderson (assistant coach) and Jonas Fritch (Case's friend). I was given a scholarship, came down, stayed, married a North Carolina girl, it's great. You get into the Big Four rivalry in a hurry. In four years on the team we never lost to Duke and Wake Forest. The competition is terrific, all these years since Coach Case came down. It rivals anything we ever had in Indiana. In Indiana it has always been high school play, in North Carolina it's college, but today we have North Carolina high schools providing the talent. I think I can shoot with anybody, but they're bigger. They can all jump. In my time there were 2-3 who could shoot, today everybody can shoot."

Come 1949, and more Case comments to Frank Weedon: "By this time we were playing all our games in Memorial Auditorium downtown and selling out for all the games. We even rented Duke Indoor Stadium and sold out a game with Pittsburgh. It was apparent that we would be in Reynolds Coliseum for the start of the 1949-50 season, so we took a trip West with the idea of getting some intersectional teams to play in Raleigh the next year." The new arena was going up, and it brought an invitation from Coach Peck Heckman of Louisville, who beat the Pack in Raleigh 72-71. He wanted to form a "super conference" of teams with basketball facilities of 7,000 or more, a national league not to interfere with present conferences. Invited, in addition to Louisville and N.C. State, were Kentucky, Butler, California, DePaul, Indiana, Michigan State, Minnesota, Michigan, Purdue, Stanford, St. Louis, Texas, Washington and Notre Dame. Nothing, obviously, ever materialized. The Pack lost eight games, no post-season.

Reynolds Coliseum was completed, the 1949-50 season would make Raleigh the basketball capital of the world. Immediately, at once. Reynolds Coliseum drew more people than any other place in the country that first season, and it would keep that going for a decade. It was hard for an outsider to come to this newest stop on Tobacco Road and win. Case's all-time record in Reynolds was 156-34. Except for 1952, he just didn't lose at home. He started the Dixie Classic in December 1949, the Big Four against the outside world, and the Wolfpack not only won the first one, but seven of the 12 played before the holiday spectacle was chopped down by the 1961 point-shaving scandals and other assorted misdemeanors.

There was one game in particular which emphasized Tobacco Road. LaSalle in 1951 returned a Wolfpack trip to Convention Hall in Philadelphia, and two high-rated teams were in battle. Ken Loeffler coached LaSalle. Among the top-notch officials working in Reynolds was Lou Bello. The effervescent Bello recalled recently, during a break in his TV work: "I was the referee. They were coming down to Raleigh, the basketball mecca, outdrawing anything New York had, and also Philadelphia, and the big paychecks Coach Case was paying. The teams sat underneath the baskets then, and it was late in the game, close game. There was a close call, Loeffler didn't like it, and Ken left his chair and walked the length of the court. It was timeout, and I remember being at State's end. Ken walked up to Case and said, 'I'm going to take my team off the floor and forfeit the game.' Case replied, calmly, 'You do and you don't get paid.' Loeffler just walked back to his seat." He also walked the railroad tracks from the campus to downtown afterwards, after losing 76-74. The next day Loeffler called

The two kings of the South, Adolph Rupp of Kentucky, left, and Everett Case of N.C. State. They battled constantly. Rupp would not play in Raleigh, but on this occasion, 1951 NCAA East first round, alumni presented Case with a new Cadillac, as shown, with Rupp's team playing the second game, and he was there.

it "the biggest steal since the Louisiana Purchase." He was, he must have forgotten, on Tobacco Road.

Bello, an astute observer of the game to this day, talked about Coach Case's "new" game in the state: "Not only did he bring in the fast break, the one-hand shot and speed, speed, speed, next thing he came in with was the pressing defense. I happened to have the first ball game when he tried that in Reynolds, against Wake Forest. Coach Murray Greason came to our dressing room at halftime to ask, 'Do the rules change on the press?' In the press they were touching, tagging all over the floor. Coach Case was so far ahead of everybody else."

But Coach Case seemed to stay involved with NCAA disputes over the playoff selections. Only eight teams played in the nationals, meaning District 3 included both Southern and Southeastern Conference champions, as well as Navy as independent. As the 1950 season neared its close, Coach Case offered to play Kentucky in a district playoff, pointing out that the Big Seven (now Big Eight) and Missouri Valley winners met for their district spot. But on February 28 Coach Rupp bluntly declared no playoff was needed, that Kentucky indeed was the only team qualified. The Baron said, "We're the defending champions. We beat Villanova and Bradley, and he (Case) didn't. Villanova beat him on his own floor. He has no more right to challenge us than any other school in the entire South. We're either good enough to represent the district or we're not good enough." Meanwhile, Case charged that Kentucky had tentatively agreed to play the dedication game in Reynolds Coliseum that 1949-50 season, but backed out. The NCAA replaced Rupp on the district committee with Roy Mundorff of Georgia Tech. Gus Tebell of Virginia was chairman, Eddie Cameron of Duke committeeman. The Wolfpack won the tournament, Ranzino the first unanimous all-tournament pick in years. Duke players talked about Sammy. Dick Crowder: "That guy is the greatest shot I've ever seen." Ceep Youmans, guarding Sammy: "Early in the game, when he was playing in the middle, he started to shoot, I knocked the ball from his grasp, he flipped the ball with the other hand, and swish. What can you do with a guy like that?"

And N.C. State got the NCAA bid with Rupp screaming. On March 4 Chairman Tebell announced: "State agreed to play Kentucky any time any place when we suggested the most logical conclusion in our district would be a playoff. However, Kentucky declined to meet State in a playoff and Kentucky asked to be selected outright. The committee felt that under those circumstances, State should be selected." State turned down the NIT. In Madison Square Garden Ranzino and Dickey combined for 57 points to beat Holy Cross 87-74, then playing CCNY in the Eastern finals. The two giants battled to the final two minutes, tied 14 times, but Ranzino and Dickey had fouled out and CCNY managed to survive 78-73. In the third place game the

Wolfpack beat Baylor, which had upset UCLA in the West, Coach John Wooden's second season. CCNY won the NCAA title over Bradley, making it the only time a team captured both NIT and NCAA. Then, a broken-hearted Coach Nat Holman had both crowns removed with player convictions in the point-shaving scandals of 1950. Both final games were involved.

One result of the 1950 squabble, however, was a revision of the NCAA tournament. The State-Kentucky confrontation was paramount, but so was the fact Bradley, NIT runnerup, had to go back for an NCAA playoff with Kansas. The 1951 field for rising NCAA playoffs became 16 teams with conference champions automatic. The Southern had one, so did the SEC. By 1952 there was the regional concept that exists today, and the first one was played in Reynolds Coliseum. Oddly enough, it brought Kentucky to Raleigh, finally.

"I think one of the games that stands out most in my memory," Coach Case wrote later, "and so many State fans have said they remember the most, was our 1951 NCAA tournament game against Villanova. We had lost to Villanova twice during the regular season and since Sammy Ranzino, Vic Bubas and Paul Horvath played varsity ball as freshmen, they weren't eligible as seniors for NCAA play. We pulled one of the big upsets in those days when we beat Villanova with Bill Kukoy, Bobby Goss and Bernie Yurin filling in for the seniors. Reynolds was packed to capacity, with Kentucky also playing in the regional."

It was bigger than that, actually. First, the seniors ineligible. The NCAA permitted freshmen to play varsity ball, but then they couldn't play that fourth year in NCAA playoffs. The rule died soon thereafter. The Wolfpack won the conference tournament, beating Duke and Coach Case saying: "Whew, I sure am glad this tournment is over. When you face a guy like Dick Groat, you just can't relax." State accepted the NIT so the seniors could play, but lost to Seton Hall. Guard Lee Terrill and forward Bobby Speight remained on the starting Pack for Villanova. They played "alley cat" ball, full-court press for 40 minutes, and beat Villanova 67-62. Of Terrill the coach said: "Probably the best game of his career, and it was just what we needed the most. He didn't get the big points, Kukoy and Speight did that, but it was Lee who kept the offense rolling, who kept setting up the plays and defense, which were our only hope to win." They went to the Garden, but lost to Illinois and St. John's, coached by Frank McGuire, to place fourth.

Undoubtedly planned for the evening, between the games that night, Coaches Case and Anderson came to midcourt. Alumni and friends presented a new Cadillac to the head coach, a new Oldsmobile to his assistant. The two cars were driven onto the court, where the second game teams were warming up. Adolph Rupp and

Kentucky watched the presentation. Smiling. His team played Louisville, whom it never played in season back home. Kentucky won 79-68.

The Pack won the conference again in 1952, beating Duke in the finals for the third straight year. It made the NCAAs for the third straight time, and this 1952 East Regional was in Reynolds. A State-Kentucky game on Reynolds hardwood was a distinct possibility, but — it didn't happen. Kentucky beat Penn State, but Coach Frank McGuire's St. John's Redmen ousted State 60-49. McGuire, beating Kentucky the next night, went on to Seattle and played for the national title, then came to Chapel Hill the next summer.

Always an entrepreneur, Case brought Rio Grande College and scoring sensation Bevo Francis to Reynolds in December 1952, along with Dickie Hemric and Wake Forest against Olympic champion Peoria Caterpillars. Bevo got 34 but lost to State, then beat the Deacons at the buzzer. Coach Case wrote: "Some keen competition among Big Four teams in 1952-53. We lost four games to Wake Forest, Duke and Carolina by a total of five points. And Wake Forest ended our Southern Conference tournament success by beating us in the finals by one point (71-70). The sensational shooting of Billy Lyles won it for them." The Wolfpack had won six straight conference titles since Case arrived, within a couple months they would be part of the newly formed Atlantic Coast Conference, and remain the big kid on the new block.

This new league saved Coach Case from a lot of headaches on his projects. He fought the tournament schedule which felt it needed the top seed in the 9 p.m. game each day to draw. The ACC changed the top seed to the 7:30 game. By the 1980s the season winner, or top seed, played the opening game of the tournament as a reward, thus getting more tournament rest. Case and other coaches also battled the rating system in the 17-member Southern Conference. In 1952 N.C. State was 12-2, West Virginia 15-1, but they did not play each other. Duke was 13-3, Clemson 11-4, but they did not meet. Coaches wanted an 8.5 scale for the regular schedule — if a team played the No. 1 conference team, final standings, it got a 17; a game with the bottom team, one point. Also, averaged out, 8.5. Also the out-of-state coaches protested the housing in Raleigh for the tournament. They were roomed in N.C. State dormitories. Complained Maryland Coach Bud Millikan: "After all, who makes this tournament? It's the boys. Those kids look forward to this tournament trip as something special. They like the idea of staying in a hotel and in a new city for a few days. They lose all that under the present setup."

But on the ACC floor there was the same, hell-bent-for-championship Wolfpack and coaching staff. They captured the first ACC tournament in 1954, edging Wake Forest 82-80 in overtime, the second of two great battles between these Wake County rivals, marking the exodus of one conference (Southern), the genesis of another (ACC). Coach Case said after the excitement: "Let me tell you something. This was the toughest tournament a team of mine ever had to play, and why? We had to face Carolina, Duke and Wake Forest on three straight nights, and that's almost an impossibility if you're aiming to win, and we always do." Carolina slowed it, final 51-50. Duke entered the fourth quarter tied at 61, rallied within 79-75 late. Coach Case was snorting after the finals: "We got a 16-point lead in the third quarter, and what do we do? Folks have criticized us for holding the ball, so this time we decided not to do that. What results? We let up the pressure of the full-court, which folks have also criticized us for, and that gives Wake Forest the chance to rally. This is one time when we should have definitely held the ball and slowed down the game. Hang the criticism." State placed third in the NCAA East Regional.

Phil DiNardo and Cliff Dwyer replaced Mel Thompson and Dick Tyler for 1955, joining Ron Shavlik and Vic Molodet, and the Pack repeated as ACC champions. In the tournament finals Shavlik got 24 points, 21 rebounds. The Pack was No. 5 ranked nationally but on NCAA probation. In 1956 Molodet and John Maglio did a lot of soring from their guard spots, beat Wake Forest in the tournament finals when the starting Wolfpack played all but one minute, Nick Pond subbing for Maglio. But Shavlik was playing with his left wrist in a brace, having broken it in late season. The Wolfpack lost to Canisius in NCAA first round play, going four overtimes before the verdict.

The first decade of Everett Case in North Carolina had concluded. In these 10 seasons of conference play, seven in the Southern and three in the ACC, his record came very close to perfection: six straight SC titles and three straight ACC, reaching the finals also in 1953. Tournament games only: 29-1. His Pack claimed six of seven Dixie Classics, game total 19-2. Overall, the Wolfpack had 267 victories, 60 defeats, an average season of 26-6. No coach anywhere ever dominated a conference like this, except possibly John Wooden on the Pacific, and the league had no tournament.

Jackie Moreland was an unfortuante recruit from Louisiana, resulting in the NCAA's greatest penalty ever, four years of probation for all N.C. State sports. It kept Coach Earle Edwards' conference champion football team out of the 1958 Orange Bowl. The basketball Wolfpack did not reach the tournament finals in 1957 and 1958, its first absences since Case came to Raleigh, but the 1959 game was another matter. Tournament final game, that is. The AP had Carolina No. 5, N.C. State No. 10, in UPI they were five and seven. On probation, the Pack, if it won, could go nowhere. The Pack edged South Carolina, when it should have lost, then beat Virginia 66-63. Coach Frank McGuire suggested to reporters, after Friday semifinals, Carolina

Fast break was the Wolfpack theme, and Vic Bubas drives from his guard position along the baseline for goal against Duke.

might not dress the starters, they needed the rest (for the NCAAs). They did play, but got considerable rest. Fans booed and jeered; one broke into the Reynolds transformer room and pulled the light switch, breaking it. There was darkness for eight minutes, the game finally resuming under dimmed lights. State hit 62 percent the second half, won 80-56. Coach Case said "They staged the greatest pregame dressing room demonstration I've ever seen. They wanted this."

Vic Bubas, who had replaced Anderson as assistant, left the staff to take the head job at Duke 1959-60, and Lee Terrill advanced. The 1961 scandals hit the Wolfpack in 1961; Coach Case was shocked and broken by his players being involved and indicted.

Case's team did not play in another tournament final, reaching the semifinals only in 1960 and 1963. Never more feisty and determined, the ol' Gray Fox entered the 1964-65 season which he had announced as being his final one; he would retire in March.

His successor, hand-picked, would be Press Maravich. The veteran coach recently talked about Coach Case and his new job: "A long time ago, before I even went to college, I heard about Everett Case who brought basketball to the South. He was very instrumental in developing the popularity of the game. He knew the best basketball was played up in Indiana, rated the number one state in the union for basketball prospects. Gradually, North Carolina came into being, and now (1983) there are just as many good basketball players as any other section of the country. My son Pete matured in Raleigh in his high school ball.

"That year (1962) I went back to Puerto Rico to coach the national team because Frank Howard (Clemson AD) wasn't paying me enough money. It was there that Coach Case called me. His assistant (George Pickett) was going into business, he asked me if I would be his assistant. At the time I was only making $5,000 and I took the job, quick. I had a six-year contract, which nobody knew about...three years before he supposedly was to retire, three years as head coach."

Case was not in the best of health at the end of the 1964 season. Coach Maravich said recently: "I knew long before the start of practice (1964-65) that he didn't feel good. Matter of fact, the first year I was there with him, I kept trying to convince him to give up the game because of his health. I kept telling him, if he kept in the game, basketball was going to take his life. Yes, I talked with him about it many times. I'd say, 'Coach, I don't want the head coaching job as long as you're here, but I don't think you're going to be here very long the way you are feeling. You're letting this game kill you, and it's not worth it. But if you still want to coach the three years and then retire, God bless you, but you must think about it.'"

They opened with Furman at home, 73-60, Case's 19th straight opening game victory. He greeted dynamite sophomore Eddie

Biedenbach, tall Larry Lakins and transfer Pete Coker. A few nights later, on the first road trip, they made the short drive to Winston-Salem and Wake Forest. The Deacons were up 18 early, but within seven minutes after halftime, State had engineered a 23-9 scoring run. It was down to two with eight minutes, still four with 55 seconds. Wake won 86-80.

It was just too much for the coach. Coach Case said, the day he retired, the Monday following the Wake game: "I felt terrible after our win over Furman last Tuesday, but I felt I would give it one more try. I didn't say anything to anyone about it. But the game in Winston-Salem did it. I had to get a chair and sit down. I thought I was never going to go home. I don't feel badly except during a game when the excitement gets me. There's no emotion in anything like in the game of basketball."

Maravich recalled: "That's when he almost went, over at Wake Forest. He was really sick, and he called me that next morning (Sunday) about 6 o'clock at home. I said, 'What's the matter Chief?' And coach said, 'Press, I just can't take it any more. I've got to step down.' That's exactly what happened. I only wish he had done that the first year I got there."

The announcement was made Monday, by March the 1964-65 Wolfpack had fought on to capture the conference title with a great tournament over Virginia, Maryland and Duke. The latter, No. 6 ranked nationally, was beaten when Larry Worsley came off the bench to replace foul-troubled Billy Moffitt, played 35 minutes and scored 30 points. The conference at its December meeting had voted to establish the Everett N. Case Award for the outstanding player in the tournament, and Worsley received it . . . in a standing ovation with his old coach, Everett N. Case, making the presentation. The players clipped the nets, as per the custom Case brought from Indiana, and when they got down to the final, single thread, they went to the press table and hoisted Coach Case to their shoulders to finish the job. Crowd roar, by then, was deafening. Coach Case managed to say: "I've never been happier. The last taste is always the best."

It was the last conference tournament Everett Case would see in person. He died April 30, 1966.

Coach Case had made out a new will on January 20, 1966, and signed it Everett Norris Case. He provided income for his older sister, Etta Blanche James as long as she lived. There were cash provisions to members of the coaching staff, plus originating a scholarship fund at N.C. State, then distribution of the trophies.

And then the most unusual paragraph ever inserted in such a document. It read: "9. All the rest and remainder of my estate shall be divided by my executors into 103 equal units which I give and bequeath to Willis Casey (3 units) and to former basketball players at

North Carolina State University as follows (with units to be received by each): McComas 2, Katkaveck 2, Sloan 3, Dickey 3, Bartels 2, Cartier 3, Ranzino 3, Bubas 3, Horvath 1/2, Harand 1/2, Cook 1, Terrell 3, Jackmauski 1, Stell 1, Holt 3, Morris 3, Kukoy 2, Pickett 3, Brandenburg 3, Speight 3, Adams 1/2, Kincaid 1/2, Appelbaum 1/2, Yurin 1/2, Tyler 2, Thompson 3, Stevenson 1, Scheffel 2, DiNardo 2, Molodet 3, Bell 2, Pond 2, Seitz 1, Shavlik 3, Dickman 1/2, Waters 3, Stepanovich 3, Hopper 1, Kessler 1/2, Pucillo 3, MacGillivray 2, Clark 1, Richter 2, Englehardt 3, Atkins 1/2, McCann 1/2, Hoadley 1/2, DiStefano 1/2, Lutz 1, Key 1/2, Wherry 3, Whitfield 1, Auksel 1/2, York 2, Gossell 2, Greiner 1/2 and Robinson 1/2."

A fiery and active Wolfpack bench, Everett Case makes a point.

7
Dixie Classic

The Dixie Classic, 1949-1960, was, in the simplest terminology possible, a classic. It was Everett Case's legacy, it was something the basketball fans of North Carolina happily and eagerly squeezed in between Christmas and New Year's, then talked about in the intervening 51 weeks.

It was, again, simply put, North Carolina versus the World, as far as collegiate basketball was concerned. It was the entrepreneurial of the ultimate, and Everett Case was the master of ceremonies.

The Big Four schools teamed together in the Reynolds Coliseum extravaganza, matched against four outside teams, selected by Case, sometimes chosen years in advance. At times, of course, that led to weaker entries, but some of the natives did not carry loaded pistols in those days either.

Everett Case took the idea and made it reality. Dick Herbert, then sports editor of the *Raleigh News and Observer*, recalled a bull session: "Reynolds Coliseum was going to be completed fairly soon. One Saturday I was at Everett's apartment at Red Beam's house, Butter Anderson (assistant coach) was there, along with Jonas Fritch (longtime friend from Kirkland, Indiana) and Willis Casey (then assistant athletic director). We were talking about the new coliseum. I said when they finished it, who's going to run it? I said if they would give it to me for one week when school was not in session, I'd run it for them for nothing for the year. Everett perked up and wanted to know, 'What'd you do? What'd you do?'

"I said I'd get the Big Four teams and the four best teams in the U.S. to come in here and have a tournament. Somebody wondered what we'd call it, and I said, 'Well, it's in Dixie and the South.' Then Butter added, 'In Indiana it's the Indiana Classic.' Everybody said, 'That's it, the Dixie Classic.'

"Everett took it from there and made it a great one. Number one, at that time of the year, it would be good for each team to play three games in preparing for the season. Everett also insisted that the best

58

officials in the U.S. be obtained. It made Raleigh the basketball capital of the nation."

There was no game limit on the NCAA schedule then (now 28), the holiday three-game tournament was excellent. Each team played through winners and losers brackets, so that on the final day the four games settled 1st, 3rd, 5th and 7th places. Only the sizes of the trophies were different, each team got all expenses and 1/10th of the tournament net (each team one share, coliseum two).

It was instant success with the fans. Other cities copied it, or tried to duplicate. Said Roy Clogston, the Wolfpack athletic director: "We're just in a bunch of basketball fans here in North Carolina. They will come out for good basketball and we intend to give them just that. The first day of the tournament proved the point beyond our fondest expectations. We had about $22,000 worth of advance ticket sales, but Wednesday we sold over $10,500 worth of individual tickets. Why, we sold out of night tickets at the coliseum box office late in the afternoon and had to close the office until we got some more from the field house."

True, such gate dollars don't sound like much in today's college basketball market, with $70 ACC tournament books (Greensboro 1984) and $42.50 NCAA finals (Seattle 1984). Dixie Classic prices met the times of the late 40s. Willis Casey, now AD, was the tournament director for the 12 years of the holiday event, and he talked about this during a break in the ACC spring meeting at Myrtle Beach: "The Dixie Classic became a social event, always the Dixie Classic and the conference tournament. In my mind, and this might be heresy, I don't think anything was the social event the Dixie Classic was. Three days, 12 games, and if you were a fanatic, you got all you could handle. That first Dixie Classic had tournament books costing $5 and $3. For all three days, I mean, choice seats, 12 games, and that was 40 cents per game for the most expensive tickets." Even so, officials were not quite sure about fan reaction. They got Walker Martin, a prominent Raleigh businessman and civic leader for decades, to buy 500 tickets to help out. He gave them as Christmas presents.

At the start each team got about $4,000; by the event's unfortunate cancellation in 1961, a share was worth $10,000. Still a bag of peanuts in today's market, with TV bonanzas and all. In the Dixie Classics Ray Reeve, venerable originator and announcer for the Tobacco Sports Network, did four games a day for three days over 50-60 stations. The entire state listened.

Coach Case dominated the show, not just in planning or the luncheons held by the Wolfpack Tipoff Club—with Harry Stewart as president and emceed by Billy Carmichael, Jr., probably the No. 1 fan in the university system. Case's Wolfpack teams won the first four Dixie Classics, took seven of the 12. North Carolina won three, Duke

59

Dixie Classic's first MVP, Dick Dickey of N.C. State clips Reynolds Coliseum nets in December 1949.

and Wake Forest one each. Those testing Tobacco Road came up with zero.

The Big Four gave the visitors a taste of Southern hospitality but did not extend it to the playing court. Three times the Big Four teams won all the first day games, thus segregating the brackets, the Insiders and the Outsiders. Overall, in the 12 years, the Big Four record against outside teams, not counting those among themselves read like this: N.C. State 21-4, Duke 13-9, Wake Forest 13-10 and Carolina 12-10. Of the 24 championship game spots in the 12 years, only seven outsiders ever made it.

It was agreed, probably between Coach Case and himself, to experiment with the rules in the very first Dixie Classic, a forerunner to the 1983 ACC experience possibly. In the last two minutes of a 1949 game, a team which was fouled had the option of a free throw or ball possession. The Dixie Classic was played with two shots on a defensive foul and keep the ball in play. Officials were Lou Bello of the Southern Conference, Arnold Heft of Washington, Frank Bender of the Big Ten and Red Mihalik of the Middle Atlantic.

All that was left, late that December 1949 with Reynolds Coliseum finally completed — although the Southern Conference would not award the conference tournament to Raleigh again until the following season (1951)—was to play the games. Each day, now remember, a doubleheader in the afternoon, clear the arena, a doubleheader in the evening. The Wolfpack always played in the afternoon, an obvious drawing card, until the finals, that is.

That first one the Wolfpack ranked No. 9 by the AP preseason, which did not pick up weekly rating until January. (The UPI began its rankings a year later.) Rhode Island State and Penn State rode the train to Raleigh, West Virginia and Georgia Tech came in cars. Tech had the top scoring team in the country, 83-point average, with Bill Cline of Salisbury its star. Tech beat Wake Forest, then Sammy Ranzino recorded 33 points as the Pack downed RI State. The first afternoon had drawn 10,500 paying fans. That evening West Virginia edged Carolina 58-50 and Penn State upset Duke 51-48, with 9,600 fans.

Thursday, the second day December 29, drew 7,500 and 9,000, and both State and upstart Penn State worked their way into the finals. In Friday afternoon games, for the lower spots, Duke offset a final shot to beat Wake Forest, and Rhode Island took overtime against Carolina. Penn State had been the eighth team invited, and it was the last to lose, beaten by Capt. Dick Dickey (the first MVP) and State 50-40 before 11,500 yelling fans.

Following this inaugural trend, the second DC witnessed another Wolfpack win recorded over Tulane, Wake Forest and Colgate. The opening pairing was interesting, matching Everett Case and Cliff Wells of Tulane, an old Indiana high school compatriot. They had once played a high school game that ended up something like 4-2. Coach Ben Carnevale came down with Navy, beat Wake Forest for third place.

But Dick Groat stole everybody's attention in that DC. Dick Groat, the guy who played shortstop for the Pittsburgh Pirates and the St. Louis Cardinals in his usual championship form, was an all-American at Duke in both basketball and baseball. When he played his final home game against Carolina in 1952, all the Groat heroics were saved for the finish. He came into the last minute with 45 points, two off Ranzino's record (47) for most by a Big Four player, short of his own school mark (46). At 50 seconds his jumper flicked off the rim, 10 seconds later a long one-hander missed target. At 30 seconds Duke fouled, and Coach Harold Bradley elected not to take the free throw but keep possession. At 25 seconds Groat was fouled, free throw, 46 points. Now, at the buzzer, Groat, quick as a mountain cat, faked a closely guarding Tar Heel, broke toward the middle, dribbled back 'tween two Tar Heels, took a layup, and, yes, the ball crawled in. Dick Groat had his 48 points, two records and 8,000 Blue Devil fans yelling.

But back to the Dixie Classic for another Groat Great Moment. His coaches agreed he would not mix his two sports seasons, and naturally there was no baseball in December. The 1950 DC did not have Duke playing for the big trophy. Rather, that Saturday afternoon, they met Tulane for fifth place, and Duke was behind 56-27 at halftime, still down 70-50 with 10:32 minutes remaining. Down 20 with 10, right? Give up? Groat began hitting, 24 the second half, more than the Tulane team. It was Tulane 72-68 with 1:52, Groat three straight goals. At 1:12, Groat broke to the left of the foul circle, flipped a jumper, tied at 72. Duke intercepted at midcourt, Scott York passed to Dayton Allen for a layup and a 74-72 victory. Groat had been great. Another interesting item for statistics bugs of the game: Tulane took 105 shots, made 30; Duke 100 shots, made 31, Nobody takes that many attempts today, or shoots a lousy 31 percent.

There were many games the fans of later days remembered. Coach Case always talked about the 1952 semifinals with Holy Cross, when he sent the Pack into a full-court press the second half to overcome the Crusaders' lead. Or of 1954 and the final game with a strong Minnesota team, Coach Case recalled: "One of the great ball games ever played in Reynolds was our Dixie Classic victory over Minnesota. I still see John Maglio driving up the lane, he just laid it in the air for the winning basket. That was a strong Minnesota team we beat 85-84."

Carolina came in December 1975, on the heels of the national championship, and Coach Frank McGuire had an experienced club. Coach Case knew that, then had a decision to make going into the title game. McGuire had held the ball on Case's talented team several years before; would he return the favor? A packed house came to see, another 300 jammed the entrance doors trying to get a ticket. Tension peaked, the big crowd split its loyalty. Lou Pucillo led State's early advantage, then when the Tar Heels took the advantage, the Pack held the ball. Tommy Kearns led the scoring with 14, the two teams combined took 51 shots. Final: Carolina 39, State 30.

The first Dixie Classic drew 52,200, the 1956 event totalled 71,200. To close out the first decade (1958), tournament manager Casey said at the time: "Except for the Wednesday afternoon games (third day, consolations), we have already sold just better than 11,000 tickets for each session. No more than 1,000 tickets remain for the two sessions Monday, the two Tuesday and the finals. We will easily reach our 600,000th fan for the Dixie Classic."

Why a sudden upsurge? Logical, indeed. What a field. Cincinnati was ranked No. 1 in the country and Oscar Robertson the top player. They were to play Wake Forest at 2 o'clock on opening Monday afternoon. North Carolina held the No. 3 AP ranking, N.C. State No. 6 and Michigan State (unbeaten) No. 9. That's four of the top 10 in the country, playing in Raleigh, the nation's basketball capital. No holiday tournament ever had such a field. The Tar Heels would met Michigan State the first evening, rematch of that 1957 NCAA semifinal shootout in Kansas City. Deacon Coach Bones McKinney confronted Big O for his first shot: "We'll specialize on Robertson all right, but just what it is, you'll have to wait until 2 o'clock to find out. I will tell you this, we won't kill the game with a deep freeze." Robertson was outstanding, but it was physical. Big Ten official Jim Enright called O for charging on his second move, he had one field goal in 10 minutes, but Wake's Dave Budd had three fouls. In the second half Robertson and Budd ended up on the floor, a small fistfight occurred, rough afternoon. Big O went to the bench bleeding. Cincinnati beat the Deacons 94-70, and it was the first opening day victory for a visiting team in four years.

National attention focused on the DC that week. Top-ranking Cincinnati lost on consecutive nights to N.C. State and Carolina, and the Wolfpack then beat Michigan State 70-61 for the title again. Out of this DC, the Pack jumped to No. 1 ranking in the nation and Carolina No. 3, and oddly enough, the two rivals were to meet in regular season conference play January 14 at Reynolds. Casey managed to squeeze in 650 extra chairs for the largest crowd Reynolds ever experienced, over 13,000. Carolina won in overtime.

Coach Case later talked about the 1958 DC: "Our all-time best has to be the Dixie Classic championship that year. That was the strongest field ever, and we had to beat Louisville, Cincinnati with Oscar Robertson and then Michigan State with Johnny Green. Carolina's consolation round win over Cincinnati was a great game. There has never been a better classic."

Of the DC and that January 14 game aforementioned, Coach McGuire later commented: "I'd never seen anything like it in the heyday of Madison Square Garden. I couldn't answer my phone for three days, so many people thought I could get them tickets. And you couldn't believe it, the pressure on everybody on that floor. It was simply oozing. The players felt it, the coaches felt it. You never saw Everett or myself get out of our seats so many times. All week I had tried to minimize this game to the boys and our people. I thought the best psychology would be to make it just another game, but I couldn't even sell myself. It was there in the air for four or five days ahead, and I can certainly say we gave the people of North Carolina wonderful entertainment for a week. They forgot all their worries and the front-page troubles." In winning, Carolina moved into the No. 1 spot.

Wake Forest and Carolina captured the final two Dixie Classics, the price of a three-day book had risen from the starting $5 to $14.50, still the top bargain in college basketball, then or now.

But other holiday tournaments were getting into the headlines, and that meant resort trips for the other Big Four teams, which they couldn't take as long as the Dixie Classic existed. The others complained, too, about the host school having ticket and recruiting advantages. Then came the 1960-61 point-shaving scandals, action that would hit both Wolfpack and Tar Heel campuses. The university administration sought to curtail the ever-growing basketball emphasis, and one of the penalties for the fans of North Carolina was the death of the Dixie Classic. The first of the nation's holiday spectacles. Three afternoons, three evenings, good basketball to appease even the most fanatic fan.

Dixie Classic Scores

December 1949
N.C. State 81, Rhode Island State 64
West Virginia 58, North Carolina 50
Georgia Tech 64, Wake Forest 57
Penn State 51, Duke 48

N.C. State 57, Georgia Tech 34
Penn State 46, West Virginia 41
North Carolina 59, Duke 55
Rhode Island State 61, Wake Forest 57

(1st) N.C. State 50, Penn State 40
(3rd) Georgia Tech 63, West Virginia 48
(5th) Rhode Island State 65, North Carolina 60
(7th) Duke 54, Wake Forest 52

December 1950
N.C. State 89, Tulane 75
Wake Forest 57, Rhode Island State 53
Navy 60, North Carolina 49
Colgate 84, Duke 69

N.C. State 72, Wake Forest 56
Colgate 63, Navy 59
Tulane 81, Rhode Island State 62
Duke 71, North Carolina 63

(1st) N.C. State 85, Colgate 76
(3rd) Navy 66, Wake Forest 46
(5th) Duke 74, Tulane 72
(7th) Rhode Island State 93, North Carolina 69

December 1951

N.C. State 71, Navy 51
North Carolina 49, Southern Cal 45
Cornell 58, Wake Forest 51
Columbia 66, Duke 58

N.C. State 58, North Carolina 51
Cornell 66, Columbia 64
Duke 79, Wake Forest 74
Southern Cal 80, Navy 64

(1st) N.C. State 51, Cornell 49
(3rd) North Carolina 61, Columbia 60
(5th) Southern Cal 87, Duke 69
(7th) Navy 79, Wake Forest 44

December 1952

N.C. State 87, Princeton 63
Holy Cross 85, North Carolina 73
Brigham Young 69, Duke 68
Wake Forest 65, Penn 61

N.C. State 76, Holy Cross 74
Brigham Young 84, Wake Forest 58
Penn 97, Duke 80
North Carolina 73, Princeton 59

(1st) N.C. State 75, Brigham Young 59
(3rd) Wake Forest 91, Holy Cross 69
(5th) Penn 70, North Carolina 62
(7th) Duke 74, Princeton 59

December 1953

N.C. State 72, Seton Hall 70
Navy 86, North Carolina 62
Wake Forest 72, Tulane 65
Duke 71, Oregon State 61

Navy 85, N.C. State 75
Duke 83, Wake Forest 66
Seton Hall 73, North Carolina 63
Tulane 74, Oregon State 70

(1st) Duke 98, Navy 83
(3rd) Wake Forest 86, N.C. State 79
(5th) Seton Hall 77, Tulane 68
(7th) Oregon State 65, North Carolina 53

December 1954

N.C. State 95, Cornell 61
North Carolina 67, Southern Cal 58
Minnesota 81, Wake Forest 73
Duke 92, West Virginia 79

N.C. State 47, North Carolina 44
Minnesota 79, Duke 73
Wake Forest 96, West Virginia 94
Southern Cal 77, Cornell 58

(1st) N.C. State 85, Minnesota 84
(3rd) North Carolina 65, Duke 52
(5th) Wake Forest 93, Southern Cal 85
(7th) West Virginia 79, Cornell 71

December 1955

N.C. State 59, Oregon State 54
Wake Forest 87, Minnesota 83 OT
Duke 71, Wyoming 54
North Carolina 86, Villanova 63

N.C. State 70, Wake Forest 58
North Carolina 74, Duke 64
Minnesota 64, Oregon State 60
Wyoming 69, Villanova 68

(1st) N.C. State 82, North Carolina 60
(3rd) Duke 64, Wake Forest 52
(5th) Minnesota 70, Wyoming 66
(7th) Villanova 68, Oregon State 63

December 1956

N.C. State 84, Iowa 70
Wake Forest 74, DePaul 68
Duke 73, West Virginia 67
North Carolina 97, Utah 76

Wake Forest 73, N.C. State 66
North Carolina 87, Duke 71
DePaul 73, Iowa 72 OT
Utah 83, West Virginia 66

(1st) North Carolina 63, Wake Forest 55
(3rd) N.C. State 102, Duke 80
(5th) Utah 86, DePaul 79
(7th) Iowa 79, West Virginia 76

December 1957

N.C. State 71, Northwestern 68
Wake Forest 64, Duquesne 54
North Carolina 63, St. Louis 48
Duke 69, Seton Hall 62

N.C. State 63, Wake Forest 61
North Carolina 76, Duke 62
Northwestern 80, Duquesne 70
St. Louis 77, Seton Hall 44

(1st) North Carolina 39, N.C. State 30
(3rd) Duke 79, Wake Forest 75 OT
(5th) Northwestern 66, St. Louis 53
(7th) Duquesne 68, Seton Hall 65

December 1958

N.C. State 67, Louisville 61
Cincinnati 94, Wake Forest 70
Michigan State 75, North Carolina 58
Duke 56, Yale 53

N.C. State 69, Cincinnati 60
Michigan State 82, Duke 57
North Carolina 92, Yale 65
Louisville 74, Wake Forest 64

(1st) N.C. State 70, Michigan State 61
(3rd) Duke 57, Louisville 54
(5th) North Carolina 90, Cincinnati 88
(7th) Wake Forest 85, Yale 76

December 1959

Dayton 36, N.C. State 32
Wake Forest 80, Holy Cross 71
Duke 63, Utah 52
North Carolina 72, Minnesota 65

Wake Forest 61, Dayton 50
North Carolina 75, Duke 55
Holy Cross 63, N.C. State 61
Utah 75, Minnesota 72

(1st) Wake Forest 53, North Carolina 50
(3rd) Dayton 71, Duke 63
(5th) Utah 92, Holy Cross 84
(7th) N.C. State 57, Minnesota 48

December 1960

Villanova 72, N.C. State 63
North Carolina 81, Maryland 57
Marquette 91, Wake Forest 83
Duke 86, Wyoming 59

North Carolina 87, Villanova 67
Duke 86, Marquette 73
N.C. State 75, Maryland 67
Wake Forest 87, Wyoming 66

(1st) North Carolina 76, Duke 71
(3rd) Villanova 75, Marquette 70
(5th) N.C. State 99, Wake Forest 91
(7th) Maryland 84, Wyoming 77

8
Murray Greason

Quiet man on the Wake Forest bench. The one who sat there calmly, with the patience of Job, his legs crossed, arms folded, sometimes his hands stuffed in his trouser pockets. He was Murray Greason.

For years the lanky guy next to him was Bones McKinney, combination yoyo and elevator. Bones recalled one bench scene: "It was the ACC tournament, a Thursday afternoon in Reynolds, 1956, and South Carolina led us at the half. It was still a close game. Coach wasn't much on water, I drank it all the time and had the water bucket right next to me. In those days we had a dipper and a bucket. Coach didn't get up and down much, he just sat there and grunted and groaned throughout the whole game. Not many people know that. But this time Coach asked me for some water and I filled the dipper. About that time something happened on the floor and I stood up to yell, and emptied the whole dipper of water on his head. I stammered, 'Coach, I'm sorry,' and he just said, didn't even look up, 'Hell, I didn't want it anyway.'"

Murray Greason had been a student at Wake Forest, spindly-legged 150-pounder who was a basketball forward, football halfback and baseball second baseman. He earned 12 monograms in college. He also obtained his law degree but he wanted to coach.

When he joined Jim Weaver on the new football staff in 1933, he would come to work every morning dressed in hunting clothes. People would ask why. Reply: "So Weaver won't know what day I really go hunting." The Greasons always had beagles, always. Skeeter Francis, now of the ACC office, recalled from his own Wake Forest days as sports information director: "Murray used to sit on the front steps at Gore Gym with his dogs, in the sunshine, and go to sleep."

Wake Forest was admitted to the Southern Conference in December 1936 and played in the basketball tournament three months later. Greason's Deacons won their first tournament game, beating Richmond 33-24 but lost to North Carolina in the semifinals 37-35. The following year, with the conference leading scorer in 5-foot-11

67

Murray Greason's favorite spot, on the steps of old Gore Gym with his beagles.

Capt. Jim Waller of the 1939 Deacons who played in the first NCAA tournament. Waller here poses for a two-hand set shot of his day, but his specialty was the hook.

Jim Waller (213 points in 15 games), the Deacons failed to qualify for the tournament.

Jim Waller, indeed, was a great basketball story. A native Tennessean, he came to Wake Forest, worked his way waiting on tables, became student body president and graduated from the law school. He also perfected a hook shot which was somewhat unique in the late 30s. Waller later explained: "I'd set up three feet away, with the basket to my left. I'd get the ball, fake right, get the defensive man on my hip and then roll across the lane and hook with my right hand. I could hook the other way when they caught onto that." There was no three-second lane rule, but by his senior year there had been a couple rules changed. Waller said: "The center jump rule didn't affect my style of play but the change of balls did. The old leather ball was deader, and from where I shot, near the basket, this was a help. When you laid the ball up, it would roll around the rim more, and maybe roll in, even if you weren't right on target. The new ball would bounce off quicker."

The Deacons of 1939 were one of eight participants in a major "first" for college basketball. They played in the inaugural NCAA tournament, but it didn't come easy. The Deacons went into the conference tournament 15-3, gaining the No. 1 seed. They promptly lost to Clemson 30-28, the Tigers going on to take the title. Waller scored early, then Dave Fuller and Smith Young sparked a score-tying comeback, only to be offset by Banks McFadden's final goal. On hand at Raleigh was Ned Irish of Madison Square Garden, prepared to invite the Deacons to the NIT. But, in defeat, the Wake Forest season was obviously concluded, so Coach Greason drove up US-1 to the campus, checked in the uniforms and got ready for baseball, which he also coached. On Saturday there was a call from Harold Olsen of Ohio State, whose efforts started the national tournament under the National Association of Basketball Coaches (NABC). A deficit of $2,531 that first year brought the NCAA into sponsorship. Olsen wanted to select the best team in each of eight districts, and Wake Forest was the District 3 choice. Coach Greason accepted, got the team back on the practice court Monday, took the train to Philadelphia Thursday night.

Starters for the first NCAA game were Capt. Jim Waller and Vincent Convery forwards, Boyd Owen center, Stanley Apple and Bill Sweel guards. In the Eastern Division were Wake Forest, Ohio State, Villanova and Brown; in the Western Oregon, Oklahoma, Texas and Utah State. In the title game Oregon and Ohio State met at Northwestern University, and the "Tall Firs of Oregon" prevailed.

The Deacons played Ohio State, took a 29-23 halftime advantage on Waller's hook shots. Reported the AP: "Off to a flying start with a bewildering run of one-handed trick shots, Wake Forest eventually wiltered before an opponent that grew stronger as the game progressed. With just 12 minutes to play and 3,500 fans in an uproar,

Capt. Jim Waller, star of Wake Forest, was banished from the game on fouls and his team's brilliance vanished. Waller, a left-hand trick shot artist, had the Bucks dizzy with his amazing performance. After he left, Ohio State scored seven points in a row and erased a nine-point disadvantage." Waller got 14 points. Owens and Apple 10 each. Of Waller, the Ohio State captain, James Hull, told reporters: "He had a very accurate hook shot. In fact, right before halftime, he shot one that was about 35-40 feet. That was unheard of."

Coach Greason put the brakes on North Carolina's high ranking 1946 team. It was the Southern Conference's 25th anniversary, and the Deacons might have pulled off the greatest upset of the period. In the semifinals they beat Coach Ben Carnevale's Tar Heels 31-29, though losing to Duke in the finals. Again the AP reported: "Coach Greason's Deacons devised a tight defense that kept the two Tar Heel leading scorers tied up all night. John Dillon dropped only one of his famed hook shots and Bones McKinney was able to get in for only one goal from the field. Blond Joe Hinerman was the young Deacon who tied up Dillon under the basket, and Deran Walters stuck to McKinney like a leech. The usually high scoring Tar Heels got only three goals the second half."

Everett Case came to N.C. State in 1946-47, and on Valentine's Day his first visit to Gore Gym was something for the Deacons to remember. Having beaten the Deacons at Frank Thompson Gym in Raleigh, the "Hoosier Hotshots" were big favorites to win again, but the Deacons kept the lead most of the frenzied night, fought off a Wolfpack rally, and Red O'Quinn got a fast break for the final 44-39 triumph. High scorer for the Wolfpack? A young reserve guard named Norman Sloan, 12 points.

By 1953 Coach Case had won six straight conference titles, including a semifinal win over Coach Greason in 1950. Murray Greason became the second coach to clip the Reynolds Coliseum nets in victory, conference tournament or Dixie Classic. Case had all the others. For Lib Greason it meant a big trophy for the den, or even the living room. Wake Forest beat State College in the 1953 finals 71-70, and Coach Greason kept mumbling to himself in postgame celebration: "Let's look up there again just to be sure."

Wake Forest went into the 1953 event second seed, 12-3, a half-game behind State. The Wolfpack was nationally ranked, the Deacons hadn't made the tournament for two years. It had matched State's bench vs Wake's 1-2 punch, Dickie Hemric and Jack Williams. Both had 20-plus averages. Bones McKinney was on the bench as Deacon assistant for the first time. In the Friday night show Wake edged Maryland 51-49 and State ousted West Virginia 85-80, something reporters called "the Southern Conference tournament's greatest doubleheader in history." In the finals the guys from Baptist Hollow led until the fourth quarter, Mel Thompson sparking a State rally to lead 65-60. Billy Lyes' set shots got even, Jack Williams regained the lead, Dickie Hemric stole a pass with five seconds to go to preserve it. Quite a celebration on the floor that Case built, Murray Greason in his 20th season as champion. He quipped: "I'd rather have my luck than a license to steal. Greatest thrill in my athletic career. Yes, even a bigger thrill than catching an eight-pound bass."

Twelve months later, in the new ACC, there was another tournament finals, same teams, different result. Duke and Maryland were the top seeds, Wake Forest third, State fourth. The tournament had five players who held all-time school scoring records — Hemric at Wake Forest, Gene Shue at Maryland, Buzz Wilkinson at Virginia, Al Lifson at North Carolina and Ames Wells Wells at Clemson. In the opening game Wake Forest trailed South Carolina by 12, then Hemric tied the score in the final seconds, Lefty Davis won it in overtime. In semifinals, over Maryland 64-56, but into overtime again. Wake and State again for the title. The Wolfpack went up 16, Hemric tied it, Wake got the final three shots in regulation—Lyles set with seven seconds, Davis rebound shot (blocked by Ron Shavlik), Davis rebound shot again. In overtime State won 82-80. The Deacons played three overtimes, an ACC record to this day.

In 1957 Coach Greason's Deacons had the to-be national champion Tar Heels by a point with 26 seconds remaining. They had lost to Carolina three times in the season, and this was the tournament semifinals. Wake wins, and Carolina goes nowhere. Coach Greason was an expert on the zone defense, Coach Case considering him the best. Coach McKinney recently explained what took place in those final seconds in 1957: "We had a particular zone for Lennie Rosenbluth, who could shoot, the very best of them. We had them a point with 26 seconds. We were behind when Bob Cunningham charged Jim Gilley, and Jim made the first one for us. I yelled to Jackie Murdock (guard) to get back to the 1-1-3 zone, our 'fruit salad' for this game. That stacked up people in the middle for Rosenbluth, Gilley supposed to be deep, behind Rosenbluth. If the ball goes to the board, Jim puts his butt in Rosenbluth, Ernie Wiggins is to run corner to front of Rosenbluth. Anyway, I yelled to Murdoch to get back in 1-1-3 but in the excitement as Gilley made his second shot to put us ahead, they forgot to tell Gillie. He's over in the corner guarding Joe Quigg and we're playing a zone. They get the ball to Rosenbluth, he charged Wendell Carr but he got three points out of it and they beat us and went on undefeated."

Later that month, March 1957, Murray Greason became an assistant athletic director and gave up basketball. At his announcement interview he was asked about great individual performances over his Deacon years: "Dickie Hemric's performance against Virginia in 1955 was the greatest any player of mine ever turned in. Scored 49, I believe

Wake Forest captured the last Southern Conference tournament, and celebration was in order as the Deacons ended Everett Case's stranglehold on the conference crown 1953.

it was. Greatest individual shooting I ever witnessed was in 1952 when Ernie Wiggins hit 12 straight shots from the floor against State College. You remember, he missed No. 13 in the overtime. Jack Murdock was one of the coolest players, under pressure, any coach ever had."

When the Deacons, coached by Bones McKinney, claimed the Dixie Classic in December 1959, a major win leading to Deacon conference titles in 1961 and 1962, Coach Greason was the first on the floor to celebrate with coaches and players. That was New Year's Eve.

About 9 o'clock New Year's morning, driving alone, his car jammed into the Willow Creek bridge on I-85 around Greensboro, and Murray Crossley Greason was killed.

Coach was wearing his hunting clothes.

Number one, 32 victories and unbeaten, the national champions celebrate after victory in Kansas City in 1957.

9
Frank McGuire

Frank Joseph McGuire is an astute New Yorker who had known about North Carolina a long time, and from many and varying points of view. But when he delivered the "32 and Oh," it was the ultimate.

When he accepted the position as head basketball coach at the University of North Carolina, many of his peers expressed surprise. He insisted, and to this day, that most people overlooked the fact that he and his family spent two and a half years in Chapel Hill in Navy Pre-Flight days of World War II. He said, "I had worked in the Carolina athletic program, I knew the Billy Carmichael family real well."

But he came from the streets of New York, had played at St. John's, had coached his alma mater (five years, record 106-36). Several months before he decided to bring the family back to Carolina, his St. John's team had done wonders in the NCAA East at Raleigh. It was the first year (1952) of the NCAA format which divided the nation into four regionals, the winners going to the Final Four.

Into Reynolds Coliseum four outstanding college teams converged in mid-March — Kentucky, the No. 1 ranked team in the country which it also led in scoring (83.2 points), St. John's 22-4, Penn State 20-4 and host N.C. State 23-9. In those days the NIT was played first, teams signed up for both. St. John's played in the NIT and Coach Butter Anderson of the Wolfpack scouted them. The NCAA committee passed up NIT champion LaSalle and picked St. John's and Penn State. But there was no mob scene at the Reynolds box office, even though the price was $3-$2-$1 each night. That was a few years ago, obviously.

Coach McGuire's veteran team beat the Wolfpack 60-49; Kentucky also won. The teams came back the following night, and Zeke Zawoluk got 32 points as the Redmen defeated the highly favored Kentucky Wildcats 64-57. Said Coach McGuire: "You must remember, Kentucky beat us 41 points (81-40) during the season in Lexington. It was one of the finest basketball games (in Raleigh) from where I happened to sit on the bench with the winning team." From

Raleigh, the East winners, St. John's, flew directly to Seattle for the finals that began the following Wednesday. They beat Illinois 61-59, then fell to Kansas 80-63. Ironically, a young reserve guard for Kansas was named Dean Smith.

By mid-summer McGuire, who had accolades as national coach of the year, was attending a coaching clinic in the New York Catskills, along with Ben Carnevale, long-time friend who had coached Carolina in 1945-46. Carnevale related this story recently: "Frank and I were very close, and we were together at Kutchers. I got a call from Chuck Erickson (UNC athletic director), who was at an NCAA golf tournament at Northwestern, and he was looking for a coach since Tom Scott had resigned. Frank had just taken St. John's to the finals and he was considering making a change although he loved New York, and I said, 'Frank, would you be interested in Carolina?' He said he'd like to talk with them. I think Chuck felt that I might be interested in returning, but I couldn't leave Navy at the time, too many benefits built up. I did say this, Carolina was the only other coaching job I'd ever take, although I would go into an administrative job."

McGuire was at the North Carolina Coaching Clinic in Greensboro in late July, spoke at the Rotary Club where a couple influential alumni became interested. Ed Hudgins Sr. called Erickson. Joe Murnick of Raleigh made a phone call to McGuire. McGuire recalled, "For my son Frankie, who was palsy, North Carolina was the ideal place, near the ocean, a pool in the back yard, living in Chapel Hill would be better for him than New York. It was just what I had to do at the time." In August he attended the press–coaches' golf tournament at Findley Golf Club for interviews.

Coach McGuire won 17 games the first season, a job well done, but then came two mediocre ones, a game over .500 and a game under .500. It became 18-5 in 1956.

How did he get the 1957 national champions?

McGuire recently: "They always ask me, how did you get the fellows to go to North Carolina? I mean the fellows from New York City. I said, well, I use the subway, Eastern Airlines. I got a nice letter from the president of Eastern Airlines thanking me. When we played at State and we'd lose, I could leave the team with Buck Freeman, a great assistant coach, a head coach actually, and I would take the train back with the officials, Lou Eisenstein, Arnold Heft, Dr. Phil Fox, and go back to New York. I did that many times. All the high school coaches would work with me, and Harry Gotkin, my closest friend, he's 82-83 now, he could pick up a player a year ahead of any else. He knew everybody.

"Lennie Rosenbluth didn't come in right away; he went to a prep school for a year. It was tough getting into Carolina. Then Buck (Freeman) had them one year as a freshman, so by the time they came to me, they were glad to get away from Buck. And by the time they came to me, and then as seniors, that was a well-knit ball club."

Rosenbluth scored 627 points as a freshman, a record at Carolina for one season, varsity or otherwise. Then came the freshman class of 1954-55, and the other four starters of the champions — Pete Brennan, Joe Quigg, Tommy Kearns and Bob Cunningham.

Coach McGuire said of 1957's beginning: "Like every other season at the start, never did I suspect what was going to happen. They were good individually, real good, but there wasn't a Chamberlain or a Russell. I mean, they couldn't win on their own, they needed to help each other. When Tommy Kearns decided to take the ball in, he could do it, but it took more than that."

They beat Furman at home (Woollen Gym), then Clemson at Charlotte and George Washington at Norfolk. South Carolina provided a scare in Columbia, the old Snake Pit, and that took points by Kearns and Tony Radovich in overtime. After Maryland, they went to Madison Square Garden and beat NYU, to the Boston Gardens to take Dartmouth and Holy Cross. The team was well travelled by Dixie Classic time, where it beat Utah, Duke and Wake Forest. It was the first of a great series with the Deacons, four times before the close (18 points total spread).

In game No. 17 at College Park, Coach McGuire had given up: "I really had, I had given up. We were losing by four with about 30 seconds, and I could see no way. New York kids are scrappy, and I was afraid what might happen at the end, so I called timeout. I told them, don't lose your composure, we're losing but we might play them again in the conference tournament. Just don't have anything go wrong, with the players, the fans, anybody. Well, we stole the ball twice and won it in overtime." It was two overtimes, in fact, with Rosenbluth fouling out the first. McGuire added: "After seeing this coming, I wasn't afraid of anything myself from then on. These guys were ice. Like Rosenbluth telling me after that Maryland game, 'Coach, we only have 15 more to go.'"

The ACC tournament in Reynolds Coliseum brought three more, plus another major score. Wake Forest for the fourth time in the season, semifinals before 12,400 yelling people. Wake Forest from 11 down, Jim Gilley at the foul line, two free throws, both good, Deacons up 59-58 with 57 seconds remaining. Get the ball to Rosey, obviously. They did, Rosey shot from the foul line, good, fouled, three-pointer. Carolina won 61-59. South Carolina provided a walk through the finals.

Tuesday night after the tournament, very little time to sit around and rest, NCAA opening round in Madison Square Garden, playing Yale. It was tied at halftime, Johnny Lee of the Bulldogs had a bundle, also three fouls. At that time the visiting press sat at tables adjacent to the teams, and the North Carolina reporters were next to the Tar Heel bench. McGuire later: "I called timeout in the second half early, and I looked around and there are no players in the huddle. You guys have them over at the press table telling them Lee has three fouls, get him to foul out of there. What coaches." Carolina won 90-74, and Johnny Lee did foul out after 25 points. Then wins over Canisius and Syracuse in the Palestra, which was the first live TV of college basketball in the state of North Carolina. Three stations did it.

It was on to Kansas City, unbeaten and ranked No. 1 with Kansas, which had lost early in the season, No. 2, and Michigan State as Big Ten winners were the opening opponents for the Tar Heels. Coach McGuire was more confident: "All along, I said that if we didn't lose a game in the regular season, we would drop one in the conference tournament, and I meant that. But when we won at Duke, and we hadn't won there in ages, and when we beat Wake Forest in the final seconds at the tournament, well, I figured we'd be in Kansas City."

N.C. State Assistant Coach Vic Bubas had said of Rosenbluth: "The best shooter the Big Four has seen in my day." Quite a compliment, and Rosey was usually double-teamed (getting 35.2 percent of the team's 75 points). Michigan State was ready. Johnny Green, jumping jack sophomore who had joined the Big Ten champions at midseason, led scoring and rebounding as Michigan State held halftime margin. Regulation ended deadlocked. In first overtime the Spartans were ahead 64-62 with Green on the free throw line, 32 seconds. He missed, Carolina rebounded, Pete Brennan hit back of the foul circle. Second overtime, Tar Heels played for last shot, got it, missed. Third overtime, three regulars fouled out (Brennan, Quigg, Cunningham), Rosey hit outside, Kearns two FTs, Bob Young rebounded, Roy Searcy got last two rebounds, 74-70. McGuire, at confession: "We were just pure lucky. Nine times out of 10 we would have lost one like that."

Twenty-four hours later, Saturday night, it was Wilt Chamberlain and Kansas, team and 10,000 fans. Some 300 Tar Heel followers were joined by Gov. Luther Hodges and two cheerleaders. In the hotel that afternoon, pregame meeting, Coach McGuire reviewed the plan: "We didn't play Kansas, we played Chamberlain. In talks I never mentioned Kansas, it was Chamberlain, always Chamberlain. I had been sitting in the hotel lobby all day listening to those Kansas people, 20 points, 18. I was getting a little hot and when I went up for our meeting, I said, 'I don't think we should show up.' I said to Tommy, 'Are you afraid to play?' He answered, 'No, coach.' He could see I was mad. So I said, 'Okay, you jump against Chamberlain.' That actually happened. When we talked just before the game, we went over our scouting report, set up the triangle, every time Chamberlain got the ball, form a triangle around him, just so. When the game was ready, Kearns went right out to the center. I never told him again, not after the afternoon meeting, never said one more word, but Tommy remembered. Then he put the act on, like bending over and jumped. I couldn't believe it." For those who really don't know, Kearns was 5'-11", Wilt Chamberlain 7'-2".

Something else was on the coach's mind at tipoff. McGuire: "They were confident, our fellows. The night before, Michigan State had us beaten if Green makes the foul shot. We were lucky. Kansas had beaten my St. John's team five years before, that was in my mind, here we go again, we get to the finals, and there's Kansas. Who's second? Who ever remembers second?"

The Tar Heels' triangle contained Wilt, he got only 13 shots all night, and the game went 55 minutes, another three overtimes. Down quickly 19-7 Kansas changed its own defense to man-for-man, and when Quigg went outside, Wilt followed. It kept the middle open. Kansas was ahead 44-41 with 1:15 left when Rosenbluth committed his fifth personal foul, in regulation, mind you. Again Danny Lotz and Bob Young came off the bench. First overtime: Wilt tied the score, then batted aside Kearns' attempted jumper at the buzzer. Second overtime: no scoring, Kansas missing final shot. Third overtime: Kansas led 53-52 as Wilt blocked shots by Kerns and Quigg in the final 10 seconds, But Quigg was fouled. At the free throw line with six seconds, he tied the score, then put Carolina ahead 54-53. Kansas' pass was in to Chamberlain but Quigg knocked the ball aside, Kearns scooped it up ... and tossed it as high as he could. When it came down, the game was over. Coach McGuire remembered his own insides: "I could see it, the last five seconds, I could just visualize. They would throw the ball way up over the basket, and Chamberlain was there, and he'd dunk it."

Carolina had won the national championship, the first in the ACC. They had won it with the "Flaming Five," as the regulars became, in foul trouble in both games, and the bench, which wasn't there, came in and saved it. Lotz, Young and Searcy. Late that night, or early in the a.m. hours by then, the team met in Coach McGuire's suite 1012. Everybody said something, even each member of the press. Governor Hodges admitted why he couldn't sit on the team bench the second half: "I heard one coach yelling something and then the other coach yelling something, and I wanted so badly to yell a few things myself. I didn't think it would be proper for me to be doing that from the bench so I just went back to my seat upstairs."

The coach had seen many things change in the ACC. He went over several of them over breakfast during the ACC spring meeting recently: "When I got to Carolina, they told me the conference played home-and-home with local entertainment. I didn't know what local entertainment was. We would drive three cars to Charlottesville, I drove one, Buck one, the team manager one, and the smokers would crowd in that third car first. Nobody wanted to ride with the coaches. When we got there, I asked where we were sleeping and they took me upstairs (old Alumni Gym), on that running balcony track, showed us the

Emotions on the Tar Heel bench, Coach Frank McGuire excited and disappointed. Lee Shaffer, All-American, and assistant Coach Kenny Rosemond share the moments in 1960.

cots. I got out of there, went to the Hotel Charlottesville and Chuck (Erickson, AD) almost fainted when he saw the bill. Next trip was to Maryland, and around Washington, two cars went this way, the manager another way and barely got to the arena. Jim Tatum was football coach, he was a big man. After we won the NCAA championship, he came to my office there in Woollen and said, 'You know, Mac, I've been against you so much, this basketball instead of football, and now I want to join you. You know what, I broke a chair the other night watching you in Kansas City.' Jim and I went all over together, speaking to alumni groups, and recruiting. I got six linemen in Pennsylvania for him that year. Everett Case and I were real close. He never had a contract at State until I got one. Frankie and I visited him one Sunday afternoon, and he said let him know when I got a contract. I did, and he got one, too."

Late in the summer of 1961, McGuire took the NBA coaching job with the Philadelphia Warriors, and his star was Wilt Chamberlain. But the next year the Warriors moved to San Francisco, and McGuire wanted to remain in the East. He returned to college ball at South Carolina, where he retired in 1980, and now serves as college consultant for Madison Square Garden. His record at three colleges for 30 years: 550 wins, 235 losses. One of five coaches who have taken three different schools to the NCAA playoffs. One of five with two different schools in the Final Four.

As for the 1957 national champions, coming with that "32 and Oh," Coach McGuire looked back: "It was a shot in the arm for the ACC and the state of North Carolina . . . Everett (Case) got it started but when you win a national championship, it was the thing that did it."

10
Terrible Times

No state probably ever experienced more horrendous nightmares in its college athletic program than North Carolina did in 1961, in basketball, too.

A long string of circumstances, some interwoven but some simply carrying their own weight in disorder, began in January and never seemed to leave the sports page. When it did, it made the front pages where the hard news is supposed to be. One sports editor wanted to hire a legal reporter for his staff.

It had absolutely no connection with the major calamities of the year, but the North Carolina freshman basketball team could not use Billy Galantai because the conference declared him ineligible for making false statements on his first eligibility papers.

Then in January the NCAA announced one-year's probation for the University of North Carolina, the penalty for excessive entertainment expenses in recruiting basketball players during the Dixie Classic in Raleigh. Chancellor William B. Aycock said the penalty, a year ineligible for the NCAA playoffs, was "for errors in judgment rather than for a deliberate violation of rules."

Two weeks later, in early February, Chancellor Aycock asked for permission not to play in the conference basketball tournament "in the interest of fair play to the other teams in the conference." It was reluctantly granted. Twice before, a team on probation had continued tournament participation.

In mid-February Duke beat Carolina 81-77 at Duke Indoor Stadium, and in the final eight seconds a free-for-all brought both teams to the floor. ACC Commissioner Jim Weaver suspended Art Heyman of Duke, Larry Brown and Don Walsh of Carolina for the remainder of the regular season. With Carolina not playing in the tournament, Heyman's suspension was lifted so he could play the event.

Coach Frank McGuire of the Tar Heels recalled recently: "That was a game with a lot of tension. You know how it is at Duke, the students so close to the floor. With about 50 seconds that game, I called

83

timeout. I told the team, you come right back to the bench the moment the game is over, no matter what happens. They let the crowd on the floor and you have to walk through them to get to the dressing room. I didn't know there was going to be a fight. Larry Brown and Art Heyman, two Jewish guys from New York fighting. That can be very dangerous. And it was almost funny. I kept them on the bench after the game, waited until the crowd got off, then we all walked down together. It was different. Where did you ever see a team stay on the bench after the game? Never, but we had to. I think that's discipline, too."

Then came the bombshell. Nobody believed that the point-shaving scandals, which hit Madison Square Garden in 1951 and returned in another generation of collegians, 1961, would spread beyond the metropolitan centers, mainly New York. That's where "the action" normally took place, but the backroads of the nation were more cosmopolitan in the decade. It was not beyond the realm of operation to shave points in Raleigh and Chapel Hill as well as Madison Square Garden.

From March 21, when Chancellor Aycock announced representatives from the New York district attorney's office were in Chapel Hill, it was almost a daily story following the ever-growing scandals in college basketball. Some fixers were arrested and indicted, many players were. Five state players, two at Chapel Hill and three at Raleigh, were involved in the surprising, astounding developments in the state of North Carolina. They brought SBI investigation, which had been originated by Wolfpack Coach Everett Case who thought something was just wrong in the way several games took place. They brought state legislation to increase the penalty for bribery or attempted bribery, but the bill's originator, Rep. Stedman Hines (D-Guilford), made this early statement: "It is difficult to legislate morals."

And then the administrators of the Consolidated University of North Carolina took action which would shock every citizen of the state, and especially the basketball fans who felt they had grown to a voting majority. In the aftermath of all the athletic problems, the trustees had to make a decision between (A) discontinuance altogether or suspension for a fixed time period of the basketball program, or (B) curtailment of the program through scholarship and schedule limitations.

They chose the latter, which cancelled the ever-popular Dixie Classic, 12 years at Reynolds Coliseum and the stage on which teams from Tobacco Road earned national reputations. Students at N.C. State marched in protests, necessitating state highway patrol and city police units to keep order. Newspaper editorials supported the move. Today, in hindsight, the Dixie Classic's death might have been too big a price to pay, although, like the Big Four Tournament of the 70s, it would have fallen sooner or later since it was played in Reynolds Coliseum, home of the Wolfpack.

84

The scandals were scandalous, in every detail. They began on March 21 when Chancellor Aycock reported two men from the New York DA's office were on campus to investigate charges of game-fixing. On March 29 Lou Brown, a member of the Tar Heel squad, was accused of being a contact man for New York gamblers, who had been indicted, and Brown withdrew from the university; Aycock added: "under other than honorable conditions." On May 5, Doug Moe was "indefinitely suspended" from the university for failing to report bribe offers, although he never participated. By mid-May three N.C. State players were arrested: Stan Niewierowski, Anton Muehlbauer and Terry Litchfield. All had played in the summer leagues in New York's Catskills, along with Lou Barshak, a New York student at Los Angeles State College, the man who arranged the fixes with the Wolfpack players, supposedly $1,250 per game. The games involved in point-shaving were George Washington, Georgia Tech, Duke and North Carolina. The Wolfpack won the first two. Litchfield had to return $250 when one game didn't turn out to the fixers' satisfaction. Niewierowski and Muehlbauer got $250 bonuses "for throwing" the Duke game, the SBI charged. The SBI, working with the New York district attorney, had Niewierowski arrested in New York and held for extradition.

In New York the scandal surpassed the 1951 episode when 33 players from seven colleges were involved. By May 25 the new matter touched 28 players from 17 schools, covering 39 games. When Ray Paprocky, the NYU star, confessed to taking $2,300 to shave points in four games, he included the Wake Forest game. The DA's office requested a hearing with Billy Packer of the Deacons, and Packer voluntarily went to New York, met with DA officials but was never called before the Grand Jury. He was never indicted.

In North Carolina stiffer penalties for attempting to fix athletic contests went to the floor of the General Assembly, which passed the measure increasing penalties for bribery or attempted bribery to one to 10 years in prison, a fine of from $3,000 to $10,000, or both. North Carolina district solicitor Lester Chambers spent much time in New York working with the DA's office. Gov. Terry Sanford pledged a probe of far-reaching scandal in the state, and said: "We are going to consider every game. If gambling lines lead to other sports, we will follow those lines."

Then on Monday, May 21, Governor Sanford presided at the meeting of the university board of trustees at the College Union on the State College campus in Raleigh. He convened the session at 11:08 a.m.; there were some routine subjects as always. President William Friday read the seven pages of his report marked "Intercollegiate Athletics," which took 16 minutes. Chancellor William Aycock of Chapel Hill and Chancellor John Caldwell of Raleigh made brief statements, about two minutes each. Then there was 40 minutes discussion, and one hour 12 minutes after introduction of the subject, the trustees approved what the chancellors and President Friday recommended.

President Friday's report, in full and in detail, was as follows:

"I come now to the subject of recent prominence, namely basketball. These events have caused us serious embarrassment. They have administered a new shock in a part of college life where we have come dangerously close to being shock-proof, but we determined to take action that would be clear in its purpose and specific in its application, and we have done so.

"There has been a gratifying willingness on the part of all concerned to assume a share of the blame and responsibility for what has happened. It is clear, however, where the responsibility for action rests. Accordingly, in company with Chancellors Aycock and Caldwell, I shall present to you our decisions in this matter.

"At the outset, I wish to recall certain actions which were taken earlier by the board of trustees with regard to athletic programs.

"In 1954, on the recommendation of President Gordon Gray, the board of trustees authorized placing the administration of intercollegiate athletics into the hands of the chancellors affected, subject to the authority of the president. In February of 1957, I reaffirmed the stand taken by President Gray, and the board approved this action.

"I wish to acknowledge that the clear delegation of authority to the chancellors in the matter of athletics, coupled with careful efforts on their part, has brought significant improvement in the admininistration of athletics on the campuses. I would note especially improvements steadily and judiciously instituted in overall arrangements by Chancellor Aycock. From the beginning of his office, he has worked diligently and forthrightly to bring all elements pertaining to the total athletic program under fair, efficient and constructive management.

"Also Chancellor Caldwell, who came to us more recently, upon learning on May 12 of the involvement of the State College basketball players, moved unhesitatingly and decisively and left no doubt as to his capacity and readiness to deal with the problem.

"In May 1954 North Carolina State College was placed on probation by the National Collegiate Athletic Association and denied the privilege of participation in the NCAA basketball championship play for one year for violating regulations concerning the recruitment of basketball players.

"In November 1956 State College was again the object of punitive measures imposed by the NCAA for irregularities connected with the recruitment of a prospective player by the name of Jack Moreland. State College was placed on probationary status for a period of four years.

"In January 1961 the NCAA placed the University at Chapel Hill on probation for one year in basketball for violating regulations governing the entertaiment of prospective student-athletes.

"On March 29, after receiving evidence of the participation of Louis Brown in bribery, Chancellor Aycock permitted Brown to withdraw from the university under conditions 'other than honorable.'

"On May 3 Chancellor Aycock suspended Douglas Moe for 'initial misstatement and subsequent concealment' of relevant facts.

"On May 12 Chancellor Caldwell was informed that members of the State College basketball team had participated in the briberies. Anton Muehlbauer and Stan Niewierowski were not, on that date, enrolled in State College, and Chancellor Caldwell has forbidden them to re-enroll. Terry Litchfield, who was enrolled during the spring term, was promptly dismissed by Chancellor Caldwell, and he will not be permitted to re-enroll.

"In addition, the Atlantic Coast Conference has found it necessary on three occasions within the last five years to impose a fine or disciplinary measures affecting one of our teams.

"This, then, is a summary of recent actions and involvements of our institutions under NCAA and ACC regulations governing intercollegiate basketball. In the discharge of duties pertaining to their respective institutions, and in meeting my own responsibility, Chancellor Aycock, Chancellor Caldwell and I have conferred frequently in the last few days. We have been deeply conscious of the implications of these events for the character and standing of the university as well as for the unfortunate students. In our resolve to counter scandal with saving remedies, we have been reassured by expressions of genuine concern and eager support from faculty members, students, alumni, members of the press and others who hold dear the traditions of this university, and hold its integrity most dear.

"As we consider the problem before us, it became clear that we must choose one of two general courses of action:

"(A) We could discontinue altogether or suspend for a fixed period of time participation by our institutions in intercollegiate competition in basketball.

"(B) We could move forthright to eliminate or correct conditions that have discredited the sport, in order that we might continue a program of intercollegiate competition in basketball.

"The chancellors and I have decided to follow the second alternative for the present. Our aim is to save athletics by de-emphasizing certain practices and removing certain influences which have been detrimental to college sports and taken away from them the very qualities which make them valuable as a part of education. Our position is a positive one. We aim to restore sports to sportsmanship. We aim to conserve for our students their rightful privilege of taking part in wholesome athletic competition and protect them, as the university must, from exploitation.

"I, therefore, report the following for your information:

"(1) One of the students who has admitted his own involvement has stated that he was first approached last summer while working on a summer job and playing basketball in the Catskill Mountains. We have decided, and the directors of athletics under the directing of their chancellors will advise every basketball player at each of our institutions, that none is to engage in any organized competition of any kind during the summr months. The penalty for doing so will be loss of eligibility for the following season.

"(2) We have examined the program of athletic grants-in-aid and considered whether to continue awarding them in basketball. We believe that the policies and administration of this program are in a sound state, and merely to discontinue the grants in this sport would be a backward step. We do not wish to return to the condition of former years when the control of financial assistance to athletics was frequently out of hand and sometimes demoralizing.

"(3) Our basketball teams of recent years have been formed of a disproportionate number of students from regions of the country distant from our state and from our conference. While this, per se, may have nothing to do with the predicament with which we found ourselves at this time, it is nevertheless confirming evidence that we have recruited these players with a view primarily to their skill as performers and without regard for the desirability of fielding teams which are more representative of the normal composition of our student bodies. The necessity for being quite clear and specific on this point has caused us to decide that, effective with the freshman class of 1962, not more than two athletic grants-in-aid will be awarded in basketball in any given year at each institution to students from states outside the Atlantic Coast Conference area. The same principle will be applied in recruiting for football.

"(4) We have considered the extent of participation by our basketball teams in holiday tournaments and intersectional competition. We have decided that for State College and the University in Chapel Hill, beginning with the season of 1961-62, intercollegiate competition in basketball will be limited to: (a) the 14 games required by conference rules; (b) the ACC tournament; (c) the National Collegiate basketball championship; (d) not more than two additional games this season and every season thereafter with non-conference teams in other than Atlantic Coast Conference or NCAA championship tournament play. Among other things, this means the immediate discontinuance of the Dixie Classic.

"Holiday tournaments, of which the Dixie Classic is a prominent example conducted at a time when college is not in session, exemplify the exploitation for public entertainment or for budgetary and commercial purposes of a sports program which properly exists as an adjunct to college education. These tournaments subject the students, the coaches and the colleges to unnecessary demands and unwise distractions.

"The chancellors are now in the process of rearranging the basketball schedules to accord with this policy.

"In the light of the foregoing, it is appropriate to say something about the status of coaches in their appointive positions in the university. Privileges of tenure, according to clearly formulated policies which have been approved by the board of trustees and in keeping with established usages, are accorded to university personnel, including athletic coaches who are so entitled by the performance of academic duties and the attainment of faculty rank. Other personnel, including the president and chancellors and other administrative officers, are not accorded tenure status by virtue of these appointments.

"Within this context I feel that it is important to reiterate that all of our athletic coaches are expressly assured that their appointments and their continuation in their appointments are not conditioned upon the obligation merely to win games or to achieve national standing for our teams. The coaches, of course, enjoy the unquestioned security of their contracts, which are administered in conformity with the procedures for other university appointments which are made on a contract basis.

"In conclusion, I wish to say that we will in these and other particulars continue to build on improvements already under way at the hands of the chancellors. The objective of maintaining athletics at their optimum value for education has engaged the best efforts of many educators in America. By the nature of its mission and its place in society, the university cannot do less than face up to persistent and difficult problems with determination and enlightened effort. To that end we shall strive to keep an intercollegiate basketball program worthy of the aims and purposes and an example of the university."

That was quite a policy statement. Two veteran coaches read it closely. Major impact was the cancellation of the Dixie Classic which had built the reputation as the nation's No. 1 holiday event in the sport of basketball. It had drawn 713,800 spectators in its dozen years, about 25 percent of N.C. State's total attendance which led the nation annually in the 50s. Its demise robbed the city of Raleigh and the fans of the whole state.

There were immediate reports of either Wake Forest or Duke attempting to continue the tournament, without N.C. State and Carolina, of course. Both expressed interest in possibly playing but not hosting. Charlotte and Greensboro were openly suggested as sites, and Illinois, one of the 1962 teams already committed, contacted both Wake Forest and Duke about possible continuance in a two-day, four-team affair. It did not materialize. Asked if he thought the action meant the Dixie Classic was dead forever, Chancellor Caldwell of State replied he had "given no thought whatsoever" to ever reviving it. As for Chancellor Aycock at Carolina, he said: "As long as I am chancellor at Carolina, I foresee no Carolina participation in the Dixie Classic."

It meant immediate reduction of the 1961-62 schedule. State dropped LaSalle, UCLA, Southern Cal, Michigan, Villanova and George Washington, and its first reaction was to withdraw from the North-South doubleheaders in Charlotte (with North Carolina, South Carolina and Clemson). It later retracted that decision. Its two "outside" games were Tennessee at home and West Virginia in Greensboro. Athletic director Roy Clogston notified Duke and Wake Forest of the new gap in their schedule, no Dixie Classic three games. Carolina withdrew from the Kentucky Invitational, cancelled games with UCLA, Southern Cal and LSU. The two Pacific Coast teams had contracted to come East in 1962-63, playing Carolina and State in doubleheaders in Greensboro and Charlotte. The Tar Heels retained two "outside" games, Notre Dame in Charlotte and Indiana in Greensboro. Virginia had already moved its "home" conference game with Carolina to Greensboro.

The schedule restrictions were gradually lifted, totally removed by May 1964 when permission was granted for the two schools to conduct a four-team Christmas event. They invited Utah and West Virginia for December 30-31, 1965, but the public did not react favorably. N.C. State then organized the Triangle Classic in 1966 with three outside teams, later attempted doubleheaders with Duke and two outside teams. Any ghost of the Dixie Classic was doomed to failure.

Dutch Muehlbauer went to work in Greensboro on Wednesday, May 10. He wanted to make some money to pay his expenses for summer school at State College, so that he could return to the basketball team for his senior year. His job included basketball classes at the Greensboro YMCA, teaching young boys. He did not show up Friday morning, he never started his Y classes for boys. The SBI picked him up Friday and took him to Raleigh.

It was Mother's Day (May 14) in Brooklyn, but no happy occasion in the Bedford Avenue apartment of Stanley Niewierowski Sr. Stan Jr. was captain of the 1961 Wolfpack. The elder Niewierowski told a reporter how the New York DA's office picked up his son Wednesday, and he hadn't been home since, and the parents were not allowed to see him. He sobbed, "Yesterday was Mother's Day, but Mrs. Niewierowski wept and wept and wept. She cried her eyes out. I am a heartbroken father, I am a sick man. But I can't see him. They won't even tell me where he is, they just say in protective custody. If I had only known something was wrong."

The State and Carolina coaches had made every effort to warn

90

their players of the pitfalls of the racket. Coach Case said at the time: "Every year we have had the SBI and city detective Bob Goodwin come out and talk to the squad about the consequences of accepting bribes and about how the gamblers try to approach the players. We did not have a session prior to the Georgia Tech game, but the next day I got them out here." He had been suspicious. He called for the law. At Chapel Hill Coach Frank McGuire, who had coached in New York City at the time of the 1951 scandals, had a scrapbook which he made his players study. He told me: "You remember, we discussed the scrapbook of the '51 scandals in 1958 and it was then that we planned to do some official action through the conference. However, with all these precautions, we were not successful in combating these small-time fixers."

Saturday midnight, on that weekend that rattled the whole state, Everett Case took my phone call and wanted to talk about what had happened, saying that he had reported to SBI Director Walter Anderson early in the season: "Maybe this was the same organization that they had already caught in New York, maybe with two different outlets; I just don't know. The George Washington game was a token affair, just an easy assignment to edge them on. But the Georgia Tech game was a real one. We were listed on the books to win by six points, but the fix was so that we would win by less than six. The score hit six on the nose. The Duke game was a dump all the way, and Carolina was supposed to be a shave deal but I don't know what happened in that one. It seems there were a couple of phone calls involved there."

The downcast coach continued with some very pertinent comments, for which he was crucified in the New York press: "Have we created a Frankenstein? The recruiting is too vicious, the rivalry is too vicious, we're so close together in this state and everybody wants to win. I appreciate that, of course. I am now convinced that the trend must be to play our basketball with North Carolina boys. I think it is true that this sport is the weakest in our state but it has improved. Nothing to compare with football or baseball or golf or track, of course. I have thought for some time, we have to change our mode of thinking. Maybe the sense of values of New York boys is all screwed up. I don't know, but the North Carolina boys would certainly be loyal. I'll admit that maybe our boys cannot do some of the important little things on the basketball floor. I also imagine we would not hold our ratings against outside competition, but maybe we've been too much in the national spotlight. I'd take my chances. I'd welcome the chance to coach it."

Coach Case was burned for that statement; the New York press murdered him. It was the worst weekend of his life, and I think it speeded his death. He was never the same.

Meanwhile, the ACC spring meeting at Sedgefield (May 1961)

brought several reactions to what had been transpiring off the court, rather than in the court. North Carolina made a proposal that the team leading the regular season standings be declared the official conference basketball champion. Withdrawn, no support. The financial report showed that the 1960 tournament had grossed $93,710, the 1961 event without North Carolina dropped to $76,997. The ACC basketball committee sought approval to allow a second ACC team in the NCAA playoffs should the NCAA rules change to invite one as an "at large" entry. No action. The ACC freshman basketball schedule was limited to 16 games, all of which had to be played on campus. Smaller cities were bidding for games, like Siler City which had a packed house the year before—and saw Carolina's Dieter Krause deck Duke's Art Heyman to conclude a good pushing session. But there was one positive note about 1961. The ACC bylaws, as had the old Southern Conference, never actually stated that the basketball tournament winner was the conference champion, just the NCAA representative from the league. It was altered to add "and the winner shall be the conference champion."

Frank McGuire in August left Chapel Hill to take the position as head coach of the Philadelphia Warriors in the NBA, and Dean Smith was elevated to head coach of the Tar Heels.

11
Bones McKinney

Horace Albert McKinney has touched every base.

Every basketball fan in the state of North Carolina knows Bones McKinney. He's been down Tobacco Road so many times so many years, wearing so many hats, he's got to be the plantation owner, at least.

He's remembered from a Durham High School team that won 69 straight . . . to an N.C. State sophomore who made all-Southern . . . to Fort Bragg enlistment, and playing service ball . . . to Carolina's 1946 White Phantoms which almost won a national championship. . . to the first NBA all-pro selection, with long-time friend Red Auerbach . . . to the Southern Baptist Seminary and coach at Wake Forest College . . . to the Carolina Cougars' first coach in the ABA, for the most money he ever got in his life . . . to ACC television, where every fan got to see him . . . to after-dinner talks, at which he still comes without peer.

And in April 1983 he helped out an old friend, Neill McGeachy, in running an ACC all-star series, which totally surprised him. Bones McKinney should know better, being surprised, that the basketball fan in the state of North Carolina is anything else.

Recently McKinney told of his latest exploits: "We had these three games with the N.C. State seniors, just back from Albuquerque and other players in the ACC, plus a couple pros who got home early. Ralph Sampson didn't play, but he was on the bench with me every night, flew back and forth so he could go to class at Virginia. He said he was my assistant, I told him that's one thing we didn't need, any more coaching. We sold out the Winston-Salem Coliseum, the Fayetteville Coliseum and Catawba College in Salisbury. I got to the Winston building about 5:30, and they were lined up outside to buy tickets. They hadn't opened, the parking lot was full. They put up end zone seats. When I went out to start the game, it was not only packed but they were standing four and five deep in the aisles. They turned people away, somebody said a thousand. Some people turned tickets back in, they had no place to stand. I was there when Ohio State, Havlicek and Lucas came in, and we didn't have that kind of crowd. Must have had 9,000 in there, and you can't seat but 8,200. It was the same in Fayetteville and Salisbury.

"These basketball fans we have. Thing that got me, in addition to the big crowd, they tore up two tables in the autograph session at Winston-Salem afterwards. Two strong tables, trying to get to those players. They didn't get out of there until 11:30 signing autographs, game was over a little after 9. I mean, grown people. I didn't know State had so many fans. People nowhere else in the world could have done that. An exhibition game, mind you."

There were scores like 101-99, 120-116 and 119-116, the latest surprise for many who, by now, should never be surprised. It was the latest chapter in the Saga of Bones McKinney, a story herein which will let Bones tell the events as he did one afternoon just before yet another after-dinner talk.

Bones will talk, and a few facts will be interspersed from time to time to establish continuity.

"When I was on that Durham High team, with Paul Sykes coaching, I had stayed out of school two years so that put me two years older than the others. We had Bob Gantt about 6'-4", but he played 6'-6" because of his size. I was 6'-6" then, but didn't weigh much, but I was still 6'6". Gordon Carver played one of the forwards, and we had a sub for him who was 6'-6". The Loftis brothers, as good a backcourt as you could find in those days. We lost our first game to Wake Forest Freshmen in our gym, which was on an auditorium stage, and then we won 69 straight. You just drew back the curtain on the stage and that was it. We beat Wake freshmen twice every year, Duke freshmen twice, Carolina freshmen twice. We never played State freshmen."

The team won the South Atlantic Classic at Washington & Lee, the Duke-Durham Tournament of Champions, then the Eastern States at Glen Falls, New York. The young stars graduated with the streak still going, the new bunch added four wins to it. Four of those schoolboys went to Duke, Bones to State.

"I have never really been able to explain how I went to State College, the others to Duke. Duke didn't really ever recruit me, and Bob Warren was coming up at State where Doc Sermon was retiring, and he just sold me on State. He took me to the textile school and introduced me to the dean, and Duke didn't hustle me that much."

McKinney as a sophomore made all-Southern in 1942, scoring 30 points in the final season game with South Carolina, and the other Durham boys led Duke to the Conference championship. World War II took Bones to Fort Bragg.

"We played a lot of basketball games, won the Southeastern AAU couple times. We had Hugh Hampton and Cedric Loftis, and back then in college if you played 22 games, somebody thought your heart would get large. We played 45 games a season."

Then it was to Carolina after the war.

"I got in touch with Ben Carnevale when I was getting out of the Army. Bob Warren was not coming back to State, going to Washington & Lee when he was discharged. I was going to W&L with him but they had a coach coming back, or something, and it didn't work out. That's when I got in touch with Carnevale. I had coached against him in the service, we had played 2-3 games. Another confession. Carolina was probably my number one choice when I got out of high school, but I went to spring practice over there one day. One man didn't turn me on. I'm the type of guy, you pat me on the back and I'll go to the ceiling for you. But this guy chewed me out, told me I was being silly about not making my decision right then."

The 1946 Carolina team had talent, was selected to the NCAA where it reached the championship game with Oklahoma A&M (now State). There it lost 53-50. What happened?

"I thought that was a real good team until I looked at some game film couple years ago. I couldn't realize how bad we were, but we were a pretty good team in those days. In Jim Jordan, a real good outside shooter. Jim White a good passer. Jim Paxton a fine backboard man. John Dillon who could shoot the eyes out, as good a hook as I've ever seen. We were a good club, and we could have beaten Oklahoma A&M if I had played decent. I guarded Bob Kurland, you know, seven-footer, and I was going to give him his 22, 23 points. But I didn't get but five, and he couldn't come out there and get me. I couldn't make one. We could have beaten them to death. If we had ever gotten ahead, knowing what we know now, we would have just stood out there and held the ball."

The NBA was just getting started when McKinney left Chapel Hill, first taking a job at Hanes Hosiery in Winston-Salem. But Bones couldn't turn down such fabulous pro offers.

"That's right, they finally offered me one of those great contracts in pro ball, and I signed with Washington for $7,000. I was going to Chicago, Arthur Morris had called me. I had played against the guys in Washington, Ferrick, Orlando and several others, and they got Red Auerbach to call me. He called me the night before I was going to Chicago, said stop off since I had to change trains in Washington. Planes in those days were just service planes. Red met me and I went to practice that night at George Washington University, as backup center to John Mahnken, who played at Greensboro ORD. I saw right quick I could make that ball club, and I wasn't sure about Chicago. After practice, we went to a bar and had a drink, and until then, mine was always just out of a bottle. I didn't know about bars. I had heard of a whiskey sour, so I ordered a whiskey sour. I had three and went to the toilet, and there was Auerbach. And that's where I agreed to a contract, in the toilet. I thought, this was great, you can play and you can drink, too."

The Deacons who started Coach McKinney's Wake Forest team along championship row. Left to right, Dave Budd, Billy Packer, Len Chappell, George Ritchie, Twig Wiggins and Charlie Forte.

Washington had a 49-11 record that season, 1947. McKinney was selected all-pro. The next season he injured his ankle, missed 10 games, but in 1949 he made the second all-pro. But to this day he's more proud of making the top 10 because the league had lots of top players by then. He coached Washington part of a season after Auerbach went to the Boston Celtics, then joined Red again. While he was the Washington coach, he signed the first blacks in the NBA, Harold Hunter from North Carolina College and Earl Lloyd from West Virginia State.

McKinney returned to the state after the 1951-52 season, enrolled in the Southern Baptist Seminary at old Wake Forest in Wake County. Murray Greason wanted him to be an assistant coach, which he did until he succeeded Greason after the 1957 season.

"I think 1959-60 was the best club I ever had. I had Lennie Chappell, Dave Budd, Twig Wiggins, and I had Billy Packer and George Ritchie in the backcourt, and I had substitutes then. We had Duke bad two times that year, but I'll tell you what beat us in the tournament finals. It was Vic Bubas' first year (at Duke), we had just destroyed them at Duke and at our place. Budd had been told by Jim Weaver (ACC commissioner) that if he got in another fight, that was it, and we played State in the semifinals and he got in one. Weaver suspended him, and people knew that Weaver suspended him with the understanding the conference faculty people would overrule him about 5 o'clock the next afternoon, so we knew he was going to get booed. Part of my pregame talk was, 'Well, Dave, no question what they're going to do, but you take it like a man and hold your head up.' We were ready to go then, ready to fight. Well, when we went out, they started to boo and then to applaud, and they finally gave Budd a standing ovation. I'll never forget that spotlight they used to throw on each player, it stayed on him. We had come to play, and they took it out on us. We never did. Billy made two for 11."

The Blue Devils won the title against the Deacons, and for five years it was McKinney and Bubas in the title game. McKinney won in 1961, then took the championship in 1962 by beating Virginia, South Carolina and Clemson.

The 1962 Deacons went to the NCAA Final Four, lost to a great Ohio State crew.

"That was quite a season. They came down to Winston-Salem in December, the number one team in the nation, and they clobbered us 84-62. But I said then, 'If Ohio State plays real well the rest of the season, we will meet again.' I meant, I just knew we could do it. But one time in mid-season we were about nine and eight, then we won 12 straight. We started to play, won the ACC, made the NCAAs. Some close ones. I remember playing Yale in the Palestra, we were 11-point favorites. We were down to the final seconds, two seconds in fact, tie score, our ball out of bounds at midcourt. I called timeout, told them to let Billy take it out of bounds. When the referee handed him the ball, all three men at the foul circle were to run to Billy like we were trying to get the ball to him. Billy would lob the ball to Chappell, because that guy, Schumacker I think, about 6'-4", couldn't possibly get the ball. Everything went perfect, Billy tossed the ball just right, and Chappell coldcocked that guy, just laid him out. Of course, they called a foul, one and one, still two seconds. He goes to the foul line and crosses himself, and I said, 'Now we find out who's right.' He missed, they got the rebound, put it back up, missed again. We beat them by 10 overtime.''

About that 1962 team which had Len Chappell and Frank Christie forwards, Bob Woollard center, Billy Packer and Dave Wiedeman guards.

"It was a fine team, I thought they got more out of it when they started to play, than they really had. Not as good a ball club as that other one, not by any means. Ohio State was a better basketball team. We could have beaten them earlier, but they got better as the year went along, too.''

After losing to Ohio State, the Deacons met UCLA in the third place game. Before game time, Everett Case tapped Bones on the shoulder and reminded him, the ACC needed a win to obtain the bye in the NCAA playoffs. ACC teams had been rushing from tournament finals to NCAA first round, sometimes tired. The Deacons beat UCLA 82-80, gained the bye not relinquished (until NCAA format changed).

About Lennie Chappell:

"I don't believe I ever taught him anything about shooting. Really had a good hook shot, but for a big man he had the finest touch of anybody I've ever seen. Shooting great, and he could run, too. He never hurt anybody on purpose, but I know he hurt a lot of people accidentally. He could jump, never was a good passer. Thing that hurt him in pro ball was the thing that I told him so many times. I would say, 'Lennie, you can't play defense.' He never was a good defensive player, but one thing he could do, he could shoot that basketball.

"He was from Portage, right outside Johnstown, in Western Pennsylvania. I visited him six times during the season, and it was an 11½ hour drive each way. That summer before he came to Wake Forest, I got him a job at Kutchers Country Club, rather Auerbach got him the job (in the Catskills). There was a clinic up there and Frank McGuire was going to the clinic, and in those days, signing just meant, hey, buddy, how are you. I had to leave our camp at Broadstone (near Grandfather Mountain), go down to Winston-Salem and get Charlie Bryant some money to go to Kutchers and stay there until Frank left.''

About Billy Packer:

"Well, I first saw Billy play in the Palestra in the state championship game for Bethlehem. Yeah, he was a little star of Bethlehem. His daddy was basketball coach at Lehigh, but I didn't know that at the time. I saw him in that tournament and he was pretty good. Actually, I got his name off the blackboard at Duke. Coach Hal Bradley let me use his office phone to call home one day, and when he closed the door, there was this list of his recruits up there. I didn't write them down because that would have been sinful, but . . . Two days after we signed Chappell, we got a note from Billy. We already had Charlie Leonard, Bob's brother, and Dave Wieldeman so we didn't need another guard. I thought it was a Dear John Letter anyway, but it was his signed grant-in-aid. I thought, well, we got three guards now and we'll work something out. Leonard was a good baseball player so in July he signed a baseball contract. It did work out.

"I have said I played Billy all the time so I wouldn't have to listen to him on the bench. He really didn't talk that much, but he always had suggestions. I tell the story, Billy wouldn't take it out of bounds because he couldn't throw it to himself. He did a good job of running the club. We didn't have a point guard in those days, I don't know where that came along, but I understand some coaches, if they don't have a point guard these days, they want to cancel their schedule. I can't believe that, but we let a man run the club and I guess that's what a point guard is supposed to do. Billy was unselfish. He had a great sophomore year. You know, he's the only sophomore to win MVP in the Dixie Classic. Never the same after that."

McKinney left Wake Forest after the 1965 season. He returned to the game as the Carolina Cougars' first coach when Jim Gardner bought the Houston franchise and moved the ABA team to North Carolina. He asked Bones to coach.

"That's the most money I ever made and the last job I ever had. There's not a lot of coaching to be done, until you start to win and they start to pick up a little togetherness. It's the most frustrating experience I've ever been through. You didn't know what time they (players) would get there, and half the time they could deal with the general manager instead of you. It was a miserable situation. The first year (1969-70) I really liked it because everybody knew we didn't have anything. They had won 23 games the year before in Houston, and we won 42 and lost 42, and ran an offense just like we ran in college. We broke off the fouls at one end, we went on the fast break, but the next year the bottom went out. True, it was the case of the employees making more than the employer, that was part of it. You've got to have complete authority, and they've got to know it, and not many of them do. You take a man with an ironclad contract. What can a coach do? How can a coach suspend him?"

In 1971 the ABA all-star game was in Greensboro, drew a record crowd of 14,407 and was on national TV, but the club lasted only through 1974.

Bones McKinney was a hot name, and Charlie Harville recommended him to C. D. Chesley for ACC basketball television. He also did work on the ABA network after being coach, also on TVS in college games.

"When we played an early game at 2 o'clock on Saturday afternoon, and I thought it was ironic that Ches' memorial service in Linville was 2 o'clock on Saturday afternoon, I hated to play because we wouldn't have any fans there. You had to play everything at 8 o'clock at night, except the Dixie Classic. Like football games used to be at 2 o'clock Saturday afternoon. That was it, and the fans didn't adjust quickly. But it wasn't long, people came out and people watched TV."

What was the Dixie Classic?

"Everybody thinks it was a success from opening day. I had a broken hand and Auerbach sent me down to scout, maybe it was 1950. I didn't call for a ticket, I just rode the train in there, caught a cab to Reynolds Coliseum, bought a ticket and sat down in the end zone, nobody there. It wasn't that big a deal. It was doing better by the time I joined Murray (Greason), and within no time people treated it as the conference tournament in winter time. People took their vacation at that time, and it was different than the conference tournament. I never played for last place but one time. We played Yale, and I said, 'Lord, you get us out of this and I won't get us in this mess anymore.' We finished seventh, and I tell you, those little trophies they gave out, you could put in your watch pocket. Vic Bubas and I called them salt shakers."

In hindsight, should they have called off the Dixie Classic as reaction to the 1961 scandals?

"No. I think it would have died eventually like the Big Four did. But then, like the year we played Duke the extra game in Greensboro, 9,000 some fans, we made more money in that game than three days in the Dixie Classic. Most we ever got was $10,000. But I don't think calling off the Dixie Classic accomplished anything. We couldn't play in the NIT, I remember years ago, because they had had all those fixes in Madison Square Garden. I said, 'Well, I know a man who got caught cheating in history at Wake Forest, why don't they just not teach history anymore?' I think it looked good at the time, like it looked good for San Francisco to drop basketball a year ago."

Bones McKinney might average 200 talks a year, and he's got a history book full of stories. What is his own very favorite?

"This is the way I tell it at a banquet. We got a boy named Bob Woollard, six eleven, not a strong person. We got him from Fork Union Military Academy, he's from New Jersey. We brought him in,

100

and I didn't know if he could play, but in my day, if a boy was 6'-11", you brought him in. The first time we took him to the weight room, we put the bar on his shoulders, not any weights, just the bar, and he went right on down to the floor (laughs).

"But we worked with him, did a good job, and with my assistant coaches, by his sophomore year he wasn't bad. As a junior, pretty doggoned good. Part of my job at Wake Forest, we were poor at Wake Forest, was to sit on the front steps and watch the new students come in because we needed to find two fellows with good cars. With good tires on them, because we had to have some way of traveling. And then Dr. Tribble, the college president, had a nephew he wanted to make the team. That's three already that's not going to play (laughs).

"Now, Woollard's senior year, Bill Hull on the football team, a tight end, later played with the Dallas Cowboys, came out for basketball since he didn't have to go out for spring practice, being a senior. He beat Woollard out, so we didn't work Woollard a lot. So he wouldn't eat a lot, because we didn't have the money (laughs). Time passed and we get to the NCAA East Regionals, and I took five of them on Thursday — in those days we played Friday and Saturday nights — and took the five who were going to play and told the assistant coaches to get the two boys who had the cars, Dr. Tribble's nephew and two boys who didn't eat a lot and come up late (laughs).

"Just come to the coliseum in Charlotte. I didn't know who they had brought. I told Hull, there's a boy named Stith, an all-American, who played for St. Bonaventure, you hold him to 25 points and we can win. So about five minutes in the second half, Hull hits his tummy, that means, coach, I'm tired, take me out. We were just down five points and I said, 'Lord, what am I going to do? I can't play.' (laughs). I look down the bench, there was Dr. Tribble's nephew, one boy with a car, the other boy with a car, and way down at the end was Woollard. He's talking to the cheerleaders. He didn't know what he was going to do during the game but he knew what he was going to do afterwards (laughs).

"I went down there and knelt in prayer, mostly, in front of him, slapped him like that (whack on nearby table) and got his attention right away. Told him ol' Hull was tired, needed two or three minutes rest, just go in there and play two or three minutes like I know you can, deep in your heart, and gave him a slap and he knocked me on my tail when he charged by me to the scorers table. But he forgot who he was going in for, so he came back, and I wrote it on a piece of paper for him (laughs).

"The first time Stith shot it, Woollard blocked it, and picked off the ball. He gave the outlet pass to Billy Packer. When Billy tells it on TV today, he says you ought to pass here or pass there, but when he played for me, he wouldn't give the ball to his mother (laughs). Billy

Please, people, let's do the play this way (see floor).

makes it, we're down by three. In nine minutes 54 seconds Woollard blocks four shots, gets 11 points and 10 rebounds, and we went from five down to five up. That's what you call coaching (laughs).

"I wasn't going to take him out. I knew he might die, but I thought dying for me was a good reason (laughs). So I called a timeout. You see Duke, Carolina, State, they all run to the huddle. Not with me. That's the worst odor I ever smelled (laughs). It's terrible, they're spitting on the coach, garlic, BO, everything else. Just five players, and when I looked up, four had their heads turned, and Woolland was sucking what air was in there. What he wanted to know was . . . 'Coach, how much time before two or three minutes are up?'"

And the house breaks up.

You must have made a million, Bones.

"Auerbach gave me the usual rookie salary at Washington my first year in the pros, $7,000. I made the all-star team and got a $500 raise. I made it again the third season, got another $500. Today that would be worth about $500,000. At the Celtics I never signed a contract, just a handshake with Walter Brown, the owner, until the league called and said I couldn't play in the playoffs until I signed a contract. That year (1952) they paid me $10,000, two more than I'd ever made, Mr. Brown added, "I'm going to give you $1,500 more because Edna is not up here and you're going back and forth some.' It amounted to $11,500.

"That summer I came to the seminary and took a newspaper route at Wake Forest. But I had to give that up because I couldn't go to school, work my paper route and study, too. I was sitting in New Testament History and Murray Greason (coach) came in with his hunting clothes on and said, 'Bones, you want to help with the basketball team?' I said, 'Coach, I'd love to,' and he said, 'Well, I can't tell you how much but you've got to go down in the morning and see Jim Weaver (AD).' I thought about it that night, I figured they'd pay me $4-5,000 but the least they could possibly offer was $750. It was November 9 and it would take me $50 a week to get through and it came to $750. Imagine how I felt the next morning and Mr. Weaver said in his office, 'Bones, we're on a Baptist budget, and this money we're paying you is coming out of the Deacon Club, and all they've got is $750.'

"At the end of the season I went on the payroll at $3,300. They upped it to $4,500, then $4,800, and when we moved to Winston-Salem, I got $6,000. I got to $7,000 as assistant, and when I became head coach, I got $8,000. When I won the Dixie Classic I felt I was in the position of Everett or Frank McGuire, and they were making $11,500. I told the college I needed $11,500 also, or they could have the job, and I got it. That's all we got, too, we didn't have those basketball camps and TV shows.

Bones McKinney, after his college coaching, became the Carolina Cougars' first coach when the ABA came to the state. He coached well, and he also clowned, this time for Bob Verga, Cal Fowler and Gene Littles, who obviously has seen it before.

"Most money I ever made, with the Carolina Cougars, $35,000, three-year contract, no cut. Jim Gardner offered me $32,000 and two years, and I said the other. I was dealing in high cotton. I told the children when I left to go to Rocky Mount to see Jim Gardner, if I come back with a six pack of Pepsi, you will know I signed. It was late when I started back, trying to stay awake, and I thought about it coming into Raleigh. I got the six Pepsis out of a machine and found me a carton to put them in, and I walked into a family cheering when I got home."

12
Vic Bubas

Victor Albert Bubas missed classes that first year on discharge from the 1st Infantry Division, so he worked with his father who owned a hardware business in Gary, Indiana, and he played some AAU ball.

He was a teenager.

Vic Bubas scored the first field goal in venerable, reknowned Reynolds Coliseum on the North Carolina State campus in West Raleigh at age 21.

Vic Bubas was a head college coach at age 31.

Vic Bubas retired as a basketball coach at age 41.

"I didn't know anything about North Carolina basketball," the commissioner of the Sun Belt Conference, Bubas' current position, said recently in the Florida sun, "but I knew something about Everett Case as every boy in Indiana did. I had been in the service and Everett's N.C. State team had been to the NIT the previous year. I got out of the service (1947) too late to get in school, but Everett heard about me and came to Gary."

A long-time association, which went deep into friendship, thus began.

"He paid my way down to Raleigh," Vic recalled, "but strangely enough, he said, 'Why don't you stay at my house rather than the hotel?' Everett was pretty smart, he knew I wanted to coach and he really dwelled on the fact that if I was a good student, behaved myself and tried as hard as I could in basketball, that he would try as hard as he could to get a good coaching job for me, but I had no idea he would keep me on his staff."

Bubas was in Coach Case's second recruiting class, 1947-48, and the Wolfpack returned to the NIT his freshman year. Not with great success, however. It had taken third spot the year before, this time came up against George Mikan and lost to DePaul. Bubas made the starting team as a sophomore, the sixth man on the all-conference team, then having a fine tournament and selected first all-tournament. He would make the two selections three straight years, his teams having a 111-24 record, or 82.2 percent winning.

One of the Case selling points, with all the recruits, was the big steel structure which sat on the campus during World War II. Plans were rejuvenated, Reynolds Coliseum was being constructed. Bubas recalled the home floor for the Wolfpack on his arrival: "Old Frank Thompson Gym. Well, a nice home court advantage. Nobody wanted to play there. If we had played all our games there for four years, we would have been close to being undefeated. But Gore Gym, over there at old Wake Forest, I think may have been even tougher. Everything was so close, the Wake Forest football players sitting right behind your bench. People say, if there is such a thing as a home court advantage, it's the fans and the closeness that makes it that way. It's not the configuration of the floor, even if it's a couple feet smaller, it's the fans breathing down your neck that makes the difference."

But Reynolds Coliseum, in the late 50s the leader in college basketball attendance, showplace of the South, was getting ready for Bubas, or at least something he had in the back of his mind.

"That first game in Reynolds was exciting to me," he said, "because for the first two years I literally went to the coliseum construction every day and counted how many bricks they put in that day. We just couldn't wait to get there, and it was exciting because when I first went down there, the steel work was up, designed before the war for about 8,000 people, and it had been enlarged to 12,000. Bigtime basketball was coming there, it was exciting."

First game in Reynolds was December 2, 1949, the opponent Washington & Lee in a Southern Conference game. Vic Bubas scored the first goal, but it was an almost gargantuan task. Bubas, with that sly grin of his, explained: "I had no intention of passing that ball to anybody at the start. I took a shot and missed it, got it back on the rebound, knocked down about eight people to get the ball back, missed it again. I put it up the third time and it went in. Coach Case took me out, sort of smiled when he did, and he said to me, 'Hey boy, you really wanted that first bucket.'"

The Wolfpack, from Case's arrival, captured six straight Southern Conference championships in tournament play, and Bubas was on the middle four, and three times the finalist opposing the Wolfpack were the Duke Blue Devils.

Bubas' final collegiate game as a player was in the NIT which the Wolfpack entered before playing in the NCAA. The latter bid was diluted by the announcement of an NCAA regulation which permitted freshmen to play varsity ball but not for four years in NCAA play. Three of the Pack starters, Bubas, forward Sammy Ranzino and center Paul Horvath, were ruled ineligible for the NCAA. Coach Case made some hurried changes: Bill Kukoy for Ranzino, 6'-9" sophomore Bobby Goss for Horvath, Bernie Yurin for Bubas. Strong Villanova was the first round foe, but the game was in Reynolds. Coach Case played "alley cat" ball for 40 minutes and won. Villanova got one shot inside. Student Bubas sat there on the bench and marvelled. He recalled that night quite well: "Villanova? Sitting on the sidelines? Tough because you've been there all the time, and you're really pulling for your team-mates, but it is really hard to all of a sudden be extracted by that kind of thing." He had contributed, in workouts he played the "role" of Larry Hennessee, Villanova's star.

On graduation Bubas joined the coaching staff as freshman mentor. Butter Anderson was the assistant coach, but Coach Case was able to hire a third person for the first time. Bubas in four years with the freshmen had a record of 65-10, three times winning the "mythical" Big Four Freshman championship, and there was no tougher collegiate league anywhere. When Anderson went into private business, Bubas moved up (1956).

It was a down-to-earth experience on the Wolfpack staff. Bubas: "I tell you what, I spent eight years there and for the first six, Coach Case was demanding, exerted a lot of pressure. State was used to winning all the time, you felt the pressure of recruiting, the pressure of coaching with him, for him. But the last two were entirely different. It had nothing to do with Frank McGuire coming to Carolina. It seemed like Everett, after six years, said, 'Hey, I got this guy in the kind of shape I want him, how to think, what to do and so on.' My last two years as an assistant, I almost had the decisions and privileges of being a head coach, without the responsibilities. That's pretty neat, to have that experience of going through, of seeing a lot of things he would approve. In fact, there weren't many things he would turn down after I'd been there that long. Tremendous experience for me."

There were offers at other campuses. Bubas: "Several situations did come my way. I turned down the Clemson job. I wanted to be the head coach at the University of New Mexico and was turned down. Also I was in the final three or four, whatever that means, at Ohio State. They took Fred Taylor and he did a great job for them. After that, the Duke job came along, and maybe God was trying to take care of me."

Harold Bradley resigned after his ninth season (1959) at Duke, and Bubas was hired. Bubas again: "Eddie Cameron (athletic director) talked with me, and when I first heard there were 200 applicants for the job, I thought, 'Oh, my word.' Then it got down to five and I knew I was in that group. Eddie called one day in early May, 'Why don't you meet me and Carl James (assistant AD) on the highway at this little restaurant between Durham and Raleigh?' I said okay, I thought he was going to talk about some more interviews or something. I walked in, sat down, and Eddie said, 'Well, I think we ought to get on with this recruiting, don't you?' I said sure, he didn't say you had the job or anything like, he sort of stunned me."

Recruiting began that moment. Bubas: "First man was Art Hey-

In a new jacket, as head coach at Duke, Bubas with his first Blue Devil captain, Howard Hurt, who was selected for the new coach's first two seasons (1960 and 1961).

man. Right after the press conference, announcing my job at Duke, I headed for New York. Fred Shabel remained as my assistant, lucky thing for me, too, to have a guy who understood Duke and would work hard, really a blessing. Fred told me Art had not made up his mind and wanted to talk to me. I knew that Art had indicated to North Carolina that he wanted to go there, but I wanted to talk to him, and when I did, both Art and his dad said they were very much interested. One thing led to another, and that was quite a stormy recruiting session, but I was glad we got him and Art proved to be a helluva player. That was the start of the program; Art brought another dimension to what we were doing. He was sort of a tough New York kid, and when he got to Duke in the fall, our guys weren't over in the gym in off-season, so he came to my office and said, 'What's going on? Don't these fellows want to win?' I knew what he was talking about, pretty soon he gathered everybody up prior to official practice, and next thing I knew they were going at each other like it was mid-season. I mean, black eyes, cuts and bruises prior to October 15, and no coaching going on. Art kind of opened their eyes to what it took."

It also opened a stream of blue chippers — Jeff Mullins and Jay Buckley in the fall of 1960, Hack Tison 1961, Jack Marin and Steve Vacendak 1962, Bob Verga 1963, Mike Lewis 1964 and so on.

Bubas was reminded of some who got away: "We almost had Bill Bradley and Rod Thorn. We had Bradley, I just made a mistake. Once a guy signs, you don't want to bug him every week. He didn't sign the national letter but in the spring Bill indicated to us he was coming. Then he went to Europe, and we had not been in contact. When the day came for him to come to school, I got a call from his father notifying me that Bill was on his way to Princeton, and I thought he was calling to tell me what time to pick him up at the Raleigh-Durham Airport. Needless to say, that was quite a shock. And it might have cost us a national championship."

His first Blue Devils were not quite ready for the NCAA playoffs, although they made a surprising run to the East Regional finals. Opening the 60s decade, the ACC did not have a top 10 ranked team for the first time in ages. North Carolina was No. 16, Wake Forest No. 18, and Duke's break-even conference record put it in fourth spot. It beat South Carolina 82-69, North Carolina 71-69 (after losing in season by 22, 26 and 25). Wake Forest in the finals held a one-point lead on Bill Packer's goal, then Doug Kistler regained the lead and Johnny Frye's four free throws concreted a 63-59 triumph. Vic Bubas had never lost a conference game, four years as a player, his first year as coach. But he had his feet on the ground. In postgame interview: "There are two men I want to thank, Everett Case, my old coach, and the other guy, the one I beat tonight, Bones McKinney. I am deeply grateful to Everett because of the training he gave me. No words can say what he's done. And Bones, I have spent many, many hours with Bones and from him I got many ideas. Some of them I used tonight in beating him. You know, it seems I've always got a horseshoe in these conference tournaments." As ACC champions, the Blue Devils made the NCAAs, beat Princeton and St. Joseph's before losing to NYU. Bubas and McKinney would meet in five of the first six conference tournaments in the 60s. Vic won four of them.

Duke went into the 1963 conference tournament No. 2 in the nation, just behind Cincinnati. The Blue Devils went through the league 14-0, only the second to achieve that (North Carolina 1957). Heyman and Mullins led 89-70 over Virginia, 82-65 over N.C. State, 68-57 over Wake Forest. In the East Regional they beat NYU and St. Joseph's, and it got the Blue Devils to their first Final Four.

Coming in, the Blue Devils led the nation in field goal shooting, 51.3 percent, but they hit only 37.8 that first evening in Louisville with Loyola Chicago. Getting one field goal in 11 minutes, they fell behind 14-31, and it was humiliating. Only Heyman could hit, the Loyola fast break ate up the Duke defense. But they rallied from 17 down to within 71-74 with 4:20 remaining. Then Loyola hit the next 14 and won 94-75. They beat Oregon State for third 85-63, thus retaining the ACC bye which Wake Forest had earned the year before. However, had Duke lost, the Mid-Atlantic Conference's .594 would have been better than the ACC's .591. What happened with Loyola? Bubas: "Two things, really. I didn't think that year we had enough talent to win it all. We didn't play our normal game. I don't think we choked, we were a little bit too nervous. Heck, I was nervous as a coach. We didn't play poorly, we just didn't play up to our potential."

The following year (1964) Duke was ranked No. 4 nationally, came into the conference tournament heavily favored, and Coach Bubas commented: "I feel like a duck on Lake Mattamuskeet." Fans in the state knew what that meant. But they beat N.C. State 75-44, North Carolina 65-49, and there was Wake Forest again. Jeff Mullins led the 80-59 victory. Coach Bubas had gone through the Big Four: "No team ever had a tougher road to the championship. Look at the road. First game, N.C. State, home court, scratching it out against the stall. North Carolina, another old rival, again scratching it out against the stall. Then Wake Forest, yet another big rival, only team in the conference to beat us this season. We took three straight Sunday punches and are still champions." In the East Regional, in Raleigh, Mullins got a career high 43 to beat Villanova, then Connecticut coached by his former assistant, Fred Shabel. Of Mullins the coach said; "I can tell you what, if anybody here tonight was looking for an all-American, he saw one."

The trip to Kansas City was not uneventful. The charter plane arrived at cold, rainy KC with slick runways. On second braking the

The Blue Devil spirit: All-American Jeff Mullins, Hack Tison and Jay Buckley.

Duke charter skidded, ploughed through a soggy plot to an adjoining runway. Scary indeed, for reporters as well. But Coach Bubas was reminded of an earlier flight that season, on a DC-3 out of Morgantown, West Virginia. Under snowy skies, just out of the airport, the DC-3 hit a pocket and dropped a couple hundred feet, not once but twice. A Coca-Cola bottle, with half the drink remaining, flowed upward, straight up. Typewriters fell from the racks, players lost their cookies. The metal food and milk containers, in the rear, began floating through the air. Bubas, like others aboard, has never forgotten: "Terrible, the plane just fell out of the sky. We had things floating like you see in spaceships. One container had ice in it, headed toward Jack Marin's head and I pushed it away. Saw Max Crowder's trainers kit floating through the air, and Bucky Waters (assistant coach) pinned it against the top of the cabin. We had a trip to Vanderbilt the next Monday, but I told Eddie Cameron no more DC'3s. "They chartered a Piedmont 404.

Back to Kansas City. Duke beat Michigan and Cazzie Russell 91-80, all the more remarkable when one checked the season record and saw Duke lost to Ann Arbor in December by 83-67 in points and 61-35 in rebounds. Duke met UCLA in the finals, and this would launch the Wooden Era, the first title. Duke was the first of nine different teams challenging the Bruins in the national finals, and Duke led UCLA by three until the eventual victors unleashed their full press and ran off a 16-0 spurt en route to 98-83. Bubas on that one: "UCLA that year got a lot of credit for disrupting people with their press. You go back to the film and you can find the press did not disrupt us. We had a stretch in the second quarter when we could not buy a damn good shot, no matter who had it. We even had stick-backs that didn't go in. I don't think we were tight, they just missed. Right at that point, UCLA hit. Now they had a 12-15 point lead, we then had nowhere near the speed and quickness of UCLA. Trying to make up 12-15 points against a team which is so quick, you usually don't do it."

The next Final Four came in 1966, but Coach Bubas wanted to interrupt the chronology: "I want to mention 1965. I think we had the kind of team that might have gone all the way, but there was Larry Worsley of N.C. State who had never played a real good game until that Saturday night in the tournament championship. He went crazy, off the bench, 30 points. They earned it, for a guy to come in like Larry did and play such a game. But we had the kind of team that might have gone on and on. Almost that good." In those days, remember, only the ACC champion went to playoffs, no NIT until several years later.

The Blue Devils arrived at Reynolds in 1966 ranked No. 3 in the AP (behind Kentucky and Texas Western), No. 2 UPI. It would be the last tournament ever held in Raleigh, the conference having voted rotation. Reynolds was sold out. the Blue Devils defeated Wake Forest 107-73, then 21-20 over Coach Dean Smith's Carolina four corners, finally N.C. State 71-66. Of 21-20, Bubas said: "We had anticipated Carolina slowing up the game, we certainly didn't expect a total stall." Smith said: "But I'd like to say I was wrong — wrong because we lost. Whether we lose 121-120 or 21-20, we still lost to Duke." Mike Lewis hit free throws in the final four seconds. Optimism peaked in the finals. Bubas recently said: "I turned to the assistant coaches at one point and said, 'There's nobody going to beat us.' They were flabbergasted because that wasn't very much like me to say that. They answered quickly, 'Damn, we never heard you talk like that.' I said, 'I never had a team play like this.'" It had Jack Marin and Bob Riedy forwards, sophomore Mike Lewis center, Bob Verga and Steve Vacendak guards.

In the East Regional Duke beat St. Joseph's 76-74 and Syracuse 91-81, and Tuesday night Bob Verga was in Duke Hospital with 103 degree fever and a sore throat. Kentucky No. 1 beat Duke No. 2 in the opening game of the Final Four at College Park 83-79. Related Bubas recently: "We got Verga out of the hospital in time to go the nationals. I tried to play him, and did start him, and I guess I made a mistake, but when you have Mickey Mantle sitting on the bench, you don't leave him in the dugout in the World Series. Bob didn't play well, he said he felt okay but maybe he was just being brave. I had a sick cat on my hands." Verga took only seven shots, made two, but despite this Duke rallied within two at the four-minute mark. A layup was missed, Kentucky rebounded, scored. Duke beat Utah 79-77 for third.

The conference approved the NIT the following year, responding to a plea from the coaches for many years. Duke lost to Carolina in the finals, and got the NIT. It was a rushed affair, team meeting Sunday after the Saturday night tournament, fly to New York Sunday morning, work out in the Garden, play Monday night. The Blue Devils lost to Southern Illinois. Then came the change of site to the Charlotte Coliseum in 1968, with that 12-10 semifinal nightmare, Duke losing to N.C. State. Coach Bubas had his final game of the ACC tournament finals 1969, losing to the Tar Heels. The native of Gary, Indiana had spent 22 years in the state of North Carolina, winning basketball games and titles. In four seasons as a Wolfpack player, his team record was 111-24 and four titles. In eight years as assistant coach to Everett Case, his team record was 183-52 and five titles. For the Bubas Decade at Duke as head coach, the record was 213-67, four titles and three Final Fours. In those 22 seasons Vic Bubas recorded 507 wins and 143 losses, 13 of a possible 22 conference championships, 18 times in the final game.

At age 41 he retired from coaching, taking a position as assistant to Duke University President Terry Sanford, in public relations. Five years later he became university vice president for community relations. In October 1976 he was selected the first commissioner of the Sun Belt Conference. He is a member of the NCAA basketball committee.

Vic Bubas finds a time for some serious coaching on the bench.

Bubas, awaiting a golf game, reminisced recently in Florida: "Tired of coaching? Yes, I wanted to do something else. I wanted to win every game, went after it as hard as I could. People say, you only coached 10 years; I coached 18 years, those eight under Everett Case count for something. I also thought I could do a lot of other things. If we hadn't had the success we did, I probably would have wanted to stay in it to prove to myself we could do it. One thing I had made up my mind about—I wasn't going to stay on the bench until we won a national championship. I didn't want to do that, maybe I would have been there until I was 65, and maybe still not win it."

13
Black Heritage

John McLendon's father attended North Carolina A&T, then went out west to Kansas to raise his family.

Young John was a small player, 5-foot-8, 150 pounds, trying to play some guard position at a junior college.

"I wasn't able to afford going to the school I wanted to," he related recently. "That was Springfield College and the YMCA. My father told me to go to Kansas University so I could fulfill my reason for going to Springfield. I just wanted to get to know the man who invented basketball, and Dr. Naismith was just 40 miles up the road."

John McLendon enrolled in the physical education department at Kansas, where Dr. James Naismith was a professor: "I didn't know at the time that I was the first black in physical education at Kansas University. My father said to just go see Dr. Naismith and tell him I was his advisee. Tell him, my father sent me to major in physical education. I told Dr. Naismith that, he just smiled and said, 'Well, all right, come on.' Dr. Naismith did take a personal interest in me; he had to, because I took one in him."

With his degree at Kansas in 1936, plus a masters at Iowa, John McLendon brought Dr. Naismith's philosophy of the game to his first coaching job, North Carolina College (now Central) in Durham, North Carolina.

And the "Naismith Game" was recalled recently, on McLendon's visit to the 1983 MEAC tournament, the ambassador-at-large representative for Converse. He said, "Dr. Naismith said what he'd call the ultimate game of basketball was this—To attack when the other team gets the ball and wherever it gets it, and any time you get the ball, your offense begins at that point. He didn't like what he called half-court basketball, letting the defense run away, then the other team wait until they cross midcourt. He felt basketball was a full-court game." Coach McLendon made it just that at North Carolina College in 1937-38, and the wiry little professor of basketball would soon be joined by two other outstanding coaches, two good friends who played basketball and

Ambassador for basketball, John McLendon attends an MEAC tournament.

Coach Bighouse Gaines, who today has 698 victories to top all active college coaches, reached the pinnacle in 1967 with Earl Monroe, who set NCAA scoring records and helped capture the NCAA College Division national title, the first black school to win any NCAA sports title.

The bench of Coach Cal Irvin's A&T Aggies was always intense on the game in front of them.

football at Morgan State. Clarence Gaines, called Bighouse from his first day as a college student, came to Winston-Salem State in 1945, where he has more game victories than any other active college coach in the United States. Cal Irvin came to Johnson C. Smith in 1950, then became head coach at North Carolina A&T in 1954.

Their records are truly outstanding:

- Clarence Gaines 698-311, 37 years coach, all at Winston Salem.
- John McLendon 523-162, 25 years coach, North Carolina College, Hampton, Tennessee State, Kentucky State, Cleveland State. Retired.
- Cal Irvin 401-132, 22 years coach. Johnson C. Smith, North Carolina A&T. Retired.

Their records, only Gaines' active and his victories keep piling up, in pursuit of Adolph Rupp, Phog Allen, Henry Iba and Ed Diddle, continue almost unsurpassed in the game. McLendon, who was a fabulous 81.5 percent with 264-60 in 12 years at North Carolina College, retired in 1969 with a 523-162 mark. He coached Tennessee State to three straight NAIA national championships (1957-8-9), first coach to achieve that in any national competition. He coached the Cleveland Pipers in the old ABL (1961), first black to coach a pro team in any major league sport. Cal Irvin, at the age of 48 at the time, retired in 1971 with a career of 401-132, including a 76.8 percent winning achievement at A&T, and a long string of conference crowns.

Add them up, 698 for House, 523 for John, 401 for Cal, and no state has a richer heritage in the game.

Coach McLendon was the first on the state scene, at the Eagles who had been 0-15 the year before. He learned this at once: "Football was the big thing in North Carolina then, basketball really secondary. It was a tolerated sport, and a lot of football players played basketball, especially in our conference where they got work aids. I was probably the first in the black schools to have separate players."

The Central Intercollegiate Athletic Association (CIAA), formed in 1913, long before the Southern Conference which grouped together the white schools in 1921, played basketball from the beginning. By the 40s some innovative minds, seeing the post-season interest the white schools generated in Raleigh with the conference tournament, planned one for the CIAA. McLendon pushed it, Talmadge Hill of Morgan State was first chairman. McLendon remembered: "We asked, 'Where are our funds to get started?' The answer was, 'You have to raise them.' So we put in $100 each of our own money, and that's how we got started. Out on a limb, I'd say." First CIAA tournament was in February 1946 at Turner's Arena in Washington, D.C. Some 3,000 fans attended, and Coach McLendon's Eagles beat Virginia Union in three overtimes for the crown. The CIAA event has moved to Baltimore, Durham, Greensboro, Winston-Salem, back to Greensboro, Norfolk and Hampton, and it is a big success today in Norfolk's Scope.

Coach McLendon had different teams. The first conference champions, he claimed, were the smallest starting team in history — four players 5'-7" and under. Coach McLendon recalled, "We played the guards in pairs, called it 'two in the corner,' which is the four corners today." They ran the ball, holding CIAA scoring honors 10 times in his 12 years at NCC. McLendon again: "But we didn't score the points Bighouse did later. Our highest scoring average was about 78, but we broke the national record one night back in 1943 over at Shaw. We scored 67 points in the second half."

John McLendon believed in firsts, and he told this story about one of particular pride: "Generally, credit for the first black player in pro basketball goes to Red Auerbach and the Celtics and the honor to Chuck Cooper who was the first drafted player. But this is a true story. Harold Hunter had played with us at North Carolina College in 1945, went to the service, returned. He was my captain all four years. Harold and Earl Lloyd at West Virginia State were outstanding players in the CIAA tournament in 1950, and we had it at Uline Arena in Washington. Bones McKinney was coaching Washington, he saw them, called me to get them up for tryouts. I drove Hunter to Washington and we picked up Lloyd in Alexandria.

"We first went up to Howard University to get a few warmup shots, so when we got to the tryouts, they'd be loose. On the way down the hill from Howard, Earl said, 'Coach, wait a minute, wait a minute. I got to tell you something. Coach Caldwell (WVS) wouldn't let us switch. I don't know how to switch.' So I turned, and lo and behold, into a street that was a dead end. I parked the car, we got out, right like that, end of the street, and worked on switching. Then we went on down the hill to Uline.

"Tryouts went like this. You've seen this E. F. Hutton speaks commercial, well, everybody stopped. They had 27-28 guys working out, and they just stopped. Two black kids. Out of the crowd came Johnny Norlander, he shook hands and said, 'Welcome to the tryouts.' McKinney had Fred Scholari, one of the players, in charge. Drills, then half-court scrimmage, three on three. I got Norlander with my boys, and for two hours they tried every conceivable combination. They beat everybody all afternoon, and the general manager came down, asked me to follow him. He said, 'We want to sign the guys up.' So I said to myself, since I did all the work, got the guys here and all that, I at least ought to be the coach of the first black to sign pro basketball. That's how I got Hunter the first. Earl stepped right behind him and signed." Each got $4,000, top price for the times.

The next year or so, a family moved next door on George Street in Durham, and there was a kid who wanted to shoot the basketball in the coach's driveway all the time. It was Sam Jones, whom Coach McLendon sent to Frank McDuffie at Laurinburg Institute, then coached him, saw him sign and become an all-time star with the Celtics.

Clarence Gaines, naturally called Bighouse by one of his college

Winston-Salem State's Cleo Hill, a first round NBA draft selection by the St. Louis Hawks 1961.

professors because he's 6'-5" and 298 pounds (and bigger than a house), began his college work at Winston-Salem State in 1945 at $200 a month. All he coached were football, basketball, baseball and track, head coach, too. He raised the football team from 0-8 to 8-1, and as athletic director, hired a football coach and took over basketball only.

House has been through the door several ways. He philosophized recently: "We've had three eras, for my team, for the CIAA, for black basketball. First, back in the 40s when there was no emphasis on basketball whatsoever. North Carolina College's 1,200-seat gym was the largest in the CIAA, and many games were played on stages, in recreation centers and dining halls. Filling time between Christmas and baseball season. No outdoor courts, and most goals were torn down during the summer. Then the CIAA started the tournament, thanks to John McLendon, and we started scheduling games in December.

"Era Two stretched from that first conference tournament (1946) to the mid-60s. During that black basketball centered on the great rivalry between Winston-Salem State and Norfolk Carolina A&T. Cal Irvin and I date back to our years at Morgan State. He was a little wingback out of East Orange, and I ran interference for him. But he was better on the basketball court. We won 10 of 11 conference titles between us from 1957 to 1967. I always felt the games with A&T were the toughest, most challenging on the schedule. We both knew we'd be facing a well prepared team with excellent material, no gimmicks. We had some big, noisy, enthusiastic crowds, and that made for some great games. We also had Cleo Hill (1959-61) and Earl Monroe (1965-67).

"Era Three saw the widespread recruitment of black players in bigtime programs. In an age of affluence, bigtime colleges began playing basketball with more money at stake about the same time a lot of white kids were discovering a greater variety of activities. The black player had become available to the major college coaches, and many of them looked upon him as the solution to their needs. There's no way we—we the smaller black colleges—can offer the same kind of exposure and luxurious surroundings as the bigtime programs. They can tell a boy he'll play in front of 15,000 spectators, he'll play on TV, he'll received all kinds of publicity and fringe benefits. So for us, it's like trying to compete against steak with hot dogs."

There is competition for the interest of fans in the state of North Carolina. They are in "ACC Country," as TV tells people every night and on weekends. House called it "the Division II dilemma." He looked across town in Winston-Salem, saw Wake Forest University. House: "Wake Forest is raising $1 million every year and we're raising $10,000. That's one tenth of one percent."

But there have been near 700 victories, and one national championship. There was Vernon Earl Monroe, the most prolific single-season scorer ever in NCAA Division II. His 1,329 points for a fantastic 41.5 point average top the NCAA records to this day. House: "First I heard about Earl Monroe was from a very good friend of mine, Leon Whitley, one of our graduates. He worked in the post office in Philadelphia where they have a very highly organized Post Office League. I went up there, and here's Earl Monroe playing with Guy Rodgers and Wilt Chamberlain and the pros. It would be 105-106 degrees out there on that asphalt, and these guys running up and down. First person I'd see would be Billy Packer from Wake Forest and the whole group from the ACC. I never saw Earl play in high school. But he came with us. At the time we had a pretty good ball club, Earl didn't break in as a starter until mid-January. We put him at a guard slot, he lost the ball in the middle of the floor. We started him as a forward in the corner, with a three-guard offense."

In summer school Monroe and Paul Long of Wake Forest became good friends, and Earl joined Long's group that played basketball six nights a week, at Wake and WSS. Both had great senior seasons.

Then came the NCAA national title in 1967. House: "We adopted a pattern, the overloading part of the old Auburn shuffle. It all starts and ends with the middle man, Earl Monroe. We had the perfect 1-2 combination, William English (6'-4", 230) on the low post, and Earl's out front in the guard spot. It all started out there. To play a perfect defense on a kid with the outside movements that Earl had and the inside movement that English had, well...and if they decide to double-team Earl, there's Eugene Smiley over there, one of the best spot shooters, and James Reid, the other youngster right around the key. And Johnny Watkins, the other guard, 6'-4", whoever was scoring, he took care of him.

"In tournament play you realize, one shot, you're out. We had erred in the conference tournament, losing to A&T. We got the bid. Long Island was first in the NCAA nationals, Earl made 2-3 moves early and that was it. Kentucky Wesleyan, we had one of our best nights, fast break so well we had 17 uncontested baskets. Southwest Missouri in the finals, we could very easily have lost that ball game. One call by the officials that might have gone one way or the other, and fortunately it went our way. I think actually Reid took one off the rim and set up a break, put us in front with two minutes to go, but it was the ball game. Sure, Earl was on top of the break as usual and made the basket (77-74).

"The team developed a yell coming out of the huddle at timeouts or start of the game—'Kill, Kill, Kill.' I don't know where it actually started, not my idea, but they developed it, and the students picked it up. If you had seen the determination these guys had in their eyes all year . . . "

Earl Monroe had magic appeal with the fans, the Rams played home games in the Winston-Salem Coliseum which was usually filled. House: "Other than our student body, I imagine 60 percent of our paying public were not black people." And May 27, 1967, when Earl Monroe was supposed to graduate, Earl Monroe graduated.

North Carolina A&T was right in the center of the movement to form a new conference among the black colleges, and so the Mid-Eastern Athletic Conference (MEAC) was founded in 1970. It was a football league originally, but it has achieved NCAA automatic qualification in basketball since July 1980. Maryland-Eastern Shore made the NIT in 1974 as well as top 20 AP ranking.

Cal Irvin's Aggies captured the first MEAC championship, and then retired to devote full time to his teaching duties at the college. He was 48 at the time. He had coached under four chancellors and had won a conference championship under every one. Of his young days Irvin recalled: "There were a few opportunities that came along but nobody in those days were running around knocking down the doors of black coaches. Even Bighouse wasn't getting any offers, and neither was I. I could have gone a lot of places as an assistant with a $5,000 reduction in salary, but it wouldn't have worked anyway. I felt when I got out, that I didn't feel inferior to anybody in basketball, nobody, from John Wooden on down. I felt just that confident in myself."

The Aggies have gone to the NCAA playoffs in 1982 and 1983 under Coach Don Corbett, and they took league honors under Warren Reynolds and Gene Littles. But somehow, with A&T being the only member from the state of North Carolina, the excitement and rivalry of the MEAC have not gained the importance with the fans which the former CIAA held. Not the 14,000 crowd that filled the Greensboro Coliseum in 1971. Not the East Coast's No. 1 social event for black fans of all sports.

Cal Irvin was a giant in the CIAA long before he recorded victories No. 400 and No. 401. They came in the inaugural MEAC tournament at Duke Indoor Stadium in March 1972. Before 7,000 fans the Aggies massacred Maryland-Eastern Shore 86-67 and students and fans alike brought out banners and cards reading, "Congratulations on 400 Victories." The title win over Howard was just as exciting for the team led by two all-conference players, James Outlaw and Elmer Austin.

Irvin first wanted to be a major league baseball player, a fine shortstop. He went to Morgan State, then to Illinois for his degree and Columbia for his masters. His brother Monte Irvin became a big league ball player, Cal a college coach, first at Johnson C. Smith Uni-

Retired this year after being head coach for the Golden State Warriors in the NBA for 12 seasons, including the 1975 championship, this is North Carolina A&T's College All-American in 1960, floor general Al Attles.

versity in Charlotte, then in 1954-55 at A&T. His Aggies never had a losing season.

In the CIAA his Aggies scored five championships, winning both the "visitation" (regular season) and tournament honors. The years were 1958-59-62-64-67. There were also third place finishes in the national Division II tournaments in 1959 and 1964, as well as reaching the NIAA quarterfinals in 1977. It was something, these CIAA titles, that seemed to stay with Cal Irvin. He captained the 1945 Morgan State team that wore the CIAA crown.

He was a fighter, among the foremost among the black schools to seek NCAA Division I status. Just after he stepped down as coach to assume the A&T athletic directorship full time, he said: "How are you ever going to prove the calibre of your basketball when some of the major powers fail to give you a schedule? This is the ridiculous thing about it. I've sent out 50 inquiries and made phone calls. We didn't give a specific date, just anytime you want to play, we'll try to make the adjustment in order to try and reach this (NCAA) objective of 75 percent of our schedule." As the A&T team got better, such Division I date chances decreased. He battled for automatic qualification in the NCAA basketball playoffs: "I thought on several occasions we had teams that would have done well. With the NCAA reclassification now (1974), and all the MEAC teams leaning to I-AA football, I think Division I basketball is near."

Coach and wife Kathryn never forget one tournament final game, 1968 in the Greensboro Coliseum. Final score was Norfolk State 134, A&T 132. Kathryn Irvin recalled: "Oh, yes, that's the game that stands out most in my mind. It must be the overtimes (3) and all the points. I remember, just knowing and watching Cal's moves, he thought he had it won. Certain things started to happen, and the other team was playing equally well that night, and it was just a battle. Always, one or two points. That game sticks in my mind because, personally, I'd rather lose by a large margin than one or two. I still think we could have won it and should have won it, but that's all part of the game."

Getting the coach to recollect some of the big things, he never fails to start with Al Attles. When Attles became a head coach in the NBA (Golden State), Coach Irvin beamed. When Attles coached his team to the 1975 NBA championship, the coach was beside himself. In 1983, when Al Attles stepped out of the coach's shoes to become a general manager of the Warriors, the coach called his protege, again. Attles, a 6-foot, 175-pound guard, made the AP College all-American in 1960.

Coach Irvin reminisced: "If there was ever a team-oriented player, Al had to be the man. He could shoot, but he wasn't the greatest and he wasn't shot-oriented like they are today. Al never really took advantage of his one outstanding skill, going to the basket. He

And the man known around the world, Meadowlark Lemon, long-time star of the Harlem Globetrotters, born and raised in Wilmington.

liked to go and give it off. Everybody loved to play with Al Attles because he'd give it off.

"His players at Golden State were just like Al. Off the bench with fire in their eyes. That's Al all the way. He was a 6-foot guard but he jumped like 6-7, he could stuff it with ease. I've never seen guards who could jump like Al and Cleo Hill (Winston-Salem State). They were both from Newark and played in the league (CIAA) at the same time.

"I'll never forget one play against Morgan State. They had a man get the ball at midcourt and Al's back at our foul line. He takes off and the Morgan man goes for a layup from our foul line, and Al knocked the shot away. It's the greatest defensive play I ever saw. He had to catch up almost half the court. Al stayed hungry, he wanted to play all the time."

Attles was drafted fourth round by the Philadelphia Warriors. He didn't plan to attend the tryouts, wanting to teach in high school. A teammate, Vincent Miller, talked him into trying the NBA.

Three great coaches in the state, and the heritage began so long ago. Bighouse Gaines concluded years ago: "I'm a firm McLendon disciple. He knew where the good players were and what to do with them. People who say Everett Case was the first man to bring bigtime basketball to North Carolina are dead wrong — it was John McLendon."

126

14

The Black Athlete

Tensions were popping when the teams for the 1952 East Regional were finally announced.

North Carolina State and Kentucky, ranked No. 1 in the country and defending national champions, had qualified as their conference winners, but six other at-large teams had to be selected by an NCAA committee. It really didn't matter to Wolfpack fans, and thus basketball addicts of the state, because here was the potential of a game of all games. Everett Case vs Adolph Rupp, which had not happened since the 1947 NIT semifinals. And, if it happened, the ol' Gray Fox would catch the Baron of the Bluegrass right there in Reynolds Coliseum.

St. John's and Penn State were selected and directed to Raleigh, and Coach Frank McGuire took his New Yorkers to handy victory over N.C. State, then upset Kentucky and went on to the NCAA nationals in Seattle. Thus, the game of all games never took place, but North Carolina fans were treated to something else, somewhat unexpected, granted, but exciting.

It was warm that mid-March evening when Penn State took the Reynolds Coliseum floor against Kentucky. This was March 1952 and Penn State brought the first two blacks to play in Raleigh — Jesse Arnelle, a freshman center who averaged 18.5 points before the season concluded, and Hardy Williams, a clever guard. When Arnelle was introduced on the booming PA system, he got a standing ovation. He also got 22 points, high for the first night, but Kentucky won.

The next evening the same thing happened. Penn State played N.C. State in the consolation game, or third place, a better term with a more positive approach. Again Jesse Arnelle got a rousing response from the North Carolina fans. Coach Case threw a full-court press at the young Nittany Lions, it was no contest, but again Arnelle got 22 points.

College coaches of the state saw the reaction of the fans, who were white, more than 99.9 percent of them, and yet it would take them, the coaches and their college administrators, more than a de-

127

Lou Hudson, as outstanding player at Greensboro Dudley 1962, went to the University of Minnesota, became All-NBA.

cade to recruit the young black athletes who could play basketball so well, so very well.

Down at Barker High in New Barn, there was a gangly young player developing. Walt Bellamy grew to 6'-10" by his senior year when his team defeated Greensboro Dudley for the Negro state championship at North Carolina College (now N.C. Central). That was 1957.

Everett Case had scouting reports, naturally, and several times he had taken his story to the chancellor at N.C. State, Dr. Carey Bostian. Case, to recall his own stories years later, would expound on the talents of the young center from down in New Bern, and Dr. Bostian would inquire on how the recruiting was going. Case would then add: "There's one thing, Chancellor. He's black." The chancellor would then agree, in so many words, to this line of thinking: "I don't believe we're quite ready."

Walt Bellamy grew to 6'-11", went to Indiana University on Case's recommendation to an old friend, Coach Branch McCracken. After being selected on the 1960 USA Olympic team, which won handily in Rome and has been recognized as probably the best USA team ever, Bellamy was consensus all-American his senior year (1961), averaging 21.8 points and ranking seventh nationally rebounding. He was the No. 1 draft choice of the NBA's new Chicago entry, averaged 31.6 points per game in 1962, which only got runnerup slot since Wilt Chamberlain had his amazing 50.4 point average. Bellamy was in the NBA 14 years, averaged 20.1 points for this long career. But he had to play his college ball outside the state of North Carolina.

Five years later another potential all-American came along in the state's prep circles, playing in the North Carolina Negro High School Athletic Conference, which conducted its own activities in the segregated school system.

Lou Hudson was starring at Greensboro Dudley, his team winning the Negro 4-A state title as a junior, although losing out to Winston-Salem Carver his senior year. Hudson was a 6-foot-4, 187-pound natural-born athlete who could do everything. When his team won the 1961 state title, he scored 34 points to cap Dudley's 22-game win streak. In the 1962 state tournament defeat, he scored 41 points in vain. Coach Bill Furcron summed up his young senior in the *Greensboro Daily News:* "As good as Sam Jones and better than Happy Hairston (W-S Carver star, NYU starter). A better high school player than Walt Bellamy was when he was at New Bern. And he loves the game. Many a night I had to run him out of the gym in order to lock up." Coach Furcron predicted: "I am convinced that Louis can play major college basketball and I'm happy to say that I think he may get his chance. I even think he has a future in pro ball if he continues to improve." Both came true for Hudson, whose senior year saw a 23.6 point average, 10.8 rebounds, shooting 60.7 percent from the floor. Scouting him

First two black players selected to the Greensboro Daily News high school All-State team, recognized as the official one, were junior Gil McGregor of Raeford, left, and Daryl Cherry of West Charlotte. McGregor went to Wake Forest, Cherry to North Carolina A&T.

constantly had been Ted Owens of Kansas, Lou Roselli of NYU, Frank Truitt of Ohio State and John Kundla of Minnesota, who had been tipped off by Bones McKinney, old NBA teammates.

Lou Hudson went to Minnesota, but he almost didn't. Everett Case at N.C. State was talking about Hudson all the time, and so was Dean Smith, the new coach at Carolina, who recalled recently: "When I got the job after Frank (McGuire) left, my minister at the Baptist church told me he wanted me to get a black student-athlete as soon as possible. We talked to Lou in Greensboro, and Willie Holderness there wanted to give him a Jefferson Standard scholarship."

The Atlantic Coast Conference had voted in stricter admission regulations than the NCAA, first a 750 minimum college board, then raised to 800. It was a deterrent to the admission of black athletes, whose cause had been aided by the Civil Rights Act of 1964.

At the *Greensboro Daily News,* whose all-state high school teams were recognized as "official" in the state, Lou Hudson had been seriously considered for all-state, which would have made him the first black so honored. For some reason he was not chosen, something we still can't adequately explain. At the time the black schools had their own state association, their own Negro all-state, which Hudson led.

Lou Hudson went to Minnesota, scored 32 points in his first varsity game, made all-Big Ten in 1965 as a junior. He was a first round pro draft choice, made the 1967 all-rookie team with the St. Louis Hawks, then the all-NBA teams in 1970 with Atlanta. He played in six NBA all-star games, scored over 16,000 points in his NBA career.

Who, then, was the first black to make all-state? It came about in 1966, and there were two selections—Daryl Cherry of all-black West Charlotte High, Negro 4-A champions, and Junior Gilbert McGregor of Raeford High, state 3-A finalists. Coach C. A. McCullough described Cherry, a senior, as a "take charge player, great outside jumper, excellent on defense." He went to North Carolina A&T where he was all-CIAA as a junior. McGregor, 6'-6" and 210 pounds, was termed a "miniature Billy Cunningham," and his coach, Don Prince, said: "He just might be the hottest prospect in the whole state, a muscled athlete with tremendous spring in his legs. He's the best ever on Tar Heel soil." McGregor repeated his senior year, 1967, when he had grown to 6'-7" and 230 pounds, averaging 25 points, 23.2 rebounds, 10-12 blocked shots. His coach, W. K. Morgan, new at the school, said: "It appeared at times as if college coaches were holding a convention at some of our games." They included UCLA, whose John Wooden had seen McGregor at the Campbell Basketball Camp.

The East-West All-Star Games in Greensboro, conducted by the North Carolina Coaches Association, had not included the Negro state association schools. In 1966 the first blacks were selected —

Duke's first black player, C. B. Claiborne of Danville, Va.

N.C. State's first black player was Al Heartley of Clayton in Eastern North Carolina.

Norwood Todmann was Wake Forest's first black, started as a sophomore. He was from New York City.

David Lawrence of West Columbus and Garland Davis of North Stanley for basketball, running back Jimmy Kirkpatrick of Charlotte Myers Park in football. Davis was chosen the outstanding player and went to Catawba. The following year, 1967, McGregor and Billy Hayes of Clinton played for the East, John Banner of North Davidson and Bobby Parks of Gastonia Ashley for the West.

Coach Jack McCloskey recruited McGregor for Wake Forest, where he played freshman ball in 1967-68, on the same team with Charlie Davis who in 1971 became the first black player chosen ACC player of the year.

The University of Maryland is recognized as having recruited the first black basketball players to play in the ACC tournament, both Billy Jones and Pete Johnson, of metropolitan Washington, going to College Park in 1964-65.

At Carolina, Coach Dean Smith had a black freshman recruit in 1964-65, 6-foot-3 Willie Cooper of Elm City in Eastern North Carolina, but he did not complete the freshman season and never played varsity ball.

At Duke Coach Vic Bubas recruited C. B. Claiborne from Danville, Virginia as a freshman in 1965-66, and he played three varsity seasons, although not as starter. He played 12 games as a sophomore, averaging 1.7 points; 19 games as junior, 3.2 points; and 22 games as senior, 6.5 points. He was Wake's first black to play varsity ball in the Big Four.

At Wake Forest Coach McCloskey recruited Norwood Todmann from Power Memorial High in New York City, a teammate of Lew Alcindor's, whose scoring record Todmann broke as a senior. On the 1966-67 freshman team Todmann averaged 23.7 points, and he became starting soph guard. He was Wake's first black varsity starter.

At N.C. State Coach Norm Sloan, who came back to his alma mater the year before, recruited Al Heartley, a quick guard from Clayton in Eastern North Carolina, in 1967-68. He became a second all-tournament player as a senior.

First truly outstanding black player was Charlie Scott, 1966-67, another New Yorker who came down to Laurinburg Institute for his senior year and was valedictorian of his class there. Frank McDuffie Sr., institute president, has told the story that he called Carolina's Dean Smith several years before to tell about a young prospect, Jimmy Walker (later all-America at Providence) and two "other high scorers." Said McDuffie: "I told him they would carry him to the national championship."

Scott, however, did not take the direct line to Chapel Hill. Davidson Coach Lefty Driesell reviewed what happened: "We had Charlie Scott signed. There were no grants-in-aid then, but he committed to us early, then changed his mind later on. Coach at Lenoir Rhyne, Billy

Carolina's first black to make the varsity. All-American Charlie Scott of New York City, by way of Laurinburg Institute.

Wells, told me about Charlie who had been to his summer camp and told him he liked Davidson, wanted to come to Davidson. We had an early admission policy in September, Charlie applied and was accepted in December. After that, he changed his mind. We did get Mike Maloy, another New York boy, that year, and I remember Charlie called Maloy several times. They were going to room together."

Driesell scheduled a freshman game with Laurinburg Institute for the Charlotte Coliseum, fans put up big signs welcoming Charlie Scott. Coach Smith took up the story: "Sure we had heard about Charles Scott, he was an outstanding player, but Charles announced he was going to Davidson in the fall before we got busy recruiting. We let it go at that. Then one night, Bill Currie, who was doing our radio broadcasts, told me that Scott was going to visit Duke (January), and we knew the recruiting was starting all over again. Frank McDuffie told us Charles wanted to come to Carolina."

Charlie Scott was fantastic, an integral part of two Tar Heel teams which reached the NCAA Final Four, an all-American. Scott made all-ACC three times, the first black to attain that. At 6-foot-6, forward or guard, he might have been the best player in the ACC until David Thompson came along, but he was never voted player of the year. John Roche of South Carolina got it twice; newspaper cartoons had media voters going to the polls in their Ku Klux Klan white sheets.

At Wake Forest Coach McCloskey had both McGregor and Davis on his 1967-68 freshman team. McGregor was a three-year varsity starter with scoring averages that went 12.6, 12.5 and 14. But it was Davis who became the Deacon superstar, "C.D." as the students and fans called him. Three times he was all-ACC, equalling Scott's achievement, and he was voted ACC player of the year 1971. C.D. increased his scoring production steadily—22.8 as sophomore, 25.5 as junior, 26.5 senior.

Charlie Davis, in Winston-Salem banking business today, related his initial experiences as a black player in the ACC, taking a break as color analyst for the Deacon radio network: "When Charlie Scott came to Carolina, a gentleman who lived right across the street from me, Norwood Todmann, became the first black at Wake Forest. In Harlem we were close, we had played together for years. I didn't know anything about North Carolina. When Norwood told me he was coming to Wake Forest, I had to ask him where it was. He was such a great player, I thought he'd go some place like St. John's or UCLA. He said Wake Forest, and then the ACC. I said, where is that and what is it? But when he went to Wake Forest, it almost made up my mind right then, and during the summer before my senior year, Billy Packer came up to see me play, and he and I got along real well, so my choice was pretty much set.

"More and more black players were coming to play in North Carolina, but at the beginning it was basically rough. I was a young man from Harlem, basically I had been around black people all of my life. Coming down South was a definite change for me. And I remember certain things very clearly from my freshman year. Traveling to Virginia Tech and for the first time seeing 'For Whites Only' on a shower, and walking up in the stands and seeing a lady with what I thought were three Ks on her blouse. I didn't know if they were her initials or what, I knew what I thought it stood for. At Clemson they were throwing chocolate candy bars at me, and I heard a Clemson official ask one of our coaches, 'What are they bringing that coon in here for?' But it was changing, and the entire country was changing. It was a learning and a growing experience. I had Norwood a year ahead of me, maybe he caught most of it. Charlie Scott was a great basketball player but he had a tendency to irritate people. I was more low key."

C.D. was the first black player named the ACC's player of the year.

In 1968 Charlie Scott made all-conference; in 1969 both Scott and Davis did. In 1974 David Thompson, Len Elmore and John Lucas had the votes. In 1975, for the first time, four blacks all-conference— DT, Lucas, Skip Brown and Skip Wise. Then in 1977 the full all-conference quintet was black—Rod Griffin, Phil Ford, Skip Brown, Kenny Carr and Walter Davis. All became all-American as well.

At 30 years of age, Dean Smith took over the head coaching reins at Carolina.

15
Dean Smith

Most basketball coaches were guards, but Dean Edwards Smith was born and raised to be a coach. Maybe there was no way he could ever have avoided a profession which has become avocation as well, along with occasional hints of obsession.

And he was a guard. His father was a high school coach who had the keys to the gym in Emporia, Kansas and it was only natural to spend a lot of time shooting a basketball, but not all year, as some kids in Kansas did. Dean Smith, 5-foot-8, 135 pounds, was also a football quarterback and baseball catcher.

He went to the University of Kansas on an academic scholarship, but got closely involved in the basketball program headed by the venerable Phog Allen. Dean Smith started several varsity games his senior year with the Jayhawks, his career scoring average would test no calculators at 1.6.

But he claimed his first NCAA championship award with Kansas as a junior (1952), and in the official team photograph he's fifth from the left, front row, seated with knees crossed, uniform No. 33. There are 23 players in the team photo. En route to the finals, he scored a field goal against TCU, scoreless with St. Louis, not even listed in the final two games. Dean insisted he played in that final game, which brought Kansas the title over St. John's, coached by Frank McGuire. Recently he quipped, but in all seriousness because he never forgets a thing: "It's one of my pet peeves that the box score, when it came out in Kansas, didn't have my name in it. I played the last 47 seconds, and they didn't show me in the game. Maybe I should have fouled somebody and they'd have put me down." Even today, the NCAA does not show him playing. As for Coach Allen and seven team members, they formed the USA Olympic team that won the gold in Helsinki. Dean Smith's would come later in Montreal. As a senior, his Kansas team returned to the national finals, lost to Indiana, and this time Dean Smith had a foul shot and a personal foul, and made the box score.

From the Air Force ROTC on graduation, he was commissioned

second lieutenant in 1953 and in Munich had his first coaching job, a service team that went 11-0. There he met Bob Spear who two years later became head coach at the new Air Force Academy, got Smith reassigned to the academy in January 1956 as a member of his coaching staff.

It was Kansas City in March 1957, another national finals, Kansas again in the competiton, this time with tall Wilt Chamberlain. Dick Harp, former Allen assistant, was head coach and that weekend Dean Smith did some scouting for his friend at Kansas. Among the other three teams was North Carolina. The NABC convention met concurrently with the finals, and three coaches roomed together — Frank McGuire of North Carolina, Ben Carnevale of Navy (ex-Carolina) and Bob Spear of Air Force Academy (ex-Navy). This time Spear brought along his young assistant, Smith. Carnevale told the story recently: "Frank was needing some help, along with Buck Freeman, and we were sitting together in the Catskills one summer and Frank asked if I knew anybody. I told him Bob Spear had a young man getting out of the service soon, I didn't know his name, but we called Bob in Denver." McGuire then added this: "When I mentioned I wanted to get somebody (1957), Spear said he might have somebody I would be interested in. This Dean Smith. I said, there's nobody I know named Dean. Joe, Frank, Bob, Carl, but not Dean. But what kind of a guy is he?" Then Dean Smith added this version for me: "We were having breakfast one morning in the hotel suite during the tournament, and Frank asked me if I'd be interested. I told him to talk to Bob first." The young assistant came to Chapel Hill in the summer of 1958, a year later, at age 27.

I asked McGuire what early ideas he formed about his new assistant, who remained on the bench three seasons: "I was interested in getting Dean's family set up, get his house ready, and he'd come to the office and say, 'When are you going to let me do some work?' He's a worker, he wanted to get on the road and stay there. He never let any detail go. He's more like a teacher, I guess, go over detail time after time after time. And I learned he's a real competitor. I was a good handball player, and he'd do anything off a couple walls to get a point, and like golf, he'd hit the ball five feet off the tee, then par the hole."

Everything broke loose after three seasons. Probation, point-shaving scandals, floor fights, and in August Coach McGuire took a job as coach of the NBA Philadelphia Warriors, which starred Wilt Chamberlain. Dean Smith was offered the head position at Chapel Hill, and no coach ever pondered the situation as questionable as this one. He had the chance to go to Wyoming, maybe Navy with Carnevale retiring, and he was 30 years old. He told reporters several years later: "There were so many problems at Carolina. Our 1962 schedule had been limited to 16 games (conference plus two) by the probation, and we could only recruit two out-of-state players. Plus, Doug Moe and York Larese had graduated, leaving us with only three scholarship players, Larry Brown, Jim Hudock and Donnie Walsh. Billy Cunningham was coming as a freshman, but I had to recruit him all over again because people figured when Frank left Cunningham would also leave. It turned out he was happy with Carolina and stayed with us. The university sought a new image. Chancellor Bill Aycock told me just to represent the school well and not worry about our won-lost record. He wanted no more controversy, no fights on the courts and for our players to conduct themselves like gentlemen. He also told me I was a member of the faculty and that I'd have a job as long as he was chancellor. Of course, I didn't know he would retire the next year."

That was the start, 1961-62. It was from the pits. From the 1961 team, which ranked No. 5 nationally and finished 19-4, 1,001 of the team's 1,765 points had graduated (Moe, Larese, Dick Kepley), and both Yogi Poteet and Ken McComb became ineligible. On the freshman team the two out-of-stater grants went to Cunningham and Jay Neary, in-staters Bill Brown, Ray Respass and Pud Hassell. The team went 8-9. The 1963 team proved to be one of Coach Smith's "favorites" as the years have gone by. It used the 6-foot-5 Cunningham in the middle (20.7 points per game) and had Larry Brown operate the shuffle, which Coach Smith had learned from Bruce Drake at Oklahoma State. Even then, he talked like this: "The shuffle enhances team play and all five men have shot opportunities. It also revolves players into various offensive spots. It is not uncommon to see a backcourt operative move into the pivot." It worked for years. That season it beat Kentucky in Lexington, reached the tournament semifinals, beat Notre Dame on national TV and posted a 15-6 mark.

Then came another low. Brown and Poteet were gone, Donnie Walsh was the third member of the coaching staff, Cunningham had to do just about everything. Of the Kangaroo Kid, Coach Smith said: "His timing is uncanny. This makes him appear to go higher than most other players. He has the gift of meeting the ball at just the right moment." But Carolina finished 12-12 with Charlie Shaffer and Mike Cooke as co-captains, and there were rumblings in the back room, some from alumni, some boos from students. That came to a public head about midnight January 6, 1965, when the Carolina team returned to Chapel Hill after a disastrous game at Wake Forest (in Winston-Salem). They had lost four straight on the road, holding a 6-6 record. When the team bus approached Woollen Gym, an ill-tempered group of students chanted, "We want Smith, we want Smith," and suspended from the building was a dummy of the coach, burning in effigy. Cunningham, it is related, stormed off the bus and

141

tore it down, and the coach, though angered, calmly got off the bus and talked to the students. The team, which then won nine of the next 12 games, had Cunninghm and sophomore Bob Lewis, who averaged 36.6 points as a freshman, and in the yearling class was Larry Miller.

If anything, this was the turning point. Carmichael Auditorium, seating 10,000, was ready for December 1965, twice as big as utility-useful Woollen since 1938, replacing the old Tin Can. Cunningham was gone, with scoring and rebounding records, but the balanced lineup included sophomores Larry Miller and Tom Gauntlett forwards, Bob Bennett center, Bob Lewis and Johnny Yokley guards. It was to be the last conference tournament in Reynolds Coliseum, and the Tar Heels faced the nationally-ranked Duke Blue Devils in the semifinal game Friday night. That was before TV, except for the championship game. It was to be the first "Slowdown of the Century" game in tournament play. Carolina went four corners at the opening tipoff, and Coach Vic Bubas retained his zone and let the clock tick. Duke 7-5 at halftime, Carolina up 17-10 with 10 minutes to play. Steve Vacendak tied the score at 20 with 2:09. After Carolina missed a free throw, Duke held for the final shot. Bob Verga, covered, passed underneath to Mike Lewis, fouled. Missed first, made second, four seconds, Duke 21-20. Said Coach Smith in the postgame: "But I'd like to say I was wrong —wrong because we lost. Whether we lose 121-120 or 21-20, we still lost to Duke." Carolina 1966 led the nation in one of Coach Smith's prized categories, field goal shooting. Its freshman team included 6'-11" Rusty Clark, 6'-8" Bill Bunting, Dick Grubar, Joe Brown and Gerald Tuttle.

First conference championship and NCAA Final Four came in 1967, together, the start of a three-year string which would project Dean Smith as a national coaching name. He had wondered about that level only a year or two before, but as Coach McGuire said earlier, Smith was a worker. Before that season, he admitted: "We'll have a good team that can go out there and play with anybody. And for the first time since I've been here, we have enough depth that all positions are up for grabs." He had begun to schedule intersectionally in December — Penn State, Tulane, at Kentucky, NYU, Tampa Invitational, Ohio State, Princeton. They went into January 9-0, finished atop the conference standings. Junior Larry Miller gained the Case Award as tournament MVP as the Tar Heels swept the tough road—State, Wake and Duke. They were No. 3 nationally, and in the finals Miller got 32, Lewis 26, and Coach Smith said: "We became a great team at halftime of the Wake Forest game (semifinals). We played three halves as well as we have all year but what caused it? What happens? I don't know, a coach seldom knows. Their mental attitude became stronger, they just took over.

Rusty Clark of Fayetteville became the big man the Tar Heels needed, going to three straight finals, including this action shot from the 1969 NCAA finals against Purdue.

They played the whole game with Duke just like that second half with Wake Forest."

They beat Princeton and Boston College in Smith's first NCAA regional play, but then in Louisville in the national semis (or then called the Eastern finals) the Tar Heel shooters missed and Donnie May of Dayton had an unbelievable night, 16 of 24 attempts from the floor and 34 points. Houston and Elvin Hayes beat Carolina for third spot, and Lew (Jabbar) Alcindor took his first national crown.

Coach Smith's Baptist minister had urged him, almost the day he became head coach, to get a black player on the team. Charlie Scott, to become the first black to make all-conference, moved up as a sophomore in 1968, along with Eddie Fogler, and Bill Guthridge joined the coaching staff to replace Larry Brown who wanted to play again (ABA). Carolina repeated as conference champs and NCAA finalist, beating St. Bonaventure and Davidson in the regional, then a good Big Ten champion Ohio State 80-66 in the national semifinals. It was Carolina's shot at the Wooden Era, and Alcindor naturally. They did not master the challenge. UCLA concentrated defense on the two key Tar Heel scorers, Alcindor took lob passes for easy goals, and the Bruins won by an NCAA final record 23 points, 78-55.

Miller graduated, the Tar Heels starters in 1969 were Bill Bunting and Charlie Scott forwards, Rusty Clark center, Dick Grubar and Eddie Fogler guards. They achieved No. 4 national rank, another conference crown in Charlotte, regional victories over Duquesne and Davidson, the latter on a Scott bomber at the buzzer. But in the ACC tournament finals Grubar injured his left knee in the first half and watched the rest of the schedule from the bench. This time in the Final Four they encountered another hot-shooter, Rick Mount of Purdue, 14 of 28 for 36 points and 92-65 defeat. Drake won third place, and Alcindor completed his triple. UCLA was still beating everybody in the nation in the NCAA championship game, with those centers.

Coach Smith later reviewed the first visits to the finals: "In 1967 this was a very good team although it was young. We had sophomores, and like I said, Dayton was lucky to be there after NCAA overtime wins over Western Kentucky and Virginia Tech, but Donnie May had a great night and we got beat . . . In 1968 this was probably the best team of the three. It soundly beat a good Ohio State team in the semifinals out there in Los Angeles, while UCLA had a great game against Houston. We played extremely well against UCLA in the finals, and we were doing fine until Bill Bunting and Rusty Clark got in foul trouble . . . As for 1969 this is where the matter of luck comes in. Dick Grubar was hurt in the conference tournament, and we were just plain lucky to get by Duquesne and Davidson in the regional. In the semifinals Rick Mount had an outstanding shooting night and Purdue beat us. That was that."

144

Phil Ford became national player of the year, tournament MVP his freshman year. He's working around N.C. State's Clyde Austin.

Carolina missed a 20-win season in 1970, lost to Virginia in the tournament opener at Charlotte when Charlie Scott scored 41 points, the only player ever to score 40-or-more in back-to-back games in the tournament. It's a good trivia catcher, because the games were 364 days apart. In Greensboro in 1971 they played South Carolina in one of the great tournament finishes, down to a jump ball with North Carolina ahead by one, six seconds. The shorter Gamecock got the tip, Tom Owens the layup, South Carolina the win 52-51.

They were back in Los Angeles in 1972, playing in the finals, and this time the Tar Heels had Robert McAdoo, the first and only junior college transfer Coach Smith ever accepted. He was the starting center with Bill Chamberlain and Dennis Wuycik forwards, Steve Previs and George Karl guards. In the regional they beat South Carolina —out of the ACC — and Pennsylvania and went to the finals as the No. 2 rated team. UCLA was No. 1, and the experts forecast a real battle between the nation's two giants. It never came about; Florida State toppled an error-prone Tar Heel attack 79-75, and Carolina had to be content with third place over a fine Louisville aggregation, Coach Denny Crum's first finals entry. UCLA won another; it had Bill Walton in center. They didn't change much at UCLA.

Phil Ford, freshman, returned the ACC title to Chapel Hill in 1975, winning the tournament outstanding player award and beating David Thompson and N.C. State in the final game 70-66. At the final buzzer the fuzzy-cheeked kid from Rocky Mount rolled on the floor at mid-court, over and over, pounding the floor in triumph. He concluded in postgame interview: "I guess this would have to be the best three days of basketball I've ever played. I psyched myself up because I knew the competition would be great." They lost to Syracuse in the regional on a final play still argued in the best of circles. Virginia at Capital Centre had its miracle of 1976 at the expense of N.C. State, Maryland and Carolina, and Ford injured his foot in one of those pickup games that kids play, and the Tar Heels limped through a prompt NCAA loss.

But 1977 took the Tar Heels back to the Final Four, this time in the more friendly confines of the Atlanta Omni, with a squad that added Mike O'Koren. Another state team, UNC-Charlotte, was in the quartet at the Omni, and Wake Forest almost made it. Nevada-Las Vegas and Marquette, coached by Al McGuire who had begun his coaching in North Carolina at Belmont Abbey, completed the field. John Kuester's quarterbacking directed the Tar Heels through the conference and No. 6 national ranking, then in regional play over Purdue, Notre Dame and Kentucky despite injuries. They outran Vegas but lost to Marquette.

Coach Smith was asked some time ago to review those last two national trips: "In 1972 in Los Angeles we had Florida State first, and they simply outplayed us. We were down 13 at halftime, and I was real happy about the way we came back, losing by four. Any similarity in those first four games in the finals? I don't see any.

"Atlanta 1977, well, when you get that far, the final four, maybe you should win, but . . . I'll say this, we were the best team in the country after the Far West Classic (Portland in late December), and we were again the best team in the country when we beat Maryland by 27. But we weren't the best team when Tommy LaGarde came down. He didn't get back. You remember what happened in the NCAAs. Walter Davis injured his finger (right hand, shooting hand) in the ACC tournament, and we're just lucky to beat Purdue in the first round. We might not have done that had we not been playing in Reynolds Coliseum with the home crowd. Notre Dame in the East Regional had us down 14 and Walter wasn't shooting effectively. In the final 20 seconds Phil Ford hurts his elbow. Kentucky was the No. 2 ranked team, I believe, and Davis was great. That was a big upset. Against Marquette in Atlanta, we got up 44-42, we debated. Ford that jumper from the side with about 13 minutes left, and if he had made it, we'd be up four and going to the four corners. But he couldn't shoot, as you know, and he missed. We had caught up in such a hurry that I didn't feel we had the momentum we needed."

At this point, in his office for the occasion, he asked somebody to bring us the 1977 finals film, and he turned on the machine: "There, you can see, four minutes went by without much action, back and forth, and there's Bill Buckley with a layup. Close, but I'd say a good call, no foul. Now Marquette goes into its delay, so when we get the ball next, about 12 minutes left and score tied, we go to the four corners. About then, I thought to myself, how about going into something unusual? But we had won all those other games with the four corners to get to the Omni, why change? The difference here (Marquette) was we had to pull them out of the zone. They knew Phil (Ford) couldn't shoot, so they just sat back in the zone. If we could get them out, by going ahead, we knew Bernard Toone couldn't play us in man, and we'd go back to our normal game." It didn't work that way. Marquette made free throws, controlled a jump ball with two minutes left, score 53-51. Coach Smith ended the story of the 67-59 loss: "And we had to chase."

There's no way to explain 1979 and Black Sunday in Raleigh. Carolina and Duke had finished in a regular season deadlock in the league, coming about when Smith's offense took a sabbatical at Durham in the final season game. The Tar Heels, would you believe, took one shot and trailed 0-7 at halftime (losing 40-47). His teams have certainly been unpredictable. Both were in the top seven nationally and placed them in the East Regional. Easy first round games in Raleigh assured both ACC giants a spot in the East Regional at Greensboro. Neither made it; Penn beat Carolina, St. John's hit Duke. Neither knew what hit them, and neither did the sellout 12,400 crowd. Or all those people who bought Greensboro tickets to beat the rush.

Coach Smith took his sixth excursion to the NCAA Final Four in Philadelphia in 1981, and it followed an exciting return to Capital Centre at Landover, Maryland for the conference event. The Tar Heels, ranked second to Virginia which had been No. 1 in the country many weeks, edged Wake Forest on a final shot in the semis, then staved off Maryland's serious threat in the closing seconds of the finals. Virginia, on season record, stayed in the NCAA East while the Tar Heels got to see the sights in El Paso, Texas and play Pittsburgh, then Salt Lake City in the regional beating Utah and Kansas State. Beating the home-standing Utes was an outstanding accomplishment, 15 points each from Al Wood, Sam Perkins and James Worthy.

Two ACC teams were on the floor in Philadelphia, paired against each other in the opening semifinal. Virginia from the East and North Carolina from the West. After a halftime score tied at 27, Wood began to hit from everywhere, including Independence Hall, having an NCAA record 39 points in 78-65 victory. It placed Carolina and Indiana in the finals. After an early Tar Heel surge behind Worthy, the Hoosiers went ahead by intermission. Then in the opening five minutes of the second period, Isiah Thomas turned thief and savior, thief for the Tar Heels, savior for the Bobby Knightmen and Indiana turned back Carolina 63-50 on Coach Smith's sixth appearance in the finals, and without victory.

It, a championship, would come in 1982 in the spacious Louisiana Superdome.

Carolina had just lost another NCAA championship game, this time in Atlanta to Marquette (1977). On the bench after the runnerup awards, Mike O'Koren, Walter Davis and Tommy LaGarde (leg in cast).

Another first in the Dean Smith Saga, that Carolina had never lost an East Regional when it reached the final game, prevented a record return to the Final Four in Albuquerque. Its dominance of the East began in 1967, and when the Tar Heels tipped with Georgia at Syracuse in the 1983 East finals, the light blue was odds-on favorite to capture the seventh consecutive East finals. But Georgia won, and the season was over. Had the Tar Heels of Sam Perkins, Matt Doherty, Brad Daugherty, Michael Jordon and Jim Braddock continued their East control, the national semifinals would have seen N.C. State and North Carolina playing each other in somewhat distant New Mexico.

Over these years, if Dean Smith had the question once, which he did, he got it a million times and not just in press conferences. He had not won a national title until New Orleans. He meant it when he said: Getting to the Final Four is harder than winning a national championship. There are 30 coaches who have won national titles, three who have been to the Final Four five times. Which mountain is harder to climb, the one that 30 people have climbed or the one three people have climbed?" Remember, he got his degree in math at Kansas.

Always active in national and international bodies, Dean Smith became the head coach of the USA Olympic men's basketball team for 1976 Montreal. It was a challenge from the start; people sought revenge for the 1972 robbery in Munich when the Soviets were handed the gold.After trials and votes by selection committeemen, the final USA squad consisted of seven players from the ACC, four from Coach Smith's Carolina team. Nationwide criticism became a motivating factor for the coaching staff, Smith and Bill Guthridge (Carolina) and John Thompson (Georgetown) and the players themselves. Afterwards, Smith admitted as much: "It was all the talk and all the complaining about the players selected to play for us. I received a mountain of mail about the team when it was chosen, and the heavy majority of it was critical." They didn't beat the Russians simply because the Russians failed to make the top level, beaten by Yugoslavia, but on July 27, 1976, in the Montreal Forum, with large and small American flags waving, the USA won the gold, defeating Yugoslavia in an undefeated run 95-74. The starting team had been Scott May of Indiana and Adrian Dantley of Notre Dame forwards, Mitch Kupchak of Carolina center, Phil Ford of Carolina and Quinn Buckner of Indiana guards. And as Lord Killanin, the Olympic president, draped gold medals around each neck, Kenny Carr of N.C. State gave the Irish lord a soul handshake.

It was total vindication for the selection process. Dean Smith made his point: "We were looking for those who were very team-oriented, dedicated and intense. We won't find as many people as big and strong as the opponents in our bracket, so we looked for quickness and speed." For the future he recommended six team members and the coach from the NCAA champion form the USA Olympic nucleus, with the coach having authority to select the other six players without help from a selection committee. It has not been adoted yet.

Dean Smith has always had new ideas for the business, or the game, if you prefer. Early his players used the "tired signal," clenched fist to tell the coach you wanted a break. He got so excited in his first game as head coach, when Larry Brown gave the signal, Smith raised his fist and yelled, "Right, let's go, play hard." Then there was the signal from the scoring player to the man who made the good pass and you see it in the NBA nowadays. Or the team huddle at the free throw line before a shot, setting up the ensuing defense. Or the four corners, ah, the four corners. It was at its best with Phil Ford in the middle, some even it called it Ford's Corners. Some years ago Coach Smith said, "Some of this delay stuff I brought out of the mothballs from Henry Iba, then put it away again. Like the triangle-2 we've used. I remember I had planned to use it back in 1970, Charlie Scott's senior year. We were in the ACC tournament in Charlotte, and if we had played South Carolina, the top club with John Roche, we would have tried it. But, remember, we want to score with it." It not only spread the offense, it spread all over the country.

The coach says sometimes he might overschedule the team, but he believes in a strong December slate of non-conference games, against the best in the country. Or trips to holiday tournaments, even an in-season jaunt to Spain (1972) or England (1975).

Through it all, 22 seasons and a 500th victory which will come early in 1983-84, there is a Carolina system with a lot of rules and the maintenance of a certain image. The disciplined game brought this remark from the coach in the 70s: "Actually, one of the most set, disciplined offenses in the country belongs to UCLA, and they have won nine of the last 11 national titles." It was his tribute to John Wooden.

Dean Smith can call your name if he only shook your hand once in an airport. He takes time to call, more than several times, a young boy in Greensboro dying of cancer. On April 26, 1982, just home with a national title, he sat down with 1,200 students under Carolina Union sponsorship. "An evening with Dean Smith." The subject ranged from athletic grants to the new Student Activities Center, which will seat 23,000 in Chapel Hill by 1985-86, to the actual color of the uniform pants against Georgetown. Then on October 22, 1982, he aided in a University Extension Education Division seminar on "Sports and American Values," with professors from the history and English departments, conducted for a group of men in industry and business.

It was Bill Foster, when he was at neighborhood Duke, who had a banquet one-liner: "I thought the man who invented basketball was Naismith, not Dean Smith.'"

16
Davidson's Wild-cats

WILDCAT: an undomesticated feline carnivore, resembling the domestic cat but larger and stronger.

Davidson's basketball Wildcats grew to full size. Big cats indeed, in the late 60s when they almost attained, not once but on two occasions no less, the ultimate of the NCAA Final Four.

Under Charles (Lefty) Driesell as coach, they reached the East Regional finals, facing on both occasions North Carolina, which they never played in regular season. In 1968 they fell by four points, in 1969 by a last-second field goal from center field by Charlie Scott, who indeed had first committed to attend Davidson.

But basketball on the Mecklenburg County campus did not begin in the 60s, rather many decades before, reaching state-wide acclaim and attention, even though the national picture never really unfurled until the Driesell Era, still the pride of Wildcat athletic heritage.

In the 30s and pre-World War II 40s, the state had its Big Five, Davidson plus the later-day ACC schools which became the Big Four after Everett Case arrived on the scene. The Big Five represented the state champion, and newspaper headlines proclaimed that title on equal terms with the Southern Conference. Sometimes, it even got more attention.

Davidson College played its first intercollegiate games in the winter of 1909, and its first three opponents were Wake Forest (losing 17-38), Trinity, now Duke (losing 22-8) and Guilford (winning 25-9). There was a decade wherein the coach is today unknown, and the foundation of Wildcat basketball was being built by two football staff coaches serving as head basketball men, Monk Younger 1924-31 and Flake (Red) Laird 1932-37.

It was Norman Shepard, who had coached North Carolina's 26-0 Southern and national champions in 1924 before going into business, who brought the first Wildcat challenges toward Southern Conference honors. When the Southeastern schools pulled out of the old Southern Conference in 1932, Davidson had been among seven schools apply-

Bringing the Wildcats into national prominence, Coach Lefty Driesell solved all his headaches.

ing for membership to replace them. Ever cautious, the Southern rejected the petition that first year, but in 1936 Davidson, along with Wake Forest and four others, was admitted to the conference, competing for the first basketball title in 1937.

Shepard took over in 1938, and by 1943 the Wildcats came into the conference tournament No. 3 seeded. Tommy Peters, an outstanding forward, won the SC scoring title with 209 points in 11 conference games, and he was also selected to the all-tournament team. This was wartime, and Davidson's first round opponent, N.C. State, lost three regulars in the draft just a couple weeks before the tournament. Peters' 17 points were certainly needed to offset a second half Wolfpack rally, the Wildcats winning 33-30. In the semifinals Davidson played favored George Washington, which would win the title. Peters scored 19 points as Davidson led the whole game, only to be tied with nine seconds in regulation. In overtime George Peters, Tommy's brother, got the only Wildcat points as GW won 47-40.

Again in 1948 the Cats came strong. Buddy Cheek made all-conference, the first such team ever selected in the Southern, and he scored 21, while J. D. Ashmore had 17, in beating Maryland 58-51 in the Raleigh tournament. Davidson had defeated Duke in regular season, but in the tourney semis Duke won 53-37 after the Wildcats led 26-24 at halftime, then could score only three points in 11 minutes. Cheek was stopped, Whit Cobb's set shots made the only damage. It was the year a season tie for the eighth position brought 10 teams into the four-day SC tournament, and the Big Five was represented in full. Half the enlarged field came from the state. Shepard, who became chairman of the NCAA district selection committee (before automatic conference qualifying), left coaching after the next season.

Tom Scott coached four seasons before becoming athletic director, and he, too, was later an NCAA basketball chairman, except his title was national, head of the NCAA Division I basketball committee, and instigator of the first 32-team bracket in the playoffs.

Lefty Driesell, from Tidewater Virginia, had played his college ball at Duke, a reserve on the Blue Devil team that went into the first ACC tournament No. 1 seeded (1954). They lost to champion N.C. State in the semifinals, Driesell having eight playing minutes in two games, getting four points and four rebounds. In four years coaching in Norfolk and Newport News his prep record was 97-15, including a 57-game win streak and state championship.

Davidson called him, Driesell accepted for 1960-61. Lefty recalled recently: "Davidson just wanted to have a good team, not a nationally ranked team or anything like that, because they only gave me $500 to recruit. They didn't really expect too much. My anticipation was to be in the top 10, which I felt we could do as soon as I got there. As soon as I spend my $500, which was about two weeks, I went to Dr.

Grier Martin, the president, and asked for another $1,000, which he gave me. Then some alumni gave me some more and we started getting some good players."

It meant recruiting head-to-head with the ACC schools, and Driesell know all about that soon: "Terry Holland was the first player I recruited. He was an all-state player down at Clinton and he was the first player Davidson had signed in a long, long time that other ACC schools were after. Then very soon came Fred Hetzel." Holland was captain his senior year, 1964, when he also led the nation in field goal shooting accuracy, hitting 63.1 percent. Semi Mintz 1958 had been the nation's best shooting free throws, 88.2 percent. But neither Holland or Hetzel could take a conference title, thus an NCAA opportunity. Captain Holland's 1964 team, 22-4, lost in the tournament to VMI 81-82, while Captain Hetzel's 1965 Wildcats, ranked No. 6 by AP and UPI in the final polls, were beaten in the tournament semifinals by West Virginia 72-74 in overtime.

The two shots at the Final Four, both excellent opportunities to be sure, came in 1968 and 1969.

The first of those great clubs had Mike Maloy, Rodney Knowles, Jerry Kroll, Doug Cook, Wayne Huckel, Dave Moser and Mike O'Neill. It beat West Virginia for the conference crown, then defeated St. John's 79-70 in the NCAA first round at College Park, Maryland. Raleigh had the 1968 East Regional, and Davidson advanced over Columbia 61-60, but in the physical process Doug Cook suffered a hip injury that prevented him from dressing in the Saturday finals. It put Davidson versus Carolina. For years Lefty had been trying to schedule Coach Dean Smith, to no avail; this was the first game between the two schools since 1954, when Carolina left the Southern Conference.

It was quite an exciting ball game, going in spurts (Carolina first eight points, Davidson next nine). Davidson by six at halftime, the Tar Heels pressing the second half, Carolina got lead at 47-46 and went nine up, then Davidson charged back. Mike Maloy made it 67-64 with 38 seconds, Maloy again 68-66 with 22 seconds. But time ran out. Carolina 70-66 and a trip to Los Angeles. Driesell analyzed what had hapened: "We lost to a real fine club, I'd like to see them go all the way. It would make us look good if they did. I've said all along we belonged in the top 10. We got beat by the third best, and if Carolina should win it, it would make us No. 2."

He immediately looked ahead: "All starters on my club are back next year. I'm just 35 years old. We're going to be in the NCAA finals one of these days." Almost prophetic. Ironic that Charlie Scott, who first wanted to go to Davidson, would make the finest shot of his Tar Heel career to knock the Wildcats out of the NCAA tree. Coach Driesell had recruited Scott out of Laurinburg Institute. Charlie had committed early to come to Davidson, then changed his mind for Carolina.

It had really riled the Wildcat coach, but then several years later Scott participated in the Driesell summer basketball camp as counselor.

Taking the conference title again, 102-76 over East Carolina in the tournament finals, the Wildcats downed Villanova 75-61 in the NCAA first round at Raleigh, moved on to the East Regionals at College Park. Just reverse the sites of the previous March. Mike Maloy looked forward to playing some of his street buddies from New York, facing St. John's in the opener, and Mike only achieved a career high, 35 points and Davidson 79-69.

There they were again—Davidson vs. Carolina, a spot in the NCAA Final Four at stake. Davidson came in 27-2, Carolina 26-3. Doug Cook, who missed the year before, was definitely ready. Wayne Huckel nursed a knee injury from St. John's but played. Carolina had Dick Grubar on crutches from the ACC tournament. Davidson led by five early, Carolina 47-46 at halftime, lead having changed 21 times. Wildcats up five, Carolina lost Lee Dedmon on fouls, but Scott came alive. Into the final minute, tied at 85. Coach Dean Smith called timeout with 13 seconds. Coach Driesell in postgame said: "I thought about using a zone to stop Scott, but decided to go man. I knew Scott would take the shot because he was so hot in the second half. I knew he would be taking it if he was playing for me." Charlie Scott did, 20-25 feet out, high orbit. The ball went through the nets as the clock flicked two seconds remaining, and Davidson never actually got the ball back into play, trying desperately to get a timeout. On national TV it was quite a Saturday matinee—Carolina 87, Davidson 85. Driesell complimented the man he once recruited: "The key was Scott. I'm not sure the greatest defense in the world could have stopped him (10 of his last 13 shots). He really rose to the occasion."

The next day, Sunday, Driesell announced on his TV show over WBTV Charlotte that he was leaving to accept the job at the University of Maryland. Over the air he said: "I didn't reach a decision until 4 a.m. this morning, and five minutes before that I was still going to stay at Davidson. It was the toughest decision I ever had to make." In nine seasons—176-62, three conference titles, two real, real, shots at the Final Four.

Terry Holland succeeded his coach. Recently, Holland, now head coach at Virginia, said in recollection: "At the time he (Driesell) was recruiting me, Davidson had won 4-5 games the previous season and he kept saying Dvidson could have a very fine basketball team and obtain national ranking. He was a little over-enthusiastic at the time, I thought, but he still convinced me that could have a good team I would be proud to be associated with, and that was the big question in my mind. While he had big dreams, those dreams were fulfilled."

Holland's first team 1970-71 won the conference title, lost to St. Bonaventure in the NCAA first round. His five-year mark was 92-43, including an NIT appearance in 1972.

Fred Hetzel, All-American, divided his time between his basketball, his books and his motorcycle.

Terry reminisced recently: "We did well in the ACC area then. I doubt if there were any ACC teams ranked ahead of us in the good year, it was certainly equal to the ACC. We scrimmaged several ACC teams but we didn't get a chance to play any of them. As a coach, it was fun that you were coaching at a school of 1,000 students and you were playing over the nation against schools that had much larger enrollment and much greater support financially, and it was fun to beat the old theory, the underdog couldn't win."

17
Ever-Changing Women's Game

Admittedly, it is difficult, very difficult to graph a continued line of progress in women's basketball in the state of North Carolina.

Without question, college women are playing their very greatest today, at all levels of NCAA competition since the drowning of the AIAW (Association of Intercollegiate Athletics for Women). They are experiencing athletic scholarships toward their education, opportunities to travel coast to coast and around the world, sports page headlines from time to time, television recognition. All have been long overdue.

But in the early 50s there were the Hanes Hoisery women of Winston-Salem who captured, and gloriously, three consecutive National AAU championships which were the ultimate attainment at the time. No college play competitively, no Olympics, just AAU.

Not too long ago, over a salad bowl at the plant cafeteria just north of Winston-Salem, Eckie Jordan, the feisty, 5-foot-3 all-American and AAU Hall of Famer, was talking about basketball the way Hanes Hosiery played.

"We had the whole team try out for the Pan-American Games in 1955," she related, "and three of us made it. We played international rules, or men's rules if you wish. Coach Virgil Yow took us to South America one summer for a month, and we played men's rules. One reason we were so good, and really, we were, was because we scrimmaged boys teams from high school all the time."

Today college women play the same men's rules. Could Hanes Hosiery play these North Carolina States, Old Dominions, Southern Cals, Louisiana Techs? Eckie Jordan's quick response: "Sure, we could beat them. We would challenge anybody, that's how much confidence we had. We played their rules, and we loved it. I don't think they are as strong as we were, they don't set up plays like we did."

Be that as it may, the game will never take place. Eras never seem to get together, eyeball to eyeball.

Naismith started his game at Springfield, Massachusetts in December 1891, and a short time after, a women's physical education instructor at Buckingham Grade School had her girls on the gymnasium floor. Smith College, with Senda Berenson as the organizer, is credited with the first actual game in 1893, playing Wellesley. The game came to the South, through training programs and word of mouth. At Chapel Hill the women played basketball on a club level, records show, as early as 1900. At Guilford College the YMCA gymnasium, reported the *Guilford Collegian* (student magazine), saw "the lack of heat and lighting discourage the use of the gym in the winter months." This was alleviated in 1900, Guilford women played basketball on an intramural level.

The "Victorian Woman" was cautious; team sports were not really in vogue. At the North Carolina Normal and Industrial College (later Woman's College, now University of North Carolina at Greensboro) the athletic association presented a trophy "for a championship team known as Athletics Class." The year was 1900, the sports were basketball and tennis. The school's first field day was 1909. Then came World War I, the women's suffrage 19th Amendment in August 1920, and then the Roarin' Twenties. Mary Channing Coleman headed the physical education department at Woman's College, which in turn taught and trained most of the phys-ed high school teachers in the state. Miss Coleman believed in mass participation, and Woman's College excelled with its play days and gym meets. Miss Coleman's influence curtailed high school tournament play for girls. She was succeeded in 1947 by Ethel Martus (Lawther), and before her retirement in 1974, times had changed. So did Ethel Martus. In March 1973, when UNC-G hosted the North Carolina AIAW basketball tournament, with women athletes playing full-court and enjoying it, I was sitting next to Ethel Lawther and commented: "I wonder if Miss Coleman is turning over in her grave."

In 1963 UNC-G had its first women's team, coached by Ellen Griffin, more famed as one of the nation's leading golf instructors, and the season consisted of four games. In 1968 the UNC-G men's team was organized. UNC-G early decided to play NCAA Division III. In 1982 Coach Lynne Agee, in her first season, had the Spartan women ranked No. 2 nationally and in the Final Four at Elizabethtown, Pennsylvania. Transferring with the coach from Roanoke College were 6-2 Michele Blazevich, a 1983 Kodak all-American, and senior forward Carol Peschel, 1982 Kodak selectee. They started with freshman Wendy Engelmann, Jody Mangum and Sherry Sydney. When they reached the Final Four, Coach Agee was talking like an old-timer: "When you reach this point at the non-scholarship Division III level,

Nancy Isenhour was called the "Panther Girl" when she played on Coach Virgil Yow's mens team at High Point College 1945.

there isn't much different between the teams from the talent stand-point. Winning becomes more a matter of controlling your emotions and executing your playing style." Coach Agee threw a full-court 2-1-2 zone trap press, the old John Wooden game, at Pomona-Pitzer of California to reach the finals. The Spartans rallied to tie home team Elizabethtown and force overtime. Carol Peschel, who had 22 second-half points, continued for a 58-54 lead, but the No. 1 seeds won 67-66. It had been quite a haul, and an enjoyable one, since Miss Coleman.

Coach Virgil Yow has played a dominant role in women's basketball in the state for three decades. Even more. He was the men's coach at High Point College during World War II, where he had starred as a player. It was certainly a war year in 1945. Coach Yow recalled recently: "We didn't have many boys who could play. I guess Malcolm Sullivan was the only one, no good players in the entire conference. A 14-year-old boy named Bill Hall had taken the entrance exam and passed it to come to High Point College. He'd been in school a month or two when he came to me — he must have been 15 by then — and said, 'Coach, I'm going to make your ball club.' I said, that's fine. He answered, 'You don't believe me, do you, coach?' He'd get out there about 15 feet away and hit 'em, with nobody on him. Well, one day I got tired of listening to him and I said, 'Bill, we've got a girl who can out-shoot you.' He said to get her out here. So, when practice started that winter, I had Nancy Isenhour out for the team. Bill came out two days and quit."

Nancy Isenhour, from Stanly County, was a senior at High Point by then, and she could shoot. Coach Yow later said, "A nice little ball player, good passer, could shoot with nobody around her, real fine girl." She played on the team all season, became a celebrity, as well as a target for the women academicians. A girl on a men's basketball team. It did get attention. Quickly, the campus was discovered by *Collier's* magazine, the AP, Universal News. She was taking her bumps, I can attest to that having refereed several of the Panther games, but she wasn't scoring. Then on a trip into South Carolina, she won the game at Wofford 31-27, but in a collision she was knocked cold. More screams from the women's campuses. The Panther Girl, as Collier's called her, was the story that winter, and Coach Yow concluded: "Nancy has been the person who has kept up our morale all year. The players swear by her. In fact, it solved one problem but got me right into another one. Now, all the boys have fallen in love with her, and I have to keep that straightened out. You ought to take the train on one of our trips. The boys all eye each other to see that nobody gets more than his share of sitting with Nancy."

As a result of Nancy Isenhour and subsequent newspaper articles, Coach Yow got a call that would certainly change his life. He said: "When the people at Hanes Hosiery saw the story you had in the

Hanes Hosiery won three National AAU championships, the first in 1951 with Coach Virgil Yow and Jackie Fagg Swaim.

The touch of brilliance for all three Hanes Hosiery champions was provided by All-Americans Eunies Futch and guard Eckie Jordan, who were great.

Greensboro Daily News, they came to see me real quick. They had wanted to start a girls basketball program, they were looking for somebody to take over."

Coach Yow went to Hanes in 1945-46 and built a national champion. How was it made? Coach Yow: "First of all, you had to have a man at the company who believed we could have a championship girls team. Jim Weeks, the presdient, was that man. Every morning he would leave a note on my desk to see him at a certain time, and we talked basketball every day. He would come up in the afternoon and ask what we were going to work on today. Mr. Weeks had played with the old Celtics, a long time ago with Davey Banks, so he knew his basketball, and we talked 10-15 minutes every day. I mean, every day.

"Not a single girl on the championship ball clubs was there my first year. I did have Jackie Swain Fagg, from Sedge Garden, and we had Erma Willard. I knew we had to recruit. We went down to South Carolina and got Eckie Jordan. Mr. Weeks knew enough basketball, and he asked, 'What are you going to do about a big center?' We started looking, B.C. Hall (business manager) and I went around to Nashville, Atlanta, Florida. We found a girl in Jacksonville who was six feet, but she was getting married, said she had a kid sister who was about 6-2. So we got Eunie Futch, invited her up, and about the same time Jimmie Vaughn came from Jackson, Mississippi."

Eckie Jordon told about her introduction: "I had been out of school several years, saw Hanes play in Greenville, and decided right quick this was the team I wanted to join. I called Coach Yow, he invited me to come up for a tryout. First day of practice, something I'll never forget. When I walked into the gym, the first person I saw was Eunie Futch, 6-foot-2. I said to myself, well, that's that, no way." Hard work made the AAU record possible. Daily practice after work hours in the plant, Jordan remembered getting home at 8-9 o'clock at night. Coach Yow recalled an overnight bus trip from Norfolk, Virginia, arriving about daybreak because of a bus breakdown. The players fixed breakfast and went to work, no sleep. Coach Yow developed a winning softball team as well, but it was really to keep the basketball players in condition.

Hanes Hosiery won the 1951 National AAU championship, and in the semifinals they beat Cook's of Nashville with Lurlene Greer. Greer was recruited for Hanes then and there. The 1952 team added Greer, lost Swaim, and 1953 had few personnel changes. Jordan and Futch were the only players on the three title teams, and they also participated in the 102-game winning streak that began in 1951 and ended when Wayland College of Texas beat them for the 1954 title. Coach Yow had returned to High Point College after a 1953 season, Hugh Hampton replaced him, and the company dropped the women's basketball program the following year with management change.

Jennifer Alley, who started at High Point College, has headed the Carolina women's team since 1975, runnerup in the women's NIT in 1978.

When High Point captured the AIAW Division II national championship in 1978, Marie Riley was the tournament's outstanding player.

Coach Yow was more cautious than Eckie in suggesting the Hanes Hosiery team could beat the best college women today: "The last two teams we had, yes, we could beat the best college teams today, but remember, they aren't as old as my girls. Our girls had been out of college six and seven years, they had the experience."

Title IX brought women's basketball to its present status, or rather it opened the door. There have been organizations such as NSGWS and AIAW, excellent contributors to the growth of the game, especially the latter. They have placed North Carolina in the Greensboro Coliseum 1978. The second and third Underalls Classic, an East-West All-Star game, was played in Greensboro in 1978 and 1979. Underalls is Hanes Hosiery, incidentally.

Growing pains had settled by August 1975 when the second annual national AIAW workshop was held at Boone, 137 women's athletic directors and coaches from 37 states attending. Some looked into the immediate future. Laurie Mabry, AIAW president from Illinois State: "Five years from now? Yes, I am sure a television network will become interested, and we have already shown women's basketball can draw 12,000 in Madison Square Garden (Queens-Immaculata)." Lee Morrison of Madison College (now James Madison University), immediate past president: "We had it (nationals) at our place this year and I was glad we had it then because we won't be able to ever again. We only seat 5,000, and we turned people away. It will be so large we couldn't handle it again." Peggy Burke of Iowa, the next president in line: "The skill level of women is increasing tremendously, and it will increase more as we see the program developing in the high schools." Marilyn Gibbs of UNC-G, coach/practitioner: "Because of the strong men's competition in the ACC, will it be tougher for women to make progress in this area? This is what I'm hoping will not happen. I hope that independently — I don't mean independently, I mean give us a chance to grow in the direction an institution wishes, irrelevant of outside pressures, or what the men's teams have won." That was, remember, 1975.

Carolina began its women's varsity in 1971, a charter member of the AIAW, and the women's program was placed under a department of athletics in 1974. Coach Jennifer Alley, who had built a fine program at High Point in four seasons starting in 1974, went to Chapel Hill and her third season the Tar Heels placed runnerup in the Women's NIT in Texas. The team played an amazing 40 games (25-15), a far cry from UNC-G's four games in 1963. Coach Alley's team also beat Sweden, Holland and England to capture the Phillips International in London, a first for the state—and the nation?

At High Point, Wanda Briley succeeded Alley, and her first season proved to be a great one, a national championship. The Panthers had been seventh in the AIAW Divison III nationals in 1977, and they repeated as state and regional champions, moving to the nationals at Florence, South Carolina. They opened 104-65 over Eastern New Mexico, and 5-foot-10 Marie Riley had 19 points, 17 rebounds, 9 steals, 5 blocks and 5 assists. Now, that's some stats line. Ethel White, Robyn Cooper, Vickie McLean, Jody Westmoreland and Germaine McAuley also scored in double digits. They beat William Penn of Iowa, a team with four over six feet, 66-65. In the semifinals it was 105-77 over the defending champions, Berry College of Georgia, and the championship battle went into overtime. South Carolina State tied the regulation with four seconds to play, then Riley and White went to work in overtime, winning 92-88. Ethel White had 20 points and 10 rebounds, but Riley was again the heroine — tournament record 41 points, with 13 rebounds. Both made Kodak all-American, which was the all-tournament team at the time. The Panthers posted 30-8.

And then, there appeared the name of Yow, three young women in the Lib and Hilton Yow family at Gibsonville, second cousins to Virgil Yow. All three are major college coaches this 1983-84 season — Kay at North Carolina State, Debbie at Florida, Susan at East Tennessee.

Theirs is a story of great human interest. Kay Yow is the senior partner, a star player in prep days, including a spot in the Women's East-West All-Star game at Southern Pines in 1960. Directed by Bob Lee, it had attempted to keep girls basketball alive in spite of state restrictions, and in their first game (1958) the coaches were C. E. Hackney of Robbins (East) and Jack Kiser of Lincolnton (West), two real veterans, in the state.

Kay went to East Carolina, later remarked: "I used to go to all those Dixie Classics, and I remember wondering why women weren't involved in sports. At East Carolina there was a strong women's intramural program, but I was more competitive than that and I'm sure there were many others like me who wanted to participate on a higher level." She coached high school, then Elon College, and her teams became competitive. They won AIAW state Class B titles. Her first Elon season had a four-game schedule, in five seasons the record was 59-19. Both younger sisters played for Kay, with quite different personalities and philosophies. Debbie said recently: "I would not be in college setting today, helping people get their degrees, if it had not been for basketball." Susan, 12 years younger than Kay, put it bluntly: "I've idolized Kay all my life."

Kay Yow became the new head coach at N.C. State in 1975-76, and Susan transferred. Susan made Kodak all-American, they were called, the coach and kid sister, "Pete and Re-Pete." The Wolfpack advanced to Division I, beat Carolina and Appalachian en route to 19-7, and went to the NIT in Texas. Coach Yow had the good fortune to take a position at a major university with an athletic director, Willis Casey, committed to a strong women's program before Title IX got teeth.

The Wolfpack bench goes wild, while the N.C. State coaches get serious.
That's head Coach Kay Yow kneeling, assistant Nora Lynn Finch standing.
Finch chairs the NCAA women's basketball committee, its first and only
lead.

It was some transition for the young coach, too: "When I first came here (N.C. State), I had no concept of what it was like to run a program at this level. I wanted to strive to succeed, but it all happened so fast." She became administrator, coach, recruiter, scout, crusader and counselor. She got Nora Lynn Finch, whose Peace College team of 1977 finished second in the AIAW Junior College Nationals, as an assistant coach several years later. Finch, now an assistant athletic director, is current chairman of the prestigious NCAA women's basketball committee, its first and only one. She played at Western Carolina in the first national tournament for women, before the AIAW.

Coach Yow's Wolfpack beat Old Dominion 77-75 in overtime for third place in the strong Region II in 1977 (21-3 record), and they kept adding tournaments — the Christmas Classic at Chapel Hill, the Nike Invitational at Las Vegas, to the AIAW nationals in 1980 and 1981. Mel Greenberg's poll of women's basketball, originated at the *Philadelphia Inquirer* and carried by the AP in recent years, first ranked the Wolfpack the second week of 1976-77, and the string of being ranked is now 104 straight weeks, and counting. *Sports Illustrated* gave State its preseason No. 1 rating in 1977-78, and Genia Beasley became a Kodak all-American.

Kay coached in the first Underalls Classic, in the Pan-American Games 1983, in the World University Games 1981. She will coach in the 1984 Olympics, the USA associate coach. She philosophized recently: "Sports is a microcosm of life. It's really a challenge to maintain your perspective and help others at the same time. I find a lot of fulfillment that I couldn't get doing a lot of other things. If I weren't helping someone, I don't think life would be worthwhile. I wouldn't ever want basketball to get out of perspective. It's hard enough to keep your feet on the ground, and it's important to know that you're a small part of something big." That has driven the Yows, just as the memory that all three sisters wore jersey No. 14 at old Gibsonville High before it lost out to consolidation. The old school retired the number, and each sister claimed it was hers.

Kay Yow has seen the college game turn from the smaller schools to the major universities, which recently she called "part of a new breed in girls basketball." She has brought the nation's best teams to Reynolds Coliseum, drawing 6,000 when the No. 1 ranked Wayland Baptists came in 1978.

But the basketball fans of the state of North Carolina still have not accepted women's play, now at the college level the best in the country. Only on Olympic years does this public express any attention of merit. That is unfortunate. There are some outstanding and exciting women playing basketball in the state. Maybe some day they will even make the headlines.

Twice the Greensboro Coliseum hosted the Underalls All-American Classic, the top game for collegiate women in the late 70s. Al McGuire of NBC-TV presents the outstanding player award to Nancy Lieberman of Old Dominion.

Kay Yow has added to her working dreams: "I think it will be fantastic when the day comes that girls will dunk the ball like the boys. I would be in favor of lowering our basket a half-foot right now. I think that would make a great difference in our game."

169

Always in charge, Billy Cunningham, selected ABA player of the year 1983.

18
Carolina Cougars

They came with a red, white and blue ball, a three-point shot circle and more hoopla than Ringling Brothers; major league professional basketball was in North Carolina.

Bob Verga shot his marvelous low-trajectory goals, and Billy Cunningham jumped leagues to return to North Carolina, and Joe Caldwell accelerated the fastest first-three-steps in the game.

Larry Brown got his coaching debut in the coliseums of Greensboro (25 games), Charlotte (15) and Raleigh (2). He came within a few tough moments in the seventh game with the Kentucky Colonels of playing for all the marbles, as they say in pro basketball.

All this happened in the five-year life span of the Carolina Cougars, which experienced two enthusiastic owners with master dreams, but never, really, the total fan support which had been anticipated and which proved an absolute necessity. They played their first game in October 1969, and by June 1974 the American Basketball Association (ABA) moved on to other territories (St. Louis).

Before the actual happening of the entertaining Cougarettes and the exciting Cougars there had to be some planning. It began in California when entrepreneur Gary Davidson founded a "new" pro basketball league and made George Mikan the commissioner. Birth date was February 1, 1967; death came June 17, 1976. Carolina Cougar burial preceded the demise. Davidson spread 11 franchises around the country, except the major markets, and one of these good cities was Houston. Frank Deford, astute author for *Sports Illustrated*, had projected a regional concept for pro basketball, specifically one in the Carolinas, and Don DeJardin, then in business in Pittsburgh, took the message literally. He pursued it, ran across Bob Gardner in his travels, and Bob had a cousin named Jim Gardner down in Rocky Mount, North Carolina. Jim listened, talked Leonard Rawls and Bob Gorham into the potential, bought the Houston Maverick franchise in January 1969. De Jardin went there as general manager, mainly to strengthen the team for moving in April, the new Carolina Cougars.

Gardner would operate, a businessman who headed Hardee's, a successful quick food chain, a politician who left Congress to run for governor of North Carolina (1968) and a Republican. He garnered more votes than any nominee of his party in more than a century. Gardner wanted a state figure to coach, and he got Bones McKinney, the best. DeJardin obtained Bob Verga, former Duke star; Doug Moe, formerly at Carolina; Randy Mahaffey of Clemson; Bill Bunting of Carolina; and Gene Littles, an all-time hero at High Point College. McKinney coached as never before, closing out 42-42 with the new team. Houston the previous year had won a total of 23 games.

Pursuing the regional concept to the nth degree, Gardner and DeJardin appointed a 17-man advisory board. They sought input, they wanted recognition. The Cougars' board consisted of John Belk, Pete Brennan and Harry Nicholas of Charlotte; Ron Shavlik, Lou Pucillo and Sammy Ranzino of Raleigh; Vic Molodet, Bill Chambers, Charlie Justice and Bob Jamieson of Greensboro; John Dillon of Winston-Salem; Earl Ruth of Salisbury; Leon Brogden of Wilmington; Dr. Joe Quigg of Fayetteville; Whit Cobb of Durham; Dick Groat of Pittsburgh, Pennsylvania; and Sam Jones of Washington, D.C. There is no record, however, that the board ever had a meeting.

The ABA wanted money to talk. The new league pooled resources to bid for UCLA's Lew Alcindor (Jabbar), who said he would take a sealed bid from each league, one bid from each, period. They opened the envelopes, Milwaukee was a few thousand better. When the ABA cleaned out an office years later, there was an old certified check to Alcindor for $1,000,000. That was 1969-70. The following year the Cougars had the rights for Pete Maravich, getting out of LSU. They lost the battle to the Atlanta Hawks.

At the first season's end a few changes were in the making. DeJardin resigned, he wanted "part of the action" which Gardner would not relinquish. When Gardner bought the franchise, he became ABA president immediately. It wasn't a job people stood in line for. He wanted a commissioner, offered it to Carl Scheer, who, as a young attorney in Greensboro, had become involved with pro basketball. He handled Guilford College's Bob Kauffman in his Seattle contract, later became assistant to NBA Commissioner Walter Kennedy in New York. Scheer did not accept the ABA spot, but in the summer of 1970 he left the NBA to become president of the new Buffalo franchise. By this time Gardner had other business interests, he wanted somebody to head the Cougars. He hired Scheer as president, with a piece of the action. Scheer was also instructed to obtain, if possible, additional investors in the Cougars, and that's how he met Tedd Munchak in Atlanta that fall (1970). Munchak, who became a millionaire in the carpet business from which he retired at age 44, sought tax shelters, and pro sports was a favorite route then, as now. He bought into the

Cougars, by mid-season owned the club. Tedd's favorite expression in departing, "Stay loose," became quite familiar in pro circles.

Coach McKinney's second Cougars got off to a very poor start, assistant Jerry Steele replaced his old coach, and by this time Pogo Joe Caldwell had joined the team from the NBA Atlanta Hawks, along with Larry Miller in an ABA trade. The Cougars won only 34 games, Tom Meschery replaced Steele, who requested to step down due to ill health. Meschery's team won 35 games.

Millions were being paid by the ABA at this time, college underclassmen were being signed to pro contracts. The Denver Rockets of the ABA did it first, taking Spencer Haywood with two college years remaining. The Cougars had three good rookies in 1971-72 — Jim McDaniels (who later jumped to Seattle), Ted McClain and Duke's Randy Denton. Players jumped from ABA to NBA like it was a game of hopscotch. Almost daily. It was a known fact that a fan needed more than a game program to know the players, usually because the program had been printed that morning.

Munchak and Scheer were determined. Scheer said: "I want to bring a winner to the outstanding basketball fans of North Carolina. These fans deserve the best in basketball." Games were still being played in three cities, several also in Winston-Salem, where the Cougars' three-station TV network centered. Cougar headquarters, however, were in Greensboro, and that cut civic pride a bit thin in the other cities, although there were Cougar offices and staff in both Charlotte and Raleigh.

Larry Brown came as head coach in 1972-73. He had played his final pro ball, he declared, and he added: "I've played under Alex Hannum for two years, and I've already said what I think of that experience, the very finest. I played for Al Bianchi for two years, and I have great respect. I started under Bob McCarthy, and he's still in the league, and let me tell you what he thinks about defense. They all had different philosophies, and I hope that I can take the best of them and put them all together. But my college experience with Dean Smith was the most important of all." In the state of North Carolina he couldn't have put the words together any better. He got Doug Moe as assistant, the dynamic duo of ABA basketball, now on the bench. They coached well. They wanted a pressure defense, always on the ball, first time utilized in pro ball, and they had 9-10 players to be used regularly.

The Cougars won the Eastern Division with a 57-27 record, and made a sweep of the league's outstanding awards — Billy Cunningham as player of the year, Larry Brown as coach of the year, Carl Scheer as executive of the year. Cunningham, who had been all-NBA four times before jumping to the Cougars, starred with Joe Caldwell who had also been NBA. Other leaders were Ed Manning, Mike Lewis, until hurt, backed by Tom Owens; Mack Calvin and Steve Jones as

Coming close to an ABA championship, Coach Larry Brown works in the huddle with the Cougars, assistant Doug Moe takes it all in. Both were head NBA coaches in 1983.

one guard pair, Littles and McClain the other. A sound team, top to bottom. They came to the seventh and deciding playoff game with Kentucky. Unfortunately it was scheduled in Charlotte, trying to keep the regional concept intact. Cougar players, however, considered Greensboro the home floor, not Charlotte or Raleigh — part of the problem. The Cougars pushed the Colonels to the limit, right to the finish, but lost. It was possibly the beginning of the end.

Scheer, always nervous and a wreck by game's halftime, called that the longest day of his career, at the time. He's now president-general manager of the Denver Nuggets in the NBA. He wanted to build the regional concept, he wanted to win. He and Munchak spent that morning on the phone. Scheer went to Charlotte early, no particular reason. He talked to a reporter who tagged along: "It's a gnawing feeling. A conflict of feelings, I guess you'd say. I keep telling myself, win or lose, it's been a great year. We've made great strides. I think we've proved ourselves and we've proved North Carolina is a professional basketball state. I keep telling myself that if we lose, I'm going to walk away from the game with my head up high. But then you realize how much losing in the playoffs can tarnish a season. People generally forget what you did during the season. Then you stop and think, some teams never win it at all." The Cougars rallied from 17 down to within six, still time to win, but Kentucky did it 107-96.

Attendance had become a Cougar problem by May 73. The Charlotte Coliseum notified the Cougars it had no Friday and Saturday dates available in January and February for the coming season. They talked with N.C. State officials about playing in Reynolds Coliseum where they did play eight games (Greensboro 20, Charlotte 14). ABA officials, led by Munchak, the most active club owner and always in the middle of things nation-wide, sought ABC-TV contract, but television wanted the major markets. Munchak was confident he had been able to sell a merger of the two pro leagues, but all efforts fell apart, if they ever existed. The NBA eventually buried the ABA but it did admit several franchises, at a steep initiation fee.

Cunningham developed an ailing kidney early in 1973-74, had an operation, and Caldwell played between hurts. Consistency was left to Mack Calvin, all-league, and Gene Littles, steady as ever. The popular High Point guard was the only original Cougar, having made the ABA all-rookie team in 1970. He worked his way into a starting guard role in late January 1972, averaging 18 points per game and shooting 57 percent in those games. In the ABA expansion draft, to fill a new San Diego club, Littles thought he might be selected, but San Diego took Larry Miller instead.

In May 1974 Munchak, who had done everything possible to breathe life into the club, announced the franchise was dead. Fans, especially wives in Greensboro, attempted to campaign to save the

Cougars by selling season tickets. It occurred in Charlotte as well. Industry was called on by Scheer. The biggest fan, Munchak, finally said: "The truth is I have accomplished nothing. I get no personal satisfaction from professional basketball, and it's not because we lost. I just feel empty about agents, players and basketball management."

Big moment for the Cougars in the state, since they did not take a championship, was hosting the 1971 ABA All-Star game in Greensboro. Scheer also had a 12-station Cougar radio network going, plus the smaller TV network for road games. The All-Star game was big. Its biggest draw had been 11,932 in Indianapolis the year before, but the Cougars turned out a record 14,407 fans to see the East, with Rick Barry, Dan Issel and Joe Caldwell, beat the West 126-124.

Bones McKinney, active with the Cougars for several years after coaching, was asked recently for hindsight, which is usually 20-20: "I was one of those who believed Jim Gardner hit it right, playing in Greensboro, Charlotte and Raleigh, the hotbed of basketball. But at the time I didn't realize that they, the fans, the people, couldn't care less if we beat the Celtics, because they couldn't go to the office the next day and say, 'Well, the Cougars beat Boston last night,' but they could say, 'State beat Carolina,' and they could get a fight. They didn't really care. It was entertainment, that is about what it was. We had some fans, some great fans, but we had fans who had been turned away from the ACC and this was their only outlet."

Munchak finally sold the franchise to a New York group of businessmen who moved the team to St. Louis, a former NBA city (before the Hawks went to Atlanta). Scheer and Brown went to the Denver club together. But Munchak had gone to the ABA meeting with no buyer in prospect, and he said he was going to give the franchise to the league.

That evening Tedd called the *Greensboro Daily News* to report his action, and I asked him: "If you're really going to give the franchise to the league, why not give it to me?"

Sharp as always, he answered: "And what do you plan to send me for Christmas?"

19
Norman Sloan

For Norman Sloan, it's easy now to say: "Those three weeks in 1974. They went by very quickly."

They brought the N.C. State Wolfpack a national championship, a great one which included deliverance of the death knell for the Wooden Era, a Final Four triumph over the UCLA Bruins, and then, almost as an after-thought, a final win over Marquette for the actual title.

But Norman Sloan's years in North Carolina number far more than three weeks, and certainly many more interesting moments than just the championship one. They cover a young man who paid his own way to visit N.C. State—probably the only one of Everett Case's Hoosier Hotshots to do so—who was literally scared to death the day he went to Coach Case's office to tell him he, Norman Sloan, was going out for football instead of the round ball thing.

From the farm days in Indiana, Sloan recalled recently: "I had heard of North Carolina, the university, but not N.C. State, and the only reason I even thought about it was Everett Case. He was a big name, the biggest in the state of Indiana. My wife had a music teacher in high school there, who grew up with Coach Case in Columbus, Indiana. She took an interest in me, a little country boy, and she wanted me to go to college and she kind of forced me on Coach Case.

"Here's how he recruited me. He didn't give me a nickel for the visit to Raleigh. I rode the bus from Indianapolis, Indiana, to Raleigh, North Carolina, for my official visit, if you want to call it that, and he told me that he would take me on scholarship. The recruiting he did consisted of this—'You got to eat, you got to die and you got to wear clothes. You're tired of being a farmer, and I'm sure you don't want to go into the undertaking business, so you clothe 'em. So come here and take textiles.' That's how he recruited me. We both came out of the service about the same time, he never saw me bounce a ball."

Sloan was in Coach Case's first recruiting class, which began winning games and conference tournaments and national recognition at once in the post-war years. The Wolfpack made the NIT his first two

Norman Sloan is a member of Everett Case's first Wolfpack 1946-47.

seasons, taking third place in 1947, but Sloan wasn't getting much playing time in that talented Hoosier crew. Sloan said recently: "I became unhappy as these kids do today because there was not enough playing time. They wanted me to come out for football, so I went up and told Coach Case that I was going to play football, at an end position. Like I said, I wasn't playing that much but it was just the idea of one of his players doing something else, and I didn't know what to expect. But he agreed to it. I played two years of football because I needed that extra year for graduation, and I had changed from textiles, which he put me in, to recreation which the school had just started."

He began coaching at Presbyterian College in 1951-52, then after four seasons and another year an assistant at Memphis State, he took the head job at The Citadel. After four years, on to the University of Florida. Sloan said recently: "Like you've heard other coaches say, you felt like you were coming home when your alma mater asked you. That's where my best memories were, North Carolina State and Raleigh. I wanted to go back and be a part of it. I didn't ask what I was going to make until I got my first paycheck. I remember Chancellor John Caldwell saying to the athletic director, Roy Clogston, when I stopped talking, 'You know, I think he wants the job.' I just wanted to be back coaching basketball at North Carolina State."

With Press Maravich, who had succeeded Everett Case, resigning to go with is talented son Pete to LSU after the 1965-66 season, Sloan did return and stayed 14 years. In that Wolfpack period his teams won 266 games, 127 losses, seven times with 20-win seasons, to the NIT championship finals, and then there was 1974 standing out like Mount Everest. In his moves to three conferences, he had the distinction of being selected conference coach of the year in all three (Southern 1957, Southeastern 1961, ACC 1970-73-74), as well as national coach of the year 1974.

He remembered what Everett Case taught him, an indelible impression, about which he talked recently: "Coach Case was one of the most exciting experiences of my life. I have described Coach Case many, many times as a gray-haired dynamo. I never saw him run down, never had an average practice. Every practice was like it was the practice before a championship game, I've said many times, every meal was a banquet. He made it so exciting and so meaningful, there's wasn't anything mundane about any game or any practice. I marvelled at the energy that the man had and was able to bring out in the rest of us. He just kind of demanded it, and we all try to approach his energy level in terms of intensity as far as playing the game was concerned."

In his fourth Wolfpack season, Coach Sloan wanted to "make the offense more simplified, using more give-and-go, one-on-one situations, and post split, plus full-court man-to-man pressures, like Coach Case used to do." He added at the time, before 1969-70 season: "I feel

Sloan's team captain his first two seasons, one out with injury, was Eddie Biedenbach, showing his favorite jumper. He joined Sloan's coaching staff later.

we have the material to play this way now. We couldn't before."

Case's game, as Sloan described it: "His game was strictly running. It was simply to play for him in terms of offensives, lot of things confusing about defense. We ran one defense, man-to-man. We'd start in half-court, and if things weren't going well, I can hear him now, call timeout and this—'By God, now we're going to go, we're going to come up full court.' That was his idea, if you didn't get 'em half-court, go full court. On offense, and this is a true story, we never knew whether we were playing against a zone or a man-for-man. We ran the same offense, old center-the-opposite, and he ran one variation off it, called center-the-same. That meant the center didn't go opposite when the ball went in the corner."

Of the famed Hoosier Hotshot fast break: "We got involved in the transition, worked a lot of passes off the defense. When we got it down to half-court, somebody would one-on-one or we'd go to the offensive boards. But the fast break. There was Paul Horvath (center) in the middle, Dick Dickey on one side, sometimes Jack McComas on the other, sometimes Warren Cartier. On the sides he'd have Leo Katkaveck and Eddie Bartels. Leo would take the basketball and put it in the forward's hands and run to the corner, and Eddie would stand in the middle. The forward would throw it back to Eddie, and Eddie would hand it off behind him as Leo went by, or he'd give to the other forward in the corner. Eddie just kept standing there, every now and then take a step in and shoot a jumper. I mean, a one-hand set shot, he didn't have a jumper at the time. I still think the beginning of the thing and the end of the thing is your effort, your attitude, your intensity. I think that's what Coach Case did better than anything else."

But Sloan's return home did not begin with yells and cheers, not even victories. He inherited Eddie Biedenbach from the previous team which lost seven of the top eight scorers, and Biedenbach injured his back in preseason, requiring surgery and missing the entire season. Sloan's first recruit was Vann Williford. Biedenbach was captain again in 1968, and he might be the only player, at least in this area, to be on the school basketball brochure twice. Top scorer as a sophomore, quick hands to warrant the title "The Pittsburgh Pirate," Biedenbach recently recalled his trip South: "Actually, until I visited Raleigh at the invitation of Press Maravich, who had a good friend whose son was on our high school team, I had never heard of Tobacco Road or the Big Four or Everett Case. I wasn't a very highly recruited athlete. They had two all-states in Pennyslvania by classifications. I was on the small one, and on the last team at that, 40-50 athletes picked ahead of me. My prep coach said N.C. State was really bigtime, he didn't know if I could cut the mustard in that kind of competition. But I wanted to come south to get out of the snow." He joined Sloan's staff in January 1968.

The conference tournament 1968 was in Charlotte for the first time, color TV for the first time. And there was a game in the semifinals never forgotten, still capable of bringing curse words from TV producers. Score: N.C. State 12, Duke 10. Duke was ranked No. 3 nationally, Sloan wanted to slow it down, but not a total freeze. But that developed and Duke stayed in its zone while Bill Kretzer went about dribbling the ball, or just bouncing the ball. It was 4-2 Duke at halftime, still 9-8 Duke with two minutes left. Strategy time, the coaches called nine timeouts in those two minutes, which took longer to play than the rest of the game. Dick Braucher's rebound goal for the Wolfpack lead with 29 seconds. Coach Sloan said afterward: "It took a lot of guts to stick in there. I love them." Coach Bubas wasn't speaking.

The 1968-69 freshman team had the first black, Al Heartley, and Ed Leftwich came the following year. The Wolfpack won the ACC tournament in double overtime against South Carolina, Sloan's starting five going all 50 minutes—Van Williford, Rick Anheuser, Paul Coder, Ed Leftwich and Joe Dunning.

The 1974 national champs began to take shape with the 1970-71 freshman class, 7-foot-4 Tom Burleson, the tall kid from the mountains of Avery County. Then came David Thompson, Monte Towe and Tim Stoddard in 1971-72. Joe Cafferky, a junior college transfer, directed one team, 1973, to a 27-0 season and ranked No. 2 behind UCLA. But it was a team on NCAA probation for violations in the Thompson activity, the same as Duke. In the 1973 ACC tournament it was ruled, if both N.C. State and Duke reached the finals, there would be a game between the losing semifinals at 6 p.m. Saturday for the NCAA bid. The Wolfpack took the final game down to the final nine seconds before posting 76-74 victory over Maryland, David Thompson sinking two free throws for the winning points. John Lucas scored for the Terps at the buzzer. Burleson summed up the 27-0 and go-home season: "Happy feeling, but an empty one."

They were ready for 1974. DT had a year's varsity experience, a 6'-4" leaping phenom, a jumping jack who played the whole court, vertically as well as horizontally. His alley-oops were exciting, and, remember, the dunk was illegal then. Tim Stoddard, rugged. Tom Burleson, come of age. Monte Towe, 5-foot-6, scared people with his finesse. Another from junior college, Moe Rivers, became a starter. Reserves were Phil Spence and Mark Moeller. But they had a bumpy start, playing UCLA in St. Louis for the TV money. They got wiped out 84-66.

First thing was to win the ACC tournament, which they did, excitingly. N.C. State was No. 1 ranked, Maryland No. 4, North Carolina No. 6. DT paced the Virginia win, and then came Maryland again, third straight year for the State-Maryland finals. It became a game still ranked among the finest ever played in college basketball. For 40 minutes they ran and dared each other to greatness, and they were all even, flat level, and then for five more minutes they maintained the turbulent tempo. Finally, with six seconds, little Monte Towe made two at the foul line to insure victory, 103-100. Burleson had 38 points and 13 rebounds. State went to the NCAAs, Maryland went home, probably the No. 1 and No. 2 teams in the country.

Celebration time, with the nets clipped, for the 1974 national champion Wolfpack.

In the East Regional, on home court Reynolds, the Pack first downed No. 4 Providence 92-78 and then No. 6 Pittsburgh 100-72. The second game was a nightmare. Going super-high on a rebound, David Thompson fell off Phil Spence's shoulder and hit the floor on his head. He lay there, seemingly for hours, motionless. He was rushed to the hospital, mild concussion, but was able to return to the coliseum for a thunderous ovation. His hair had been cut close, it was called his TWA (Teenie Weenie Afro). He was ready to play the week following.

The Final Four was in the Greensboro Coliseum, a new pairings rotation had East vs West. That meant the Wolfpack's first foe was UCLA. Tom Burleson prepared for his all-American rival, Bill Walton: "I've been thinking about the matchup, and I've been looking at film and stuff. I've played against him (St. Louis) and that's definitely an advantage for me. I know the type ball he plays." DT had a score to settle with Keith (Jamaal) Wilkes. The payoff came in spades, doubled. UCLA led early, a DT alley-oop gave the Pack the margin late. At the regulation buzzer Tim Stoddard's side shot bounced off the rim. End of first overtime—Burleson, faking Walton out, got final shot in close, ball off the back rim. Second overtime—UCLA up seven, Pack rallied, DT got 76-75 State. Insurance came at the foul line, final 80-77. UCLA was beaten, after 38 consecutive NCAA tournament wins, seven straight NCAA titles. The two coaches reviewed the excitement. Sloan: "This team has been under pressure before, it never really bothers them. When we got down seven in overtime, I didn't think the game was over. Much time was left, but against UCLA we all realized that was a tremendous task." Wooden: "I thought we had the game in hand two times. In the second half (up 11) we took three shots you just don't take when you have the lead. Then in overtime (up 7) we made a crucial mistake or two, but that's to the credit of North Carolina State."

Monday night, for the record 15,829 fans in the Greensboro Coliseum and the 42 million on NBC-TV, the Wolfpack completed the task, a bit easier, for some anticlimactic. North Carolina Gov. James Holshauser, writing a tournament column in the *Greensboro Daily News*, commented: "It somehow seems a shame that Saturday's State-UCLA game had to be the semifinals. The way it turned out, it would have been a perfect finale. When the No. 1 team in the nation defeats the No. 2 team in two overtimes, it's sort of hard to imagine a fitting encore." It was Coach Sloan's challenge, to keep the Pack ready. They met Coach Al McGuire's Marquette, No. 3 ranked (State beat the Nos. 2, 3, 4 and 6 teams in the NCAAs). Two technical fouls on McGuire turned an eight-point spread quickly, late the first half. The Pack led by 16 later, won 76-64. DT was the outstanding player (and national player of year), along with Burleson and Towe on all-tournament.

Freshmen became eligible for the varsity the next year, and Kenny Carr joined the Wolfpack, along with Al Green from junior college. In the late summer the team took a 17-day trip to the Orient, then formed the nucleus of a USA team which beat the touring Soviet Nationals five of six games, one in Greensboro. They did not win the 1975 tournament, losing to Carolina and the freshman Phil Ford 70-66. Maryland, on the better season record, was chosen as the NCAA's second entry from the ACC, and the Wolfpack voted not to go to the NIT. David Thompson summed it up for the seniors: "Going out with a loss leaves you with an empty feeling."

Rebuilding began immediately. Hawkeye Whitney came, Clyde Austin and Kenny Matthews, and they played some hard battles in the conference tournament. Three new freshmen for 1979-80 were Dereck Whittenburg, Sidney Lowe and Thurl Bailey. The 1980 tournament had Maryland No. 7 in the nation, North Carolina No. 10, Clemson No. 17 and N.C. State No. 19. Duke won, and five ACC teams made the NCAAs. The Pack lost to Iowa's 70 percent second half shooting in Greensboro.

During the conference tournament Norman Sloan announced he was going back to the University of Florida, a decision which took much deliberation.

Joan and Norman Sloan still remember "Those Three Weeks." The coach said recently, pausing during the NABC convention in Albuquerque where a new Wolfpack was competing for a national title: "What happened in 1974, it's almost like you're half awake and half asleep. When you get to this point, everything moved so quickly. You have so many things to take care of. There's no such thing as pressure. I never felt one bit of pressure, we were too busy. The enthusiasm of the basketball fans in North Carolina, no question about that. I don't know that we could have won the thing if we played anywhere else. We were good, don't misunderstand, but, shoot, if we had been playing out in Los Angeles, I don't know that we could have beaten UCLA. They won three of theirs at home, it makes a big difference. Everybody you bump into on the street, the intensity is greater, more people able to be at the game, more for us than for UCLA. Of course, UCLA had won much. They had put themselves in that unenviable position, everybody wanted to see them fall."

Belus Smawley of Appalachian, early NAIA star with a jumper.

20
Kansas City Connection / NAIA

Kansas City has meant more than steaks to the smaller colleges of the state of North Carolina. It's Kansas City the site of the NAIA (National Association of Intercollegiate Athletics) national tournament, 32 basketball teams from districts all over the nation. They gather to conduct an all-week revival, a true survival of the fittest, starting Monday morning, a champion by Saturday midnight (1984 format altered).

It takes five games to win the national crown, just as Guilford College's Quakers did in 1973 when Coach Jack Jensen combined team play around the outstanding performances of Lloyd (World) Free and M. L. Carr.

Others have gone from the state to challenge right to the Saturday night showdown, Coach Jim Gudger's Western Carolina Catamounts in 1963, then Coach Danny Roberts' Campbell College (now University) Camels in 1977. Those two teams remember well.

This tournament, begun in old Kansas City Auditorium, started in 1937 when eight teams from the midwest area gathered to play for a championship. In 1938 it became a national event with 32 teams, Roanoke College (Virginia) representing this district. It was then the National Association of Intercollegiate Basketball, changed to include all sports years later.

High Point College went in 1939, North Carolina's first representative. Coach was Virgil Yow, and the Panthers dropped their first game. Quick trip. Said Coach Yow recently, settled down at his Camp Pla-Mor at Windy Hill Beach, South Carolina: "It looked pretty big to us, playing in the big auditorium and all. But it was a real chore raising money for the trip, although back then you could buy a hot dog for a nickel. We went by bus the first time, the next time we couldn't get gasoline with the war on, so we went by train." Coach Yow also chaired the district selection committee, with Jake Wade (*Charlotte Observer*) and Smith Barrier (*Greensboro Daily News*). Next time was 1942, and the coach called this the best of his High Point teams: "We only lost one game, that one by one point down at Elon. We beat them 33 points when they came to our place, then 31 in the conference tournament." They averaged 55 points a game, holding opponents to 35 and the starting lineup included four who made the 1939 trip — Bill Keene, Hilliard Nance, Jerry Counihan and Cel Malfregeot, plus guard George Demmy.

Yow had been one of the college's finest athletes when he graduated in 1930, started coaching at his alma mater in 1932. He left for the nationally-acclaimed Hanes Hosiery women in 1945, then returned to High Point in 1953. Obvious question: How had the men's game in North Carolina changed? He answered recently: "One thing, from the two-hand set shot to one-hand jumpers. I never had a boy use the one-hand jump shot the first 13 years I was at High Point, but when I came back, they all were shooting that way. Much better shooters, too. Earlier, we would have one or two boys who could shoot 50 percent maybe, but the defense would keep them covered. They wouldn't get many shots, they'd let the other boys shoot. I remember playing this team one time, they had one boy who really couldn't shoot but he was a hot dog, he just shot all the time. So we covered four of them, let him shoot. He shot 14 times in the first 10 minutes, and we got 14 rebounds."

Belus Smawley's name always comes up when historians sit down to play the game of picking the all-time best players in the state. He stood 6-foot-2, weighed 195, and he had developed his two-hand, fadeaway jumper by the time he enrolled at Appalachian State under Coach Flucie Stewart. That was right at the start of World War II, Stewart left, and by midseason 1943 the new coach, Clyde Canipe, had been drafted, and Smawley became coach and center.

The Mountaineers qualified for the KC tournament, and off they went by train. In the opening game Coach-Center Smawley got 14 points, they won 48-31 over Simpson Teachers of Iowa. The coach increased his scoring to 24 against Kansas Wesleyan in a second half rally. But senior guard Hoy Isaacs sprained his knee in that game, and the Apps lost to Northwest Missouri in the quarterfinals 46-34. Smawley was selected for the Chuck Taylor MVP award in that national, later playing pro ball for five years, averaging 13.1 points before 1951 retirement.

Jim Gudger played for Western Carolina when it won North State Conference honors in the late 30s, returned as head coach after World War II and took the Catamounts to KC in 1947. In 19 seasons, with many 20-win marks, his teams dominated the league. Henry Logan was to thrill the Reid Gym faithful, the first black on a varsity basketball team at a predominately white school in the South (1964-65).

Gene Littles of High Point selected NAIA All-American three times in late 60s.

Current head coach at UNC-Wilmington, Mel Gibson made All-American at Western Carolina in NAIA tournament 1963.

Bob Kauffman, giant for the Guilford Quakers, twice All-American, first round NBA draft selection (Seattle).

Logan was four times NAIA all-American.

The year before Logan arrived, 1963, in a newly-formed Carolinas Conference, Coach Gudger took a 10th seeded team to the NAIA championship game. Capt. Mel Gibson, today the UNC-Wilmington coach, started at forward with Gaston Seal, Darrell Murray and Danny Tharpe guards, 6'-9" Tiny Lavelle center. Gibson made first team all-tournament, Lavelle second unit. They beat Eastern Montana 64-61, Miles College 107-86, Lewis & Clark 77-57 and Fort Hays State 100-84 in the semis. But powerful Pan American was too much in the finals 73-62, despite Gibson's scoring, the tournament high with 137 points for the week, shared by Willis Reed of Grambling. That final game? Said Gudger: "Difference that Saturday night was Lucius Jackson, and anyone who has seen him play will tell you there is no college pivot man better. He completely dominated the boards all week." Of the week in KC: "We won four games, playing the graveyard shift on five straight nights, and that is quite an accomplishment because there isn't a man on the team who ever played five games in five days before. The boys experienced a week they won't ever forget." Gudger retired at East Texas State in 1983.

The state had sent teams to the NAIA with contending seeds, but No. 1 ranking came first in 1968 with Coach Jerry Steele's Guilford College Quakers. The talented crew had Pat Moriarty and Ed Fellows forwards, all-American Bob Kauffman center, Bob Bregard, Bo Whitaker and John Brooks guards. Said Coach Steele recently: "Being ranked No. 1 going in, to me is the toughest game you could possibly have. We were there, and we were not used to being in headlines of that nature. We led the whole ball game, then lost on the very last basket." They did, 80-78 to Oshkosh. Of the NAIA Ides of March Steele said, "Greatest sports event ever. You must go there sometime to see exactly what it is. You go sit in the stands with those sweet old farmers and when the teams come on the floor, like, say, Lockhurst and Guilford, they don't know one team from the other. But in about five minutes they've got *their* team and they're involved in the ball for the rest of it. The first two days are pure madhouse, eight games Monday, eight Tuesday, and then they get down to a real, fine, nice tournament."

At least Coach Jack Jensen had been through five Kansas City games before he took the 1973 Guilford College Quakers on its westward ho. As Steele's assistant, he had been in 1966-67-68. Then in 1970, after a 3-3 start, the Quakers won 29 straight and went to the KC semifinals before losing to Kentucky State's great club.

Guilford lost the 1973 league title to Catawba, won the district. They were unseeded in Kansas City. Jensen explained: "Technically, I guess, we were No. 14 but that year they only announced the first eight seeds. It had always been No. 1 vs No. 32, and so on, but they had so many routs. They revised the pairings so No. 1 met No. 17, No. 2 vs No. 18." The team had a sparse bench, but an outstanding lineup — M. L. Carr and Teddie East forwards, Ray Massengill center, Lloyd (World) Free and Greg Jackson guards. They beat Keene State of New Hampshire, Valdosta State of Georgia, Westmont of California (comeback with four late points in less than 10 seconds), Augustana of Illinois. In the finals with Maryland Eastern Shore, Free got the half-time lead at the buzzer, he and Carr scored for 99-96 final. Lloyd Free was tournament MVP, first time a freshman had ever captured that. He and Carr were all-tournament. Coach Jensen had only one word for the week: "Tired."

Coach Danny Roberts had Campbell in the finals in 1977, a non-seeded team, the first from the "bottom 16" to reach the title game. To this day Roberts is not sure about the trip: "It happened so fast it was hard to enjoy. You plan one night, practice the next day, then play that night. By Saturday I was exhausted." The Camels had balance — Don Whaley and Keys Benston forwards, Sam Staggers center, Clay Alston and Don Laird guards. Staggers, in there just to jump the opening tipoff, moved to forward where he made all-tournament; Laird made the hustle award. Coach Roberts recalled: "Things began to jell in our last regular season game at Pembroke, and then they got better each game. Clicked well together, and we hadn't expected that. Our two previous teams were better." The Camels beat Lincoln Memorial 76-75, Southwest Oklahoma 71-56, Alcorn State 77-63, Henderson State 76-52, and then came fifth seed Texas Southern in the finals. Southern's front line was 6'-10", 6'-10", 6'-6", and they hit early and won 71-44. Campbell's five opponents that week had a combined 109-19 mark for the season.

For years, a few decades ago, all the colleges in North Carolina competed in the North Carolina Intercollegiate Athletic Conference, mainly in basketball, baseball and track. That was around World War I. Then the larger schools gravitated toward the Big Five (Carolina, State, Duke, Wake Forest, Davidson) and the smaller colleges to the Little Six (Guilford, Elon, Catawba, High Point, Lenoir Rhyne and Atlantic Christian).

The gap was obvious, and something was done. Seven colleges reformed the North Carolina Intercollegiate Athletic Conference at a meeting at the Washington Duke Hotel, Durham, December 6, 1930. Appalachian joined the aforementioned Little Six. Western Carolina joined in 1933, East Carolina 1947. Dr. S. L. Marion of Lenoir Phyne was elected president, and attending that meeting were three gentlemen who would play major roles in small college athletics in the state for decades—E. G. Purdom of Guilford, D. E. Faust of Catawba and A. L. Hook of Elon.

Freshman star of Guilford's 1973 champions, Lloyd (World) Free .

They played basketball that 1931 winter, the first North State champions determined on regular season play until 1941 when the tournament was inaugurated at High Point College. After World War II, the tournament was held at Elkin, Statesville and Winston-Salem before moving to the Lexington YMCA for a long and successful run. The Carolinas Conference replaced the North State May 20, 1961, reorganizing with 11 members from both Carolinas, an affiliation which existed until more recent district realignment in the NAIA.

Among the coaching achievements of the so-called smaller colleges, one stands out for versatility. Douglas Clyde (Peahead) Walker became known for his football at Wake Forest and with the Montreal Alouettes, but in 1927 when he began coaching at Elon College he handled football, basketball, baseball and a "minimal teaching assignment." In 1934-35 Coach Walker's Fighting Christians won all three North State Conference championships—football, basketball and baseball.

NAIA Championships

(Times in national tournament in first parenthesis. Won-lost record by years.)

APPALACHIAN (5)—1940 (1-1); 1941 (2-1 quarters), 1943 (2-1 quarters), 1948 (0-1), 1950 (0-1).

ATLANTIC CHRISTIAN (1) — 1955 (1-1).

BELMONT ABBEY (1) — 1962 (0-1).

CAMPBELL (2) — 1970 (0-1), 1977 (4-1 finalist).

CATAWBA (2) — 1945 (0-1), 1982 (0-1).

EAST CAROLINA (2) — 1953 (0-1), 1954 (0-1).

ELIZABETH CITY (3) — 1969 (3-2 semis, 4th place), 1971 (4-1 semis, 3rd place), 1972 (0-1).

ELON (3) — 1952 (0-1), 1956 (0-1), 1957 (0-1).

GARDNER-WEBB (3) — 1972 (3-2 semis, 4th place), 1974 (1-1), 1981 (0-1).

GUILFORD (6) — 1966 (0-1), 1967 (1-1), 1968 (0-1), 1970 (3-2 semis, 4th place), 1973 (5-0 CHAMPION), 1976 (0-1).

HIGH POINT (8) — 1939 (0-1), 1942 (1-1), 1946 (0-1), 1951 (0-1), 1964 (2-1 quarters), 1965 (1-1), 1969 (2-1 quarters), 1979 (1-1).

LENOIR RHYNE (2) — 1958 (0-1), 1959 (2-1 quarters).

NORTH CAROLINA A&T (1) — 1971 (2-1 quarters).

NORTH CAROLINA-ASHEVILLE (2)—1969 (1-1), 1971 (0-1).

PEMBROKE (1) — 1973 (0-1).

ST. AUGUSTINE'S (2) — 1977 (0-1), 1980 (1-1).

WESTERN CAROLINA (3)—1947 (0-1), 1963 (4-1 finalist), 1972 (0-1).

WINSTON-SALEM (6)—1961 (2-1 quarters), 1962 (1-1), 1963 (0-1), 1965 (2-1 quarters), 1975 (2-1 quarters), 1978 (2-1 quarters).

The pride of Western Carolina, section as well as university, is Henry Logan, floating through the air for yet another score. All-American four times, only the second person in NAIA records to achieve that.

NAIA All Americans

Selections started 1950-51 season. Figure in parenthesis indicates (1st, 2nd or 3rd team.)

APPALACHIAN
1955 — John Pyecha (2)
BELMONT ABBEY
1980 — Billy Holmgaard (3)
1981 — David Kershaw (3)
CAMPBELL
1976 — Marshall Lovett (3)
1977 — Sam Staggers (1)
CATAWBA
1969 — Dwight Durante (1)
1982 — Dwayne Grant (1)
1983 — Maurice McDaniel (3)
EAST CAROLINA
1954 — Bobby Hodges (2)
ELIZABETH CITY
1962 — Marvin Troutman (1)
1969 — Isreal Oliver (2)
1970 — Isreal Oliver (2)
1971 — Mike Gale (1)
ELON
1964 — Jesse Branson (1)
1965 — Jesse Branson (2)
1971 — Tommy Cole (2)
1972 — Tommy Cole (3)
GARDNER-WEBB
1971 — George Adams (1)
1972 — George Adams (1)
1974 — John Drew (1)
1975 — Jim Blanks (2)
1976 — Dave Bormann (3)
1977 — Dave Bormann (1)
1978 — Lewis Young (3)
1983 — Eddie Wilkins (1)
GUILFORD
1967 — Bob Kauffman (2)
1968 — Bob Kauffman (1)
1970 — David Smith (2)
1971 — David Smith (2)
1973 — M. L. Carr (1)
1974 — Lloyd Free (1)
1975 — Lloyd Free (1)
1977 — Sam Kennedy (3)
1978 — Gary Devlin (1)

HIGH POINT
1959 — Danny Sewell (2)
1960 — Danny Sewell (2)
1965 — Dale Neel (3)
1966 — Gene Littles (3)
1968 — Gene Littles (1)
1969 — Gene Littles (1)
1974 — Pete Collins (3)
1979 — Charlie Floyd (1)
LENOIR RHYNE
1955 — Raeford Wells (1)
1956 — Raeford Wells (2)
1957 — Raeford Wells (1)
1962 — Jerry Wells (3)
1963 — Jerry Wells (2)
NORTH CAROLINA A & T
1960 — Al Attles (2)
1972 — Elmer Austin (2)
PEMBROKE
1977 — Tom Gardner
PFEIFFER
1979 — Mike Epps (2)
WESTERN CAROLINA
1951 — Ronald Rogers (3)
1952 — Ronald Rogers (1)
1953 — Ronald Rogers (3)
1963 — Mel Gibson (1)
1963 — Tom Lavelle (2)
1965 — Henry Logan (3)
1966 — Henry Logan (1)
1967 — Henry Logan (1)
1968 — Henry Logan (1)
WINSTON-SALEM
1961 — Cleo Hill (1)
1962 — George Foree (3)
1964 — Ted Blunt (3)
1966 — Earl Monroe (2)
1967 — Earl Monroe (1)
1968 — William English (3)
1969 — William English (3)
1978 — Carlos Terry (1)
1980 — Reggie Gaines (1)

21
Off Campus /
Coliseums and TV

When college basketball outgrew the campus, still the focal point of administration and student activity but no longer able to house the thousands of people who would like to witness the contests, the boom came.

There was television, live and in color, eventually — when it first brought North Carolina teams in national combat right into the dens and living rooms of millions, back there in 1957, it was black and white. Television might be the single most responsible factor in today's popularity of the sport in the state. People still talk about watching the Tar Heels in triple overtime at Kansas at midnight in 1957, or the Wolfpack all over the West at 1:40 a.m. in 1983.

And almost as important, because they spread the actual playing of the games from campus to Charlotte and Greensboro, the two major cities in the state, was the building of arenas where more people could watch. Campus facilities, except N.C. State's Reynolds Coliseum, did not suffice in the growth of the game. When the Charlotte Coliseum opened with 11,667 seats in 1955, it was the start, and quickly the NCAA utilized both the facility and Charlotte's hospitality as its first off-campus site for the East Regional. When the Greensboro Coliseum was built in 1959, with 9,000 seats, the move continued, and Greensboro's enlargement to 15,900 in 1971 was the key. It provided the site of the 1974 NCAA Final Four, the first time the nationals had been South, and it was a tribute to the fans in the state of North Carolina, which indeed was one of their selling points when they made several summer presentations to the NCAA committee.

The new, and larger, arenas provided the studio for TV, including intersectional matchups, as well as the ACC tournament beginning in 1967. It has not been held on a campus home court since, although Wake Forest plays its home conference games in Greensboro and

Georgia Tech hosts several games in the Omni. With Carolina's new 23,000-seat arena, however, the ACC tournament will undoubtedly go to Chapel Hill by 1986.

The Charlotte Coliseum had its first game December 9, 1955. Managing Director Paul Buck, the coliseum's only boss man in all the years, related recently: "The Charlotte Jaycees got interested, and they wanted either Carolina or State. Everett Case, who had his own big building, wanted a guarantee, having the champion team then, so they talked with Frank McGuire who had just come to the Carolina. He agreed to play Georgia Tech. They had to sell pretty hard to bring it about."

Then came the long-standing, though entry-changing North-South doubleheaders. It was first called the Carolinas Doubleheaders, and Buck had this recollection: "A lot of people have taken credit for this event that began in January 1959, but it was Bob Quincy who did it. He was sports editor of the *Charlotte News* at the time (now *Charlotte Observer* sports columnist), and he had the idea and put the apparatus together. We had a meeting with State and Carolina people at the old Charlotte Hotel, and Frank Howard down at Clemson said, he didn't know much about this basketball but if there was going to be any money made, he wanted to be a part of it." State and Carolina met South Carolina and Clemson, each giving up one home conference game on alternating years. But then the Gamecocks built their own coliseum, needed the home game. Georgia Tech replaced them. Four years later, Clemson had a new arena, dropped out. Furman took its place. The Citadel joined in several years ago, and the North-South, 25-years-old, continues a draw for the fans in the most populous section of the state.

Davidson has played in the Charlotte Coliseum for years. Buck said: "The holiday tournament which John Belk set up with Davidson has gone by, and then all of a sudden there was Lefty Driesell. He built the Davidson program and we were very successful as long as he was there."

When Greensboro Coliseum came on the scene (1959), Bob Kent was the managing director with an inside knowledge of basketball, which he had played and coached in West Virginia. Recently he talked about the first efforts: "W. H. Sullivan, Sr. was our commission chairman in building the place and he and I went down to see Everett Case in his office. Mr. Bill was on State's athletic council and said he wanted to bring the State-Carolina game to Greensboro for the coliseum opening. Everett answered quickly, 'Not as long as I'm coach.' There was too much rivalry there. We couldn't work out a date that first season, so I called Al Severance, coach at Villanova, where State was to play. I asked what it would take to move the game down to North Carolina, we dickered around and we offered him expenses and

$7,000. He snapped it up. They couldn't make much money playing in the Palestra at the time."

That was December 16, 1959, State vs. Villanova in Greensboro. Many other deals were made similarly, even within the conference. Virginia played its "home" games with Carolina there in 1960 and 1962, with State in 1961 and 1964. Wake Forest and Duke set up a "third" game, not to count in conference standings, for a big Saturday night in Greensboro. In the 60s Carolina played Notre Dame in Greensboro, Indiana in Charlotte one season, then Kentucky in Charlotte, Vanderbilt and NYU in Greensboro in 1965. That winter State played Southern Cal, Duke met Virginia Tech and Wake Forest played Davidson, a busy college schedule in Greensboro.

Jim Oshust came to Greensboro during the arena's enlargement to almost 16,000, largest arena south of Philadelphia, until the Louisiana Superdome. He has found changing times in college basketball, but recently he said one thing: "The basketball fan in North Carolina is the greatest. True, they're partisan, selective, narrow-viewed — I wouldn't say narrow-minded. We had the regionals in 1976 and 1979 without conference teams and we bombed out. They're television minded, they watch ACC basketball every night and the weekends. At first we could schedule certain games with the Big Four, so many for Charlotte, so many for Greensboro. Today the games are picked for balance as far as TV potential is concerned. A schedule is never engraved in stone, the clay never dries on the tablet. The game can be changed to 3 o'clock or it may even go the next day."

When the NCAA revised its tournament format, having four regional events, first on campus only, it turned to Reynolds Coliseum the first two years (1952-53). After four years in the Palestra (Philadelphia), the Charlotte Coliseum was ready, and the Queen City was the perfect host for four years starting in 1958. Sellout crowds and Southern hospitality. Quite a combination. In more recent years both Charlotte and Greensboro have hosted early round games, as well as regionals.

Biggest basketball event in the history of the state was the 1974 Final Four in Greensboro. On the court it offered David Thompson and Bill Walton at the same time, and the Wolfpack beat UCLA in double overtime. In the NCAA's new rotation system it had been East vs West for the first time, so the nation's No. 1 and No. 2 teams met in the semifinals. Marquette advanced over Kansas, and Coach Norman Sloan's N.C. State team became national champions on an exciting Monday night with NBC-TV. It was a Wolfpack which drew thousands to its practices, because NCAA tickets had been long sold. The Greensboro Coliseum had a record 9,000 fans for the free Friday afternoon practice of the four teams, a record until Albuquerque last April.

Having the finals in Greensboro didn't just happen. With the coli-

Ray Reeve, the voice everybody listened to.

seum enlargement, the idea birthed. Why not have the NCAA finals in the South? Why not in North Carolina, whose fans were the greatest? As it developed, I was the one to make the first pitch, to Bebe Lee of Kansas, as chairman of the NCAA basketball committee. That was during a USBWA all-America selection meeting in Kansas City. Then it was with Walter Byers of the NCAA, during the Louisville finals. That was 1969. At the NCAA committee's summer meeting at the Broadmoor Bob Kent and I made the presentation. It was cemented in Monterey the next year when Oshust, now the director, headed the group, which included Woody Durham and Bill Hensley, from the governor's office. Tickets were placed on sale with letters postmarked April 1, 1973. It had to be after 12:01 a.m. There were midnight traffic jams all over the state, and the coliseum received 42,500 pieces of mail, the largest single mail in the history of the state, U.S. Post Office people said. Orders were for 136,000 tickets, and a lottery had to be conducted. It was the NCAA's first such experience, but drawings have been annual ever since.

Just as important in state basketball annals was moving the conference tournament out of Reynolds Coliseum, where it had been so successful since 1951 when the arena was completed. But with the home Wolfpack winning championships regularly under Everett Case, other coaches, as early as 1954, began to push for a change of venue. With Charlotte and Greensboro having new arenas, there was a place to go. Eddie Cameron of Duke, chairman of the ACC basketball committee since the early Southern Conference days in Raleigh, faced the situation, which he recently explained: "We were the only conference in the country, except the Southern, with the tournament deciding the champion. Later the coaches didn't like that, not in Reynolds Coliseum at least. The coaches thought it was too much of an advantage for State to take the attention, to have the best seats and to entertain boys (recruits) at home. The coaches said, either move the tournament around or move it somewhere else. The committee had to listen to the coaches who felt it was too much to State's advantage."

Both Kent and Buck appeared before the committee — with a possible solution, their arenas. Cameron said, "Both were good places to stage the tournament, both men were capable directors. They were independent floors. No home floor advantage and no home entertaining advantage either. That's what brought the change on." Kent related: "We knew there was a hue and cry over State playing at home for several reasons. The conference voted to play one additional year in Raleigh (1966), then one in Greensboro (1967) and one in Charlotte (1968). I told our commission, they're being very nice to us, we only have 9,000 seats. I guaranteed them, they're going to stay in Charlotte."

It triggered the enlargement in Greensboro, the coliseum commission wanting to host the ACC tournament in the future. This also brought on the idea of the Big Four, Kent's idea which he recently discussed:

"At the time the concert business was not the greatest, we realized the Greensboro Coliseum had a basketball mentality. That's what the people wanted. Our commission liked the idea but I told them it probaby won't ever happen. The coaches would be dead set against it, the idea of playing each other twice in the season, then the tournament and all that. But I said I thought the money will do it, and it did. They took $40,000 each that first one."

TV, the great big wonderful tube which can take the fans to New Orleans and Albuquerque and Anchorage, has mushroomed more than the off-campus arenas, the latter once having a proposal for a Research Triangle dome seating 50,000, or one in the Triad about half that size. The proper governments could never get together on either project.

TV basketball in the state had a most humbling beginning, with a star actor already on stage. That was the 1957 Carolina basketball team, 32-0, the last two in the triple overtime in Kansas City. It was made for television, to say the very least.

By the time Coach Frank McGuire's team had progressed to the East Regional at Philadelphia, three TV stations in the state, along with C. D. Chesley of Philadelphia, were busy. Chesley, to become the "Father of ACC Television," set up a telecast produced by WPPB-TV in Wilmington, Delaware, with Matt Koukas, former Warrior, as announcer. Gaines Kelley of WFMY-TV Greensboro, Charles Crutchfield of WBTV Charlotte and Fred Fletcher of WTVD Durham, all general managers, completed the first arrangements. The state's first live TV basketball occurred on Friday, March 15, 1957, at 7:30 p.m. Carolina won; next time same thing, Carolina won again.

Why not Kansas City? The three station managers made frantic calls the first of the following week. It had not been set in advance, but Chesley was in Kansas City early. By Wednesday night the games were set. Carolina vs. Michigan State 8:30 p.m. Friday, in winning it was Carolina vs Wilt Chamberlain at 9:30 p.m. Saturday. They went triple overtime, the state of North Carolina stayed up to see all the action.

They were hooked.

So was Chesley. The enthusiastic ratings started him thinking "ACC basketball network." So were some other people. Sportsminded Pilot Life Insurance officials were, and Dick Andrews, vice president for public relations then and now, recalled recently: "I got as excited as anybody on those games, and Monday morning I was in O. F. Stafford's office (president) with some ideas, which he also had. We had been doing sports on radio for years, mostly high schools. We were coming to our 50th anniversary and were looking for something big. We did not get into the telecasts of Carolina in the NCAA, Mose Kiser of Guilford Dairy got into that, but we thought it might be something worthwhile. Chesley was thinking along the same lines, and we met through the *Greensboro Daily News* sports editor, whom you know, I think."

Chesley and Dick Bailey, later to own Sports Network Inc., attended the ACC spring meeting in May 1957 and met Andrews. The network began; first game had Clemson at North Carolina on Saturday afternoon, December 7, 1957, and the schedule — all Saturday afternoon — included 12 games through March 1, with 12 stations on the network. But Andrews also recalled: "Ches has a tough time selling it. He'd come to me and get a partial commitment, then go to the TV stations and tell them he had a sponsor all set, then go to the schools and say the TV stations wanted it bad, then come back to me and say the schools wanted it. We had Frank McGuire and Everett Case to several promotional luncheons, and it finally got off the air." Chesley, before his death in April 1983, had said, "I drove around to every city in the state with a TV station and talked to all the station managers. Many were receptive, but only under the condition that I lined up the sponsors, all of them. We couldn't get national sponsors interested; in fact, Pilot Life bought six minutes, half our time, and that, and only that, made it possible."

Eddie Cameron at Duke took an early interest in TV, along with Chuck Erickson at Carolina and Roy Clogston at N.C. State. Eddie said recently: "Ches met with Chuck, Roy and myself and sold us on the idea. He had a vision that it would be a good thing for the conference and the schools, and it did turn out to be a good thing. He thought we were organized enough to control it. He said we could stir up interest, to help build up attendance, and he was right. He had a hard time selling, and we in turn had a hard time collecting. Sometimes we didn't get our money for six months, but we finally got it, and each year was a big improvement. That first year, I remember, we sold the Carolina-Duke game for $1,000, that $500 each, but it was good money in those days."

Jim Simpson, now of ESPN fame, and Bill Creasy did the first game in Chapel Hill that December 1957. Charlie Harville joined the network early. Jim Thacker had the longest tenure, from 1965 until the change of ACC contracts after 1982. Billy Packer, now with CBS-TV, remains for ACC assignments after his "one-night stand" as a fill-in in 1971. He wanted his kids to see him on the tube, and Skeeter Francis had suggested him to Ches. Bones McKinney, like Jeff Mullins when he retired from the NBA, carried the local touch to the TV audience. Bones learned something quickly: "When I was a basketball coach at Wake Forest, I thought I was known pretty well around the state, even

C. D. Chesley had an ear for what North Carolina's basketball fans wanted: live TV, any day of the week, any hour of the day or night.

the whole Atlantic Coast region, but when I became a color man or analyst, or whatever you call it, really just a color man, when I went to a little country store I couldn't believe it. Like one day in Carteret County, in a little store, some guy jumped up when I walked in an said, 'You can't be nobody but Bones McKinney, I see you every game.'" Of his former boss, Castleman deTolley Chesley, Bones said: "I never met a man as professional as Ches. He presented the ACC with a gold mine. They ought to put a statue up in front of the ACC office."

ACC basketball television, with North Carolina as the key state, stations who would carry every game, exploded. By 1964 Ches was doing the tournament finals from Raleigh, for which he paid $10,000. In Charlotte 1968 he added the semifinals, and the show was in living color, price tag $30,000. Two years later it was $70,000. By 1978, when Ches helped the conference sell the finals to ABC-TV for $250,000, all tournament games were being televised. By 1981 the total conference TV package, which included Channel 17 Atlanta to all parts of the country on cable, brought in $600,000. There were some unusual TV items along these years. In 1960 seven inches of snow greeted Raleigh on opening Thursday, so WRAL-TV televised all four games live as a public service. When the tournament moved to Greensboro in 1967, pre-soldout house (no tournament ticket has been on public sale since), closed circuit TV on the big screen went to the adjacent auditorium, 3,000 more paid.

Metrosports Inc. had the TV contract in the ACC for 1981-82, the network consisted of 27 stations and 38 games, 31 of them during regular season. Metrosports paid $3 million.

Raycom-Jefferson Productions holds the current contract, three years ending 1985-86 for the total $18 million. It includes ESPN. NBC-TV again carries the ACC tournament finals on its full network.

The 1982 Nielson ratings system listed the 60 shows syndicated in five or more markets with the ACC basketball as the only sports show. It gave ACC basketball 23rd overall rating, sixth among total men viewers, fourth among men 18-49 years old. When Penn played in the NCAA second round in Raleigh 1979, beating Carolina in an upset, Penn Capt. Tony Price told a full interview room: "I always thought ACC basketball was a TV show." Steve Vacendak, Duke captain and now assistant AD, has said: "I came to Duke because of TV basketball."

Ray Reeve's Tobacco Sports Network was an integral part of college basketball in the transition days from Southern Conference to ACC. The gravel-voice expert, and he was that, gave the most accurate and interesting broadcast of any announcer in his day, and since. In his summation at halftime or game's end, he would recite the scoring for players. N.C. State had a guard named Bernie Yurin, and Ray would spit it out: "Wolfpack scoring, Ranzino seventeen, Horvath twelve, Terrill ten, Yurin eight ... "

In 1946 five or six stations in Eastern North Carolina were on the Tobacco Network, which added the basketball broadcasts. But they weren't live. Radio would kill attendance, athletic directors believed. First games were at Chapel Hill where Reeves was allowed to record and play back later ... the second half only. With Everett Case's good teams, most of the Tobacco Sports Network schedule was the Wolfpack, but not confined to just one team. Reeve's schedule grew to 8-10 games a week, with live games, as many as 80 a season. Bill Currie became the world's greatest color man, by self admission. They covered Tobacco Road, all four schools by the early 60s. Dick Herbert, sports editor of the *Raleigh News and Observer*, has often observed: "At one time Ray Reeve was the best-known person in North Carolina. His huge radio network brought out-of-state basketball into the state, to many thousands of listeners, and played a tremendous part—probably equal to what Everett Case did — in increasing the state's interest in college basketball."

There was also "broadvision" originated by the university TV station, WUNC. Carolina did some of its home games on television without sound. Fans could tune in their radios for that, an appeasement to the protesting radio people.

By the early 60s each of the Big Four schools started their own networks, which are strong today. In 1983 the Wolfpack network had 56 stations, Carolina 43, Wake Forest 42 and Duke 22. If you lived, for instance, in Burlington you could get Duke on WPCM-FM, Carolina WBAG, State WBBB and Wake Forest WBAG-FM. Or down on the coast in Wilmington, Duke on WKLM, Carolina WMFD, State WWQQ-FM and Wake Forest WGNI.

With no real large city, Charlotte the queen at 300,000 plus, there are many daily newspapers in the state, and a majority of them staff the conference tournament and the NCAA tournament games that follow. No state provides better or more coverage of college basketball than North Carolina, and that includes the smaller afternoon dailies as well as the 4-5 larger morning papers.

David Cawood, NCAA media director as well as the new TV communications coordinator, knows what to expect when a North Carolina team reaches the Final Four: "We just plan for more press tables for the working reporters, more than any other state or school that has played. Even with recent increase in national coverage, the largest group will be when a North Carolina team plays. Like New Orleans and Albuquerque the last two tournaments."

22
St. Louis Blues / Bill Foster

Bill Foster was serious as he smiled, mainly because he and the family were coming home. He had coached at Rutgers, had operated a wonderful summer camp with the venerable Harry Litwack in the Poconos of Pennsylvania.

Then he took the covered wagons West, settling in a mediocre basketball program at the University of Utah which he turned into a winning mark the very first season. Brigham Young could not have done better. It did lose the second season, but by the fourth he and the Runnin' Utes were in the NIT finals and the Foster family was back East, at least for the week.

But he and the family had a hankering, this William Edward Foster, not to be confused with William Carey Foster at Clemson who is no kin. It did give the ACC the unusual situation of having two Bill Fosters as coaches. Now the state of South Carolina has both. Foster said at the time of his return East: "Many players in the East turned us down at Utah because it was too far from home. We will not have this problem at Duke."

From Madison Square Garden, where Purdue had just beaten Utah for the NIT crown, he came to the 1974 NCAA finals in Greensboro, convened with his fellow coaches since he would become president of the National Association of Basketball Coaches (NABC) in 1976. Three days later he was back on the campus in West Durham, signed and sealed as the new head basketball coach.

"Carl James (athletic director) when he hired me enlightened me about the rivalries in North Carolina," Coach Foster said recently, during the latest NABC convention, doing well from an in-season heart attack and successful bypass at South Carolina, where he is now coaching.

"I was fully aware of it. Games on the road were tough, but they're

Moment of caution for the Blue Devil coaches en route to the NCAA finals 1978, Bill Foster, head coach, left, and Lou Goetz, assistant.

like that everywhere. You're outnumbered, no question about that, 1,000 to 50. In the ACC you have 50 complimentary tickets. If you had 50 friends left, you tried to get them to use those tickets, to people who at least would cheer for your team. You were going into a hornet's nest but I think you expected that. Rivalry among the four North Carolina schools was intense, but I want to tell you, going to Maryland was no picnic either."

He began reviewing his conference competition, and found himself saying: "Last season at one time three ACC teams were ranked in the top five teams in the nation. Needless to say, it is the nation's strongest conference. The ACC tournament has to be one of the most exciting events ever held in college sports. I have never been to the ACC but understand you have to be there to really believe it."

That was 1974 when he took the Duke job. He learned quickly, although it took him four years before his Blue Devils could get a tournament win. His first tournament was 1975, and what a weekend for a new coach to show up for initiation. There were four teams nationally ranked—Maryland No. 2 (just behind unbeaten Indiana), N.C. State No. 8, North Carolina No. 12 and Clemson No. 14. On March 1, which was the morning of the final regular season games, not a single club knew whom it would be playing the first day of the tournament, a week away. At the commissioner's office Sunday morning, Bob James drew Duke for No. 6, which meant it played Clemson instead of North Carolina.

If that didn't keep Coach Foster awake with anticipation, he only had to wait a few days. The Blue Devils had favored Clemson tied with seconds ticking off, then Tree Rollins worked in close with 27 seconds to play, made his shot, Clemson 78-76. Even that was just part of the 1975 tournament routine. Of the six games played in the tournment, all six, mind you, the total margin was 20 points, and two went overtime.

Coach Foster began to build the Dukes, since his first spring had started late with a recruiting blank. First blue chip recruit was Jim Spanarkel, out of Hudson Catholic High Jersey City. Then came the big blond giant, Mike Gminski, who passed up his senior year at Masuk High in Monroe, Connecticut in an advanced academic program. Tate Armstrong was scoring, in 1977 an amazing 31.5 points average for ACC road games, but he missed the tournament with injury.

It was also slogan time in Durham, from "The Runnin' Dukes" (1975) to "Freedom to Run" (1976) to "We've Only Just Begun To Run" (1977) to one that proved itself: "Off and Running" (1978). This Blue Devil aggregation would amaze the nation, take St. Louis by storm and come within one Kentucky player, who had the greatest shooting night of his life, of being national champions. As well as the youngest team ever in the finals, because Coach Foster settled on two freshmen (Gene Banks and Kenny Dennard), two sophomores (Mike

Gminski and John Harrell) and the old veteran, a junior, Jim Spanarkel. They drove people crazy as they entertained them. His new freshmen were Banks from West Philadelphia, Dennard from Stokes County in North Carolina. He remarked of his return East at this particular time: "The ACC has had good public relations. We were recruiting in the North and East, and of course now the Big East has made some changes there. TV has made an impact, definitely, but it's getting more regional and I think players are staying in their regions. State pride is becoming more highly involved in recruiting."

But 1978 did not begin with all that stuff in the promised land of St. Louis' Checkerdome. The Blue Devils lost to Carolina in the Big Four, to Southern Cal in overtime on a Western trip. They learned they would win on the road, a key to the whole viewpoint being Spanarkel hitting 33 points and beating Maryland at College Park, Duke's first ACC road win in six years. Bob Bender, who had transferred from Indiana's 1976 national champions, became eligible in January. At Clemson the front line (Gminski, Banks, Dennard) had 66 points and 23 rebounds, and right there assumed the name "The Duke Power Company." At home they beat the No. 2 ranked Tar Heels, and it propelled the Dukes into the top 20 for the first time in seven years. Coach Foster had used his "sixth man" well, going 12-0 in Cameron Indoor Stadium where the student body is as tough as any other body.

It was tournament time, something to look forward to for a change. The ACC format was changed, starting Wednesday and taking Friday off, so the Saturday afternoon finals (4:30 p.m.) could be on ABC-TV. The ACC would change anything for that. It was also the first time to bring outside officials in, which would prove to be a bad judgment call. Duke was No. 8 nationally by now, Carolina No. 11. Dennard got 21 in beating Clemson 83-72, Coach Foster's first ACC tournament victory. Then came 81-69 over Maryland, and in the finals it was Duke and Wake Forest, which had beaten the Tar Heels. It was Duke's first finals since 1969 and Vic Bubas, and Wake's first since 1964 and Bones McKinney. Rod Griffin sparked Wake's halftime march, then Gminski and Banks blitzed the Deacons 85-77.

In the NCAAs Rhode Island State was edged at Charlotte, Gminski rallying within one with 32 seconds, then hitting one-and-one for 63-62 with 17 seconds. The East Regional saw the Dukes come from eight down midway into the second half as Gminski blocked three shots, 84-80 over Penn. Villanova was easier, 90-72.

The youthful Dukes thoroughly enjoyed St. Louis in the Final Four. Coach Foster quipped after the ACC: "From the basement to the penthouse in a year." In the Checkerdome they beat Notre Dame, but Coach Digger Phelps' Irish displayed one of the playoffs' all-time comebacks. Pounding the board, Duke was up 16 in the second half. Coach Foster related what happened in the postgame interview: "The margin fell from 16 to 14 to 12 to 10 to eight to six (2:20 to play) to four (1:37 to play) to two (20 seconds). They began hitting us with three-on-one and four-on-one breaks, and we had to make them take a different type of shot than layups. We couldn't get them to miss, they stuck it in." Duke won 90-86, but to do so, the Blue Devils in the final 10 minutes had to sink seven of eight field goal shots, 17 of 19 free throws.

At the NCAA Sunday press conference the Kentucky Wildcat seniors marched silently to the rostrum, spoke serously as if defeat would send them to the death chamber. It was rumored Coach Joe B. Hall was out if he didn't win. In pleasant contrast were the young Blue Devils. Said Captain Spanarkel: "We want to enjoy it, all of us, not just the starters. Our bench has been great with its positive performance." Coach Foster: "I love the enthusiasm part, it is tremendous to watch. They play unselfish team basketball." The title match was billed as Kentucky power vs Duke finesse. Coach Foster was named NABC coach of the year, along with Abe Lemons of Texas, and there was a phone call threat on Gene Banks.

Duke ran out of Blue Devil magic. With Jack Givens scoring 41 points, Kentucky went up 16 in the second half, this time forcing the Dukes to the comeback. They did, Gminski's eight-footer with 11 seconds cutting the margin to 92-88. At 28 seconds Dennard made a strong move to the basket, scored, but he was called charging. It was debated. Duke's 2-3 zone had been penetrated and annihilated by Givens in the gap. Final score 94-88. In defeat Spanarkel spoke for the team: "Kentucky proved it was the best team in the nation. We just caught Givens on the wrong night. His was the best performance I've ever seen in any game in which I've played, and it happened to come in the NCAA finals."

There were high hopes for 1979, and the slogan, right, was "Let's Do It Again." Freshman Vince Taylor of Tates Creek High in Lexington, Kentucky was added. Duke was preseason No. 1 ranked, but they lost that in Madison Square Garden when both Ohio State and St. John's stopped them. By season end they had beaten rival Carolina at home in one of the odd games of the decade. At halftime the score was 7-0 Duke (final 47-40). But in the tournament finals it was Carolina again, and this time the Tar Heels did it. That Saturday afternoon Bob Bender had an emergency appendectomy. Both ACC giants were placed in the East Regional, so they cold fight it out for the Final Four. They lost in the second round on "Black Sunday" in Raleigh.

When they returned to the tournament finals in Greensboro in 1980, five inches of snow and sleet kept some of the fans away but warmed the Blue Devils in 73-72 over Maryland. Coach Foster resigned as Duke coach Sunday morning after the tournament, to accept a similar position at South Carolina on Frank McGuire's

Mike Gminski, the big man, flips goal over Villanova in the 1978 East Regionals.

retirement. Potential candidates for the Duke job were mentioned — Chuck Daly of NBA 76ers (ex-Duke coach), Eddie Sutton of Arkansas, Jim Valvano of Iona and Tom Young of Rutgers.

Coach Foster took the team to the NCAA as conference champs, and the four nationally-ranked teams were also invited. It was the first time any conference had five enties. The ACC champions were sent to the Mideast Regional, beat Penn the first round, then Kentucky in the regional, Kentucky at Lexington, Kentucky, too. Duke won 55-54, but lost 68-60 to Purdue in the finals. The Blue Devils had made the final eight, almost the Final Four.

His six years had a 113-64 mark, the final sesons being 27-7, 22-8 and 24-9. Mike Krzyzewski succeeded him at Duke, took the 1981 Blue Devils to the NIT. As for the Bill Foster finale, 1980 in March, the team had to win to make the NCAAs, almost like old times when only the champion moved on. Senior Bob Bender summed it up well, after beating the Wolfpack in the tournament first round: "We're playing now like each game is our future."

23
The Big Four / Carl Tacy

To the full enjoyment and benefit of the players and the fans, two basic ingredients of basketball in the state of North Carolina, there was the Big Four Tournament in Greensboro.

It came early in the season, sometimes by December 1, even the day after Thanksgiving, sometimes after the holidays, and it did create some much-needed revenue for the college athletic budgets. But it never caught on with the coaches, who hated it, and when times and economics, meaning the NCAA playoffs and their ever-sweetening pot, the Big Four went the way of the Dixie Classic, which is unfortunate, for the players and the fans.

Carl Tacy became associated with the name, Big Four champions, because his Wake Forest teams captured four titles, the most of any coach among the 11 Big Fours held in the Greensboro Coliseum. Tacy also had a team (1977) which came within a couple fast breaks of making the Final Four in the Omni, and then 1983 brought a Final Four attainment in the NIT at Madison Square Garden.

Now in his 12th season at Wake Forest, the quiet coach with an unassuming approach to life, even among ACC basketball coaches, knew all about the game in North Carolina and the ACC. After all, 10 years in Virginia high schools, two seasons at Ferrum Junior College and a 23-4 year at Marshall included knowledge and information about that league toward the coast.

"Sure, I had an idea what the ACC game was all about," Coach Tacy had said, the time being well after the indoctrination in the spring of 1973 when he was asked to succeed Jack McCloskey. "I had a good idea, but as it turned out, not really. I knew the brand of basketball and I liked it. There is a national recognition of ACC basketball, and it was definitely a challenge sort of thing, something every coach wants as early as possible in his career, but not too early, I might add now.

Honesty, however, I hadn't stopped to realize the road games in the conference, the intensity of the fans, the fan knowledge of the game and the support of the fans. I could just see one thing, myself in the ACC."

A problem developed overnight. "We couldn't win," said the coach, which is about as simple an analysis as possible. His teams liked to run, the way West Virginia teams always have, and he came to Wake Forest from Marshall University. When he dipped in conference play for the first time, he lost to Virginia by 13, two games in the Big Four, Carolina by 18, Maryland by 29, Carolina again by 18, Duke by 13, Virginia by 32, Clemson by 25. Isn't that enough to draw the sordid picture? Tacy: "We had to give the kids a chance to win, we had an obligation to our fans as well. They wanted some wins, so we went to the deliberate game more and more."

It came too late, a last place finish in the conference. It put the Deacons against the second-seeded Tar Heels of Chapel Hill in the opening tournament game. Coach Tacy recalled later: "I knew there would be a tremendous strain in the tournament. Playing before so many thousands of people. It was an exciting time for me as a coach." N.C. State was on probation in 1973, a team could finish second in the tournament and make the NCAAs, since then only one team could go. The days of Tacy miracles began that very first tournament afternoon.

There had been a premature moment of jubilation on the Carolina bench when Deacon Tony Byers accidentally stepped on the out-of-bounds line, giving Carolina the ball at 1:18, score tied at 46. Four Corners, Brad Hoffman jump shot for Carolina, missed, but Bobby Jones rebounded 48-46 with two seconds. But hold it. The Deacons' Eddie Payne took the ball out, not guarded closely, threw it about 80 feet over the outstretched arms of Jones and Mitch Kupchak, into the hands of Lee Foye who shot, hit. Tied. In overtime the two rivals go back to the final seconds, and Carolina had the ball. At seven seconds George Karl takes a short jumper, scramble for the rebound at seven seconds, Payne got the ball near the foul line. No timeout, just go. Payne told of the play: "Dribbled it out of traffic, quickly. Tony Byers had released and was open. He took the pass, then shot the ball to Phil Perry. Little short shot, good." Wake Forest had upset the Tar Heels 54-52 in the coach's tournament debut.

What did the West Virginian think of the ACC at that point? Answer: "Just what I had anticipated, remarkably so, playing in front of such a large crowd and being scrutinized in everything you do. I'm sure the fans got the feel of the excitement and pressure, and I really appreciate that. But I also believe that to obtain and have the full appreciation of what the ACC tournament really is, you must be in it. I realize the fans' involvement, but I can't see how you could ever fully realize what it is unless you've been in the ACC as a player or coach."

His teams played in the tournament finals in 1978, came within a shot, maybe a half-shot at the most, of making the finals in 1981 and 1982. Carolina got the last shot and won 58-57 at Capital Centre, then Ralph Sampson and Virginia won in overtime 1982.

But the Big Four, now that was something else. It had Carl Tacy written all over it. When the coaches finally persuaded the athletic directors, with all the "new" NCAA first round money, that the Big Four had outlived its usefulness at the bank, there had been 11 of them. Tacy won four, three in a row, Big Four record; six straight game victories, Big Four record; two titles in one calendar year, Big Four record.

Coach Tacy's second Deacon team played N.C. State in the Big Four finals, the Wolfpack which went on to capture the 1974 NCAA national championship. In the rotating Big Four they drew each other in the final game of January 1975, the Wolfpack with a 36-game win streak going, plus No. 1 national ranking. Skip Brown and Jerry Schellenburg took control, and Cal Stump took the boards, resulting in 83-78 triumph. In the final Wake beat Duke with a 1-2-2 zone. The following year, January 1976, the Deacons drew Carolina in the first round, and the Tar Heels were No. 3 nationally. Skip Brown again starred, the Deacons again won 95-83, but Brown missed the last 17 minutes with a bruised kneecap. He did not play the next night when the Deacons won another Big Four, beating N.C. State and Kenny Carr who got 45 points. It made the Deacons 9-0 on the season.

The Big Four was changing already, it had to be moved to the start of the season as the NCAA playoffs added another weekend on the March schedule. The conference had to get into league play right after January 1. Big Four VII matched two nationally ranked teams in the first game, No. 3 Carolina beating No. 15 State, then the Deacons edged Duke 81-80 as Rod Griffin converted two free throws with 15 seconds for 81-78, enough to offset Tate Armstrong's final Duke goal. Schellenburg, MVP for two tournaments, was playing small forward, freshman Frank Johnson at guard. Jerry and Skip Brown scored 17 straight. Deacon points against the ranking Tar Heels. It went overtime, and Wake Forest won 97-96. Three in a row.

Then came the last of the Big Fours, December 1980. Wake Forest had its junior strength — Alvis Rogers, Guy Morgan, Jim Johnstone and Mike Helms. Frank Johnson had returned after injury for his fifth (and most outstanding) season. Coach Jim Valvano walked in for his first, and only, Big Four, and lost to the Deacons 87-57. Admitted Coach Valvano: "This was shock therapy for us." Carolina, ranked No. 10 nationally, edged Duke, and then Johnson, the MVP, paced the balanced Deacons to 82-71 triumph after the Tar Heels rallied from 20 down to within seven with two minutes left in the packed and screaming Greensboro Coliseum, the crowd 15,703.

Regrettably, it was all over. The Big Four had come when Bob

It became a Carl Tacy habit, draping his team captains with Big Four nets. Skip Brown, left, and Jerry Schellenburg in the late 70s.

Kent, then managing director of the Greensboro Coliseum, presented a suggestion to the four athletic directors during the ACC spring meeting at the Homestead in Hot Springs, Virginia. He outlined a season-opening tournament, playing each other, certainly $40-50,000 per school. The coaches never really liked it, but there was the money.

Players liked it, they could toss a little tester at each other without having the results show up in the conference standings. Fans did not accept the holiday schedule at once. Only 11,196 showed up the first Friday evening, then 11,656 for the Saturday night finals. It wasn't until the to-be-national champion Wolfpack played the finals in December 1973 that the coliseum was sold out. It then became a standard thing, tickets had to be obtained through the four institutions' athletic foundation headquarters. Tickets were $35, each team take-home check was $80,000.

Before the termination, Carolina Coach Dean Smith was saying, and rightly so: "It's harder to play in the Big Four than it would be to play the No. 1 and No. 2 teams in the country, DePaul and Kentucky (December 1980), back to back. In the Big Four you're playing rival schools. You know them and they know you. We're better playing intersectional opponents." Carl Tacy, who owned the Big Four, added, "It is a tournament that's extremely hard to play this early in the season because of the tremendous competition and the calibre of teams you face. And there's always the matter of reestablishing confidence if you come out of it 0-2. That was a strong feeling among the coaches."

About this time also the NCAA tournament was expanding. It had gone to 32 teams in 1975, and more than the ACC champion. For the first time in NCAA five conference teams went to the NCAAs; they were Duke (champion), North Carolina, Wake Forest, Maryland and Clemson. The magical 20 was more important. The NCAA was paying $132,744 by 1983 just to make the playoffs. The Big Four tournament potential of coming out 0-2 became a key factor.

Coach Tacy's Deacons almost made the NCAA Final Four in 1977, and had it happened, the state of North Carolina would have had three of the four teams. The Tar Heels and UNC-Charlotte made it, along with Nevada-Las Vegas and Marquette, but the Deacons almost turned aside Marquette in the Midwest Regional finals. Rod Griffin was selected ACC player of the year, and Wake Forest got the ACC's second bid. Four losses dropped the Deacons out of the top 20 late in the season. They downed Arkansas, No. 8 ranked, with full-court pressure in the Midwest 86-80. They beat Southern Illinois, shooting 68.2 percent the last 20 minutes, in the regional 86-81, and then came Coach Al McGuire and Marquette. Al scouted well: "Ours is a rhythm game and we've got to keep the score below 70 if we want to win." Wake led 35-31 at halftime, then as the second half play opened, the Deacons came down the floor six or seven times on the fast break without scoring. McGuire changed his defense to a "triangle and 2" to cut off Griffin and Jerry Schellenburg. In four minutes the Warriors outscored Wake 14-2 and won 82-68. The Deacons had had a shot.

The immediate past season, 1982-83, was a most unusual one, in more ways than the normal Deacon supporter could comprehend as it unfolded. It began with Alvis Rogers the only senior holdover from injury. It soon fit Delaney Rudd into the backcourt with Danny Young, and Anthony Teachey became dominant under the boards. John Toms was at forward, and when freshman Kenny Green returned to school, he was a strong sixth man, sometimes starter. They moved quickly to 14 victories in the first 16 games, ranked. They lost to Carolina 80-76 in Greensboro, and the Deacons fell part. They lost the final four season games in no-contests, 107-74 to Virginia, 130-89 to State. There were reports of player dissention, rumors of Coach Tacy returning to Marshall.

Whatever, they came together to reach the NIT Final Four, a definite turn against adversity which plagued the Deacons in February and early March. In the ACC tournament they had the N.C. State Wolfpack down seven with nine minutes. With a tie score they had possession, expertly running the clock, timeout at 30 seconds. An errant pass was deflected by Sidney Lowe, the Wolfpack went in to win the game 71-70. But the defeat did not close out the Deacons. They missed the NCAA, but got the NIT, which was new life for a team and staff that needed it. Delaney Rudd, with an off-court foot injury, played hurt in beating Murray State 87-80, and the second victory came at Vanderbilt. Back home again, they beat South Carolina 78-61.

It culminated in a trip to Madison Square Garden, making the NIT elite, another first in Deacon basketball annals. But 1983, nationwide, happened to be the Year of the Red, all four teams at Albuquerque sporting that bright color, and Wake Forest ran into the red-colored Fresno State team in the NIT semifinals. Coach Tacy's team had done well in the Garden earlier, beating St. Joseph's by 13 in the Holiday Festival before losing a close game to St. John's, later No. 1 ranked in the nation. Fresno State, the nation's No. 2 defensive team in the country, kept the Deacons outside and cut off their fast break and controlled the board, and there's nothing else you can do. The Californians hit 66.7 percent from the floor, their best of the year. Delaney Rudd recovered from the shock of 86-62 to comment: "It seemed like they kept getting layups and we kept shooting 30-footers." Wake's outside shooters made only 12 of 35 from the floor.

It was recorded, an NIT Final Four was quite an achievement under any set of circumstances. Even under normalcy, Coach Tacy realized what an ACC season can be: "We were not a powerful team this season. People laugh when you say this, but the ACC is different than a lot of places. It's tough to keep a team up night after night."

24
61,162 Believers

All those eyes, 61,162 pairs of wide-awake, highly-excited human peepers, were straining to focus on another pair of important objects in the total picture of that huge barn, the Louisiana Superdome.

They tried to keep touch with the big scorebord clocks that seemed to suspend softly in space, balanced against the first balcony boards. The time of another national championship was ticking into eternity, and the conflict on the hardwood battlefield below had not been concluded, not by a long shot, which it would eventually take. Georgetown did lead, however by a narrow point.

Down the court, which seemed miniscule to those in the top rows, the Tar Heels from Chapel Hill worked their way cautiously, and Coach Dean Smith signalled timeout. Those huge clocks paused at 32 seconds. Those 61,162 pairs of eyes rested for just a moment, a well earned break, but it was not necessarily a welcomed respite. They couldn't wait, they bubbled in anticipation. Some were with bodies walking the Superdome passageways, peeping in every couple seconds to see if the combatants were at it again. They were too nervous to let their bodies sit.

Action returned, Jimmy Black, the lone Carolina senior and team captain, threw the ball in from out of bounds. A couple passes, Michael Jordan, the freshman, back to Black, to Matt Doherty, back to Black. Twenty seconds appeared up on high.

Here it was. Jordan about 16 feet out, to the left of the lonely goal floating there in space, the Superdome being that massive for a basketball game. The young Wilmington freshman took the shot that proved to be the oculomotor nerve for all those 61,162 pairs, and the ball went through the nets without a thread of difficulty. The Tar Heels were ahead 63-62, and 15 seconds later they had become the NCAA national champions of 1982. True, 15 seconds can be a millennium, and there remained some heroics and an errant toss, which James Worthy found right in his two hands, closing out the Hoyas' potential attempt at a possible victorious goal. Eric (Sleepy) Floyd, the Gastonia senior with Georgetown, did bomb a shot at the buzzer, but it was from the French Quarters, at least.

Coach Dean Smith won his national championship.

Coming into the 1982 Final Four, that had been the ever-lasting question for the Tar Heels. The coach had been to this level six times, more than any other coach except John Wooden of UCLA, but missing in his trophy room was the big cup. The players tried to answer the question at press conferences. In New Orleans, the senior, Jimmy Black: "I'm getting tired of answering that one. We'd like to win it for him, though. And for ourselves. It would mean a lot." Added sophomore Sam Perkins: "We all know he hasn't won. I lost myself last year and I know how it feels. There's been a reason each time. Things happen. We'd like to win this both for Coach Smith and for ourselves." They finally had the chance to tell that question, stick it in your ear.

On top of everything else, as if more was needed to make the trip to New Orleans more memorable, it had been a truly outstanding game for the national title. Said James Worthy, the junior chosen MVP in the final college game he would play (NBA first round): "It was great. Nobody got more than a four- or five-point lead. It was what you want in a national championship.," Then Black, who became the team spokesman along the climb to the pinnacle: "I thought it was a great game. The audience probably was on the edge of their seats, too. It's the type of game you expect in a national championship."

Frank McGuire, who had coached the first Carolina national champions a quarter century before (1957), enjoyed every minute of the action, and in the post-game celebration on the floor, he noted: "No coach in my time ever deserved an NCAA championship more than Dean Smith, and I'm glad I was there to see him win it. Yes, and another thing, I can't remember a more thrilling, a better played championship game."

Ben Carnevale, who had coached the first Tar Heel team to reach the national finals in 1946, was seated at the officials table as a member of the NCAA basketball committee. He said: "Now, that was one of the classics in this tournament."

Through it all, Coach Smith was hurried from spot to spot, to the CBS television booth with Brent Mussberger, even while the awards presentations were beginning with Dave Gavitt, committee chairman. The coach managed to get the final snip or two of the victory nets; he had hugged the huge John Thompson, an old friend and Georgetown coach; he had shaken the hands of each of the Hoya players. Actually, he was beside himself. He was doing nice things by instinct, but, maybe the first time in his career, Dean Smith was not totally organized at this particular moment.

It had been a long and testing basketball season for the head coach and his staff, Bill Guthridge, Eddie Fogler and Roy Williams. It

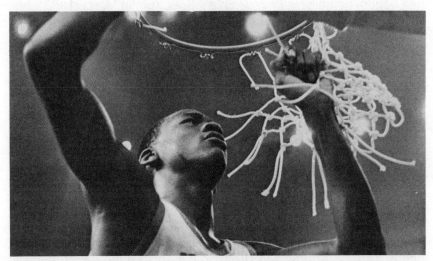

The freshman who made the goal that made the crown, Michael Jordan, gets in a few clips behind the senior, the juniors and the sophomores, after beating Georgetown for the national title.

Just concentrating on the job. Coach Dean Smith and Sam Perkins during a tense moment in New Orleans.

had begun, actually, in Philadelphia's Spectrum in March 1982 when the Tar Heels turned back conference-mate Virginia and met Indiana for the national title. Coach Bobby Knight's Hoosiers had won, but the Tar Heels returned everybody except Al Wood. They had come into a new season ranked No. 1 in the country. Few teams, other than those UCLA giants of the Wooden Era (Alcinder and Walton) had come in and gone out No. 1.

But they beat Kansas in Charlotte, Southern Cal in Greensboro before 15,171. They defeated Rutgers in Madison Square Garden, Kentucky in the Meadowlands before 18,116. Crowds followed them everywhere they went. They squeezed by Penn State in the Cable Car Classic, also Santa Clara. They opened the conference schedule in January at College Park, full-house 14,500, and after 66-50 victory, they brought this comment from Coach Lefty Driesell of Maryland: "This just might be the best North Carolina team I've ever seen."

At home against Ralph Sampson they rallied late for 65-60. Still at home, with a 13-game win streak that surprised the coach but with Sam Perkins in the infirmary because of a stomach virus, they lost to Wake Forest, the Deacons outscoring them 30-18 the second half. At Charlottesville, in a return meeting, they lost to Othell Wilson and the Big Guy. Back at home, they narrowly edged Maryland. The defense was becoming more of a factor and Matt Doherty, who thinks and talks like his coach, said: "Good defense is different than good offense. Good defense stays with you, good offense doesn't."

The Tar Heels were not razor sharp in the ACC tournament at Greensboro, beating Georgia Tech 55-39 and N.C. State 54-46. In the latter the margin was only 50-46 with 1:21 to play and the front line had to score 43 points. It was Virginia again in the title game, and this developed into that well-controversed 47-45 affair that was on national television and shook up college basketball officialdom. It actually brought about the multitudinous experiments with the shot clock and three-point goal in 1983. Dr. Edward Steitz of the rules committee said no single game in his quarter century on the board had caused as much comment. Coach Smith went to his delay with 13 minutes remaining because Virginia was shooting so well. Coach Terry Holland stayed in his zone, did not pursue because his star guard, Othell Wilson, was benched from injury the previous night. It was truly a standoff.

The Tar Heels found unexpected difficulties with James Madison University in the NCAA opening play at Charlotte, only 52-50, but in the East Regional, this at Raleigh, it was a better performing team that downed Alabama 74-69 and Villanova 70-60. The offense was generating again, Doherty's defense had been in evidence for some time, constantly.

That was how Carolina went to New Orleans. There they were matched with Houston of the Southwest Conference. Michael Jordan got the ball, over to the side, about eight feet out, took the first shot and made it. Thirty seconds had gone by. It would be two days and 6-7 hours later that he would make the last goal in the finals, worthy of a national championship. This start got the score to 14-0 in five minutes, but the Cougars were excellent ball players. In pregame interview Captain Black had said: "I can't say what type of game it will be, but we will try to take them out of their offense. They want the score to be 102-75, we'd like to see it around 65-60." The senior had a knack for being right. Carolina beat Houston 68-63, and meanwhile Georgetown played a game that Louisville didn't like either, 50-46.

Sunday became a day of regathering your wits in the Final Four, which means for the teams a quiet practice in that spacious barn with only closest friends on hand. It also takes an hour or so for mass interview with the ever-growing mass media, who in New Orleans still asked that question. Again, Captain Black: "Every article I've ever read says how great Coach Smith is but then it always goes on to say how he chokes when he gets to the Final Four. I'm getting tired of reading about it, too." Coach Smith commented: "Life is going to go on, our team is going to go on, and we're going to have a great program win or lose. But once you get here, you would like to go away with it one time. It would be fun to do it this year, I'll admit to that."

The guard, Dean Smith, was not going to make it a personal battle with the center, John Thompson. Dean quipped: "If we were to play, he'd take me inside and kill me." The two coaches had been close for years since Smith recruited one of Thompson's players at Washington's St. Anthony High School (Don Washington). When Smith became USA Olympic coach in 1976 Thompson was an assistant, along with Bill Guthridge.

The big coach had the big center, Patrick Ewing, the Washington Monument on legs. His assignment was to intimidate the Tar Heel shooters, regardless of how he did it, and no player ever carried out instructions better. Ewing scored quickly, then on the other end he blocked shots, illegally, of course, for which he was called. He was called goal tending on James Worthy once 2-2, twice 4-6, on Jordan once 6-8, Perkins once 8-12. It wasn't until Matt Doherty dropped through a driving layup that the Tar Heels actually scored by putting the ball through the nets. Ewing had four tending calls but he was intimidating, his assignment. It wasn't until reserve Chris Brust's free throw that Carolina took the lead (25-24). It had been a thinking coach's game the first 20 minutes, when the Hoyas led 32-31, the game was going to be in the 60s where both coaches wanted it. Worthy had 18 at the break, Ewing and Sleepy Floyd 10 each.

There was little or no alteration in the procedure for 20 more full turns of the clock. Perkins put Carolina up three, then two minutes later Ewing had the Hoyas up three. Coaches called time as the end neared, Carolina up one, Georgetown up one. Then it was Carolina up three, and Ewing cut in that, Floyd took a nine-foot jumper and the Hoyas were ahead 62-61 within the clock's final turn (57 seconds). The Tar Heels worked slowly down the court, then timeout at 32.

Coach Smith devised the final attack, which he explained later, much later in fact. It was in the airport in Miami the next morning, between round-about flights home. Smith: "We called our 'two play' from the zone offense, but normally it's a lob from Black to Worthy, but we knew Georgetown knows that, too, so we want to get it behind Worthy to Michael Jordan. Georgetown properly is in its zone, and Jordan or anybody is to shoot as soon as he gets a good shot. As a second alternate, the big men want to work the boards for rebounds, and James (Worthy) said he had his inside position. Third alternate, if the first two miss, foul at once."

The whole season moved around the ball, to the middle (Jordan), back to Black (right side), to the middle (Doherty), back to Black (still on the right, couple steps nearer the action), to Jordan, and he was open on the left. Jumper, nets. Later Michael Jordan said, "I thought about the possibility of my taking a shot that would win or lose the game when I was on the bus on the way over here. What if my last second shot would determine how the game came out? I guess it was a premonition." Also a good shot.

Georgetown called no timeout, the clock ticking from 15. Fred Brown dribbled to the left, had no shot. He looked for an outlet, made the pass, but the ball went straight to a surprised Worthy. Floyd had gone to the right corner, was blocked out and covered. Eric Smith had left the key, dropped down the lane. Worthy was still around the key. Later, in dejection, Brown put it simply: "As soon as I let it go, I wanted to bring it back. I wished it was on a rubber band." Six seconds, Worthy fouled, two seconds, Worthy missed, and Floyd tried a total desperation from somewhere in the distance.

It had been achieved. A national championship for the coach, but just as important, going most of the season No. 1 and coming to the Final Four highly favored and winning. The Louisiana Superdome had been converted into Blue Heaven.

25
Nineteen Eighty WHEE! Jim ValvanOH!

Hemingway would have loved covering Phi Packa Attacka.

Nick, Hemingway's Nick, would have a new character role, much like a James Thomas Valvano, just call him Jimmy, because Nick would have allowed himself to get caught in the fun like millions of North Carolinians and others around the U.S. of A.

In Hemingway's *The End of Something*, Marjorie questioned, "What's really the matter?" Nick replied, "I don't know." She prodded, and then, as the book read, Nick looked up at the moon, coming up over the hills, and answered, "It isn't fun anymore."

North Carolina State's basketball Wolfpack of 1983 was fun, fun, fun.

It peaked in mile-high Albuquerque in an adobe arena, called The Pit, where it won the national championship, but not in any old ordinary, household, run-of-the-mill manner. Not by a long shot, truthfully.

It began ... when?

When Jim Valvano took the Wolfpack job three years ago, at age 33, telling everybody he had always dreamed of being a bigtime college coach, and the Atlantic Coast Conference was bigtime. That's when it began. Valvano played a long string of one-liners, coast to coast, but field goals were the real objective, that and his new-born defense against free throws. And when the 1983 season was complete, he had filled in the gaps around three seniors, Dereck Whittenburg, Sidney Lowe and Thurl Bailey.

Rocco Valvano, his father, had been a high school coach, and son Jimmy liked what he grew up with. He played college basketball under Bill Foster at Rutgers, played in the NIT, and made the all-tournament team, got an idea that winning was an important facet of the game. His vivid memory includes the first thrill of coaching, his Johns Hopkins team beating Swarthmore. At Iona he first made the NCAAs.

When 1982-83 began, the senior-loaded Wolfpack was given a good challenging position in the conference, but still behind Virginia and North Carolina. On January 12 in Reynolds Coliseum Whittenburg, whose shooting range comes with howitzers, had an amazing first half, something like 27 points on Virginia, but then the whole season, in one play, took a flipflop. Whit, after a short jumper from the left, came down on Othell Wilson's foot and broke his own foot. Season was ended, right? Whit sat on the bench until just before the regular schedule ended. What happened to the Wolfpack meanwhile? It melted into a team and won. It beat North Carolina, and Whit took part in the net clipping, in his jeans. Coach Valvano took the positive side, as always: "We learned a lot of things without Whit. Lowe learned he could still shoot the ball, he didn't have to pass all the time. Terry Gannon came in for a lot of minutes. The others got more playing time, they learned they could win without Whit."

It was a team having fun, and growing up, and winning. In triumph at the Omni in Atlanta, the conference trophy in hand, postgame interviews resembled Johnny Carson's "Tonight" shows. The Three Seniors and Coach, hugging, kissing, joking, slapsticking, and winning. They carried that to Oregon and Utah and New Mexico, natural habitats for an Eastern college basketball team, and somewhere in Albuquerque, at the NCAA Final Four, Coach Valvano was saying, "You know, this is the furthest East we have played since the conference." No team had ever been asked to Marco Polo it as much. Maybe that became part of the mystique. The Wolfpack took to the road to win, no other reason, flat none. Nine times the season could have been over, on the road at that, and only the ninth was the finale, as national champions. On Pacific Standard Time the Pack might have been playing basketball at decent evening hours, but back in North Carolina, it became 2 a.m. Maybe the Pack figured that, it had to do something exciting to keep its fans on the line.

Albuquerque, that final weekend, was the meeting place of the nation's press, 500 or more from newspapers, magazines, journals, even people who just write letters home. The University of New Mexico even built a special building for the media, afterward turning it over to gymnastics.

Some of the Valvano background and philosophies they learned, like the following:

Lesley Visser, *Boston Globe*, quoting Valvano: "Everybody (Corona in Queens) was poor, everybody was tough. We'd go to the Garden on 50 cent tickets. It was great. We'd go to Nedick's before the game and get a hot dog, with those Boston-style cut buns, and an

orange drink. Sometimes we'd go in for a tripleheader. There is nothing like growing up in New York."

Joe Henderson, *Tampa Tribune*, talking about game strategy: "It
wasn't like N.C. State was making a big secret of what it planned to do.
Valvano said Sunday, 'We're going to play, shall I say, a slow tempo
game. If we get the tap, we may not shoot until Tuesday.' Valvano said
that his goal was to have his team in a position to win when the end
came. To do that, he would refuse — at all costs — to get into a sprint
race with Houston. He said, 'You come down to the end of the game
with a chance to win, and you see what happens.'"

Mike Lopresti, *USA Today*, on that final winning play: "You've got
to be lucky to win a championship," said Coach Valvano. "We got bent
out of shape on the last play. Then, we lost track of time of how much
time was left. All our receivers were covered, so we went to the tight
end over the middle."

Steve Daley, *Chicago Tribune*, on life in the fast lane in Ogden,
Utah (regionals): "Finding himself in Ogden last week, the New York-
bred coach made the best of the town where all-night drugstores
closed at 10:30. 'There's not much to do here,' Valvano told a group of
writers. 'We eat 17 meals a day. This afternoon we're going to have a
team meeting to discuss what we'll talk about at the next team
meeting. And tonight we're going to watch film of ourselves eating
lunch.'"

All this, and more, for a team that had to win five times over teams
which had been ranked No. 1 at one time during the seson, and all
within 25 days.

After it was all over, Coach Valvano, after the flue at the finals and
a hernia operation, could finally enjoy the celebrations, with President
Reagan in the White House, with Pam and the girls in Cary. But he has
not settled down since, and James T. Valvano never will.

The coach was enthralled with the Final Four. Coaches get that
way, especially with the first one. Players and fans reach the same levels, but it's their fun. But when Coach Valvano saw Houston's Phi
Slama Jama in The Pit, UNM's arena dug out of the sands 56 feet
below ground level, he wasn't sure of the future. He witnessed the
dunk session against Louisville: "I've never seen anything like that in
16 years of college basketball. I missed seeing their first dunk because I was being interviewed (by Brent Mussberger, CBS-TV) in the
midst of the Houston band. I fouled out. It was like a Mafia meeting.
When they shoot and miss, they become terribly dangerous because
that means they're going to dunk. They pass the ball so well inside.
They throw a hard three-foot pass, they catch it, they dunk it. I'd love a
clock on this game, an eight-minute clock."

N.C. State (regular season: 17-10) would not have made the
NCAA playoffs had it not been the ACC champion from the tourna-

Climbing to the very top, Cozell McQueen was the first over the rims in the Wolfpack victory over Houston in The Pit.

ment. Thus, there were three games which would have ended the season in Atlanta, short trip home. Each game thereafter labelled itself in the do-or-die category, each game was for the season. Nine times Phi Packa Attacka, from a different planet than Phi Slama Jama, and obviously a more powerful one, went down death row, and nine times escaped. No national champion has ever achieved as well.

Willis Casey, as N.C. State athletic director and former member of the NCAA basketball committee, made no qualifications in his salute to the Wolfpack 1983: "We won the national championship in 1974, Carolina won it in 1957 and again last year, but don't you think you can even compare the other three national titles with this one. The others won in the state of North Carolina primarily. We played the conference in Greensboro, the regional in Raleigh and the Final Four in Greensboro in 1974. In 1957 Carolina won the conference in Raleigh. Last year Carolina won the conference in Greensboro, the first round in Charlotte and the regional in Raleigh. This team hit the road, played three conference tournament games in Atlanta against three great teams. Then they went West. To win nine straight tournament games on the road against nationally ranked teams, it's never been done before, and probably will never be done again.

"And it was sudden death. I certainly gave up against Pepperdine, during the process of the game I'm talking about. Before the game, I probably had more worries about Utah, because by then we had to be thinking about going all the way but it was in Ogden, their fans were there, the high altitude and all. A lot of things made me very apprehensive about it. Now, if somebody had told me we were going to hit 81 percent the second, I probably wouldn't have felt that way."

Wolfpack fans flocked to Albuquerque where the winds off the desert blew hard and it snowed, but nothing ruined the spirit of the occasion. All four teams wore red, so The Pit was bloody looking indeed. But the University of New Mexico sports teams are nicknamed the Lobos, and the Wolfpack had the advantage there. Its former live mascot was called Lobo, because it was. The fans came with banners and placards which read, "God's Team," "Destiny — Final Chapter," "Thanks CBS and Kardiac Kids," "Packman Eats Slama Jama," and just plain "Go Wolfpack." From the 1974 champion Wolfpack Phil Spence was on the floor afterward: "Fantastic, even better than our close ones." Former Coach Norman Sloan and Joan, attending the NABC convention, were on hand. From Seattle David Thompson said: "Winning pumped me up. I know how they feel, they must be on cloud nine." He must have been, scoring 31 points in beating the Lakers that night.

Hemingway, through Nick, would have enjoyed the best things in Wolfpack life, such as the following:

229

CAST. Thurl Bailey, Alvin Battle, Lorenzo Charles, Terry Gannon, Sidney Lowe, Ernie Myers, Cozell McQueen, Dereck Whittenburg.

DIRECTORS. Jim Valvano, with Tom Abatemarco, Ray Martin, Ed McLean, Max Perry.

PRODUCER. God.

ACT ONE. Friday, March 11, Omni, Atlanta. Beat Wake Forest 71-70 in ACC tournament first round. In regular season finale the Wolfpack had floored the Deacons 130-89, and nobody believed that. Some said it was just senior day, everybody getting caught up in the flow. In Greensboro earlier, but without Whittenburg, the Pack lost to this same club by 18.

It was Wake's strategy, playing for a big play at the end, to hold the ball after Lowe tied the score at 70. The clock read 4:25. There was no conference 30-second clock by this time, so the Deacons worked off three minutes 55 seconds, called timeout. Valvano changed the defense from passing man, calling a half-court zone trap. Alvis Rogers, the man on the floor with the most experience (hardship year with injury), sort of lobbed a pass to Danny Young in midcourt. Said Lowe: "I was in between Young and Rogers, able to get a hand on the ball, saw Thurl out of the corner of my eye and tapped it toward him, which was all I could do." Ball back to Lowe, the assist man, fast break, Pack timeout. Valvano plan now: have Lowe attack, pass in if the defense attacked. It worked just like that, Lowe bounced the ball undereath to Charles and Rogers prevented a stuff by fouling. Three seconds left, two free throws coming. First missed. Charles made the second, game over, move on.

For what it's worth, Coach Valvano was quoting his philosophy already: "I've always said the first game of any tournament is the most important and most difficult. This kind of win seems to relax a team."

ACT TWO. Saturday, March 12, Omni, Atlanta. Beat North Carolina 91-84 overtime in semifinals. Whittenburg had been on the bench when Valvano ended his famine with Carolina, a great 70-63 back on February 16 in Reynolds. Whit was on the bench again when 40 regulation minutes ended tied at 70. This time Whit just couldn't hit, two for 11 shots, nothing in that personal property of his (3-point range). It was four starters and Terry Gannon.

In overtime Sam Perkins put Carolina up 80-74 with 2:13 to play, and Coach Dean Smith doesn't lose games at that position in tournaments. State missed the front end of three straight bonus chances, then Whit made two 80-76. Free throws exchanged 82-78. Carolina missed a bonus, Whit from three, 82-81 with 1:31 left. Another Tar Heel foul miss, Whit drove the baseline, dropped reverse layup, State up 83-

82 with 50 seconds. Whit and Bailey hit, six down to seven up in two minutes, and against Carolina.

More Valvano thinking, this time from the mouth of senior Whittenburg: "I was having a bad shooting game, everybody saw that, but this guy refused to give up on me. He just kept staring me straight in the eye, saying, 'Hey, you're good. Go back in the game and stick it.' He also kept telling me I could drive the baseline, so then I did that, too."

ACT THREE. Sunday, March 13, Omni, Atlanta. Beat Virginia 81-78, ACC champs. That was the team with Ralph Sampson, and the Wolfpack seniors had a 1-7 record with big Ralph, losing the last seven. Ralph and Othell Wilson charged to a 59-51 advantage with 11:26 remaining. Lowe and Gannon hit outside, cut the margin to 65-64, then Bailey went deep for three, and State was ahead. The Pack ran to an 11-1 spree to lead 75-66 with four minutes. Wilson cut it to 79-78 with 20 seconds, but in vain for Virginia. The defense blanketed the 7-4 Sampson, who did not score a single point the final 7:45 of the game. Once he went for a dunk, only to discover the ball wasn't in his hands. Gannon had stripped it down about knee level. Sampson's knees that is; Gannon's eyes.

Charles equalled his career 12 rebounds, which he had set two nights before. Gannon hit four of six from the bonus range. Bailey, game high 24, had 18 of them the second half.

Valvano had beaten Sampson and Virginia for the first time, again looked to the foul line for saving grace. Whit was there with six seconds, leading one. Said coach: "Those free throws at the end are not easy. I'm thankful Whit could knock those in. It takes a senior to do that."

ACT FOUR. Friday. March 18, Gill Coliseum, Corvallis, Oregon. Beat Pepperdine 69-67, two overtimes, NCAA first round of West Regional. Winning ACC title got no favors in the NCAA seedings, so the Pack was packed for a long trip West. Pepperdine came out of the West Coast Athletic Conference, not too well known in the East. By 2 a.m. EST, when TV and the game concluded for fans back in North Carolina, Pepperdine was a familiar name.

State missed its first 12 shots, a signal of danger ahead. The Pack was flat. With two minutes to play, the West Coast team was at the free throw line, missed. No additional scoring, most unusual, regulation tied at 47. The Waves rolled in for the overtime, up 57-51 with 1:10 remaining. This was it, trip home upcoming. Gannon two free throws 57-53, Charles inside 59-55, Bailey dunk 59-57 with 22 seconds. Again Pepperdine was at the foul line, again missed. Whit was fouled, but he, too, missed the front end of one-and-one. But Cozell McQueen rebounded with short hook, tied 59. Whit hit eight free throws in second overtime.

Lowe added his own version of Valvano: "No matter what I'm sure we will all remember this game for the rest of our lives. We were like a pitcher who doesn't have anything going for him, but still goes nine innings and gets the win."

ACT FIVE. Sunday, March 20, Gill Coliseum, Corvallis, Oregon. Beat Nevada-Las Vegas, 71-70, NCAA second round. The Runnin' Rebels of Coach Jerry Tarkanian were running in this important showdown, up six by halftime, seeking to show people why they were No. 1 at mid-season, still with the country's best record at 28-2.

Sidney Green sparked the Rebels up 12 with 10 minutes, and Vegas began to spread with four minutes. State fouled, and Vegas missed. Several times. With 32 seconds left Eric Book went to the line, one-and-one, Vegas ahead 70-69. He missed, Charles rebounded. Without timeout State got the ball to Whit, eight seconds, miss from 20 feet, ball bouncing off front of rim. Bailey rebounded, bounced off a layup, Bailey rebounded again, this shot good. The Wolfpack had won by a single. Do you need any more?

Valvano talked about letting them play when the Pack got possession with 32 seconds: "I thought about it, quickly, sure, but they were unsettled and we knew what we wanted to do anyway. If I called a timeout, it gives him (Tarkanian) a chance to get his team settled. I mean, we were looking at a team who had the lead by 12 points and all of a sudden they lose it, and the last thing I wanted to do was give them a chance to get settled down."

ACT SIX. Thursday, March 24, Dee Events Center, Ogden, Utah. Beat Utah 75-56 in West Regional. Regional play was at Weber State, 30 or so miles north of Salt Lake City, home territory for the Utes. The 11,800 crowd was the largest ever at Ogden, hundreds had to be turned away.

The Utes had done wonders in late season, but the Wolfpack led by four at halftime although Bailey was scoreless. Quickly the Utes got six straight points and the lead. Whittenburg took over, Lowe and Gannon aided, the Wolfpack hit 78.9 percent from the flour the second half. It was easy for the first time.

Coach Valvano attempted to explain the new format, an easy one: "Utah may be the real Cinderella in the NCAAs. We were never 5-7 or 7-10. And they're not the Runnin' Utes anymore either. They play ball control and they're not the kind of team we'd like to get behind."

ACT SEVEN. Saturday, March 26, Dee Events Center, Ogden, Utah. Beat Virginia 63-62 West Regional finals. Somewhat out of the beaten path for a State-Virginia game, but here they were. Fourth time in the season, Sampson two in season. State one in tournament. This was the

Big Guy's last opportunity for a national championship. Virginia didn't really consider an NIT crown (1980) as such.

Virginia led by five at halftime, shot 73.3 percent the final 20 minutes, and lost. Cavaliers got up 10, then State tied it, Sampson made it 61-59 with 1:43. Whit tied it. The Wolfpack wanted to foul, do it quickly, and that put Othell Wilson on the line, one and one. He made the first 62-61, missed the second which Bailey rebounded. Whit faked a shot, passed to Charles, fouled by Sampson. And Charles made two free throws, State 63-62 with 23 seconds. Virginia got its shots, Mullen miss, Wilson rebound but miss, and McQueen recovered the ball just in time.

Valvano was beside himself, dreaming: "I've been coaching 16 years and maybe just once a season you'd like to have a victory like the one against Pepperdine, or Virginia. But when you start stringing game after frantic game together like we have, it's special. Maybe this happens only once, we might even keep winning. Man, wouldn't that be something? And the beat goes on."

ACT EIGHT. Saturday, April 2, The Pit, Albuquerque, New Mexico. Beat Georgia 67-60 in the Final Four semifinals. Two surprise entries had come out of the East and West, and they were to meet. There were reports the Wolfpack really wanted to play North Carolina again, but Georgia took care of that at Syracuse. Do you believe that, the Wolfpack wanted to play anybody, just anybody.

Coach Hugh Durham's Bulldogs were playing in the NCAA for the first time, and they were in the Final Four. Quite an achievement. It scared the Wolfpack defense, but for no good reason. They bothered the Bulldogs sufficiently, forced a 30 percent shooting accuracy which resulted in an 11-point halftime margin, up to 18. By the end the Pack, of course, settled into a time-delay control game. Bailey and Whit had 20 points each, McQueen a career 13 rebounds and four blocked shots. Lowe 10 points and 11 assists.

Coach Valvano had seen Houston stuff Louisville in the basket and he had to be thanking 48 hours ahead: "We have got to control the tempo. We will have a better chance in a game in the 50s than in a game in the 80s."

ACT NINE, FINALE. Monday, April 4, The Pit, Albuquerque, New Mexico. Beat Houston 54-52 for the NCAA national championship. This was it, the final dream. Houston had been the dream team of Saturday, 13 recorded dunks. The Pack had to guard against what the Louisville defense did, allow unprotected space between Houston and the basket. There were three dunks in the title game, the Pack made the first and last, allowed Olajuwon the other, in defeat.

Bailey got the first to begin the scoring, Gannon joined the seniors

He's always happy, but this time in Albuquerque Jim Valvano was 110 percent.

in controlling the first half, up eight at the break. Coaches, attending the NABC, mingled at halftime and agreed, State could win in the 50s, but they knew Houston's potential. So did Valvano. Within four minutes the Cougars surfaced, getting the first 10 points and the lead 35-33. They outscored the Pack 17-2, built a seven-point margin, State had two timeouts. Houston had shut off the inside. Houston led 52-46 with 3:05. It was time to foul and test the Cougars' nerves, where they had been vulnerable all season, even in their No. 1 status. Houston missed, Whit from 22 feet, 52-50. Steal, Whit from 23 feet, tie score 52, a minute left.

Valvano later delivered his coaching strategy: "We don't care whom we foul at the end of the game. If someone makes it, we don't foul him again. If we foul Drexler and he hits a pair, we don't foul him again. If we foul Franklin and he misses, we're going to foul him again. It's an old Italian strategy my father taught me."

Poppa had taught well. Franklin at the line missed, McQueen rebounded, Valvano timeout 40 seconds. The game, at least the regulation 40 minutes, was in the hands of the Wolfpack, but they were sweaty hands, under Houston pressure. The Cougars surprisingly had backed off in their own delay earlier. Pass to Bailey in the corner brought a double-team, he got the outlet pass to Whit, and a Cougar almost got a hand on that. Time was going, Whit didn't see the clock, he just knew. He fired from 30 feet, 3,000 feet, from wherever, it was a prayer that had to be put in the air. The ball was inches short, some say a foot, but the Houston defense had come out and left Lorenzo Charles all by himself. He caught the pass, the shot, the whatever at rim level, and stuffed it. It had so much stuff it won the 1983 national championship.

Jim Valvano had no words to top that.

26

How To Celebrate / North Carolina Style

It's time we have a party. Somebody has just won a basketball game somewhere. We acknowledge, no generation, no country, no state can claim an uncontested label as the world's greatest celebrants for an athletic championship, but North Carolina basketball fans will take a back seat to no one.

They can yell fairly loud, sometimes boisterously, whether it's off the rugged stone peaks of Grandfather Mountain or the lofty sand dunes of Jockey's Ridge. They use paint like Rembrandt. They know how to totally enjoy their sports and their sports teams, and basketball has come to the fore as probably the most prestigious endeavor for which a celebration can be programmed. The word used to be "planned"; today everything is "programmed." It only takes a shot like Michael Jordan's or Lorenzo Charles' to be the oculamotor nerve.

Fans, like their football brothers and sisters, will travel with their teams, notably the ACC basketball champions of the past two seasons. Both teams and fans went to New Orleans and Albuquerque to capture the national championship, and we succeeded.

There were outstanding post-game coronations in Chapel Hill and Raleigh, and all over the state for that matter, but on campus they evolved into real jungles of jubilation. It was a Blue Chip Event one year, a Red Letter Day the next. And many students enjoyed both triumphs, because, after all, and remember it's party time, they were national championships for the state of North Carolina. Each revelled in the other's.

But, just to keep the record straight and to remind today's generation this fun-loving nature isn't confined to their genes, it was nothing new, this 1982 and 1983.

Best party of them all might well have taken place back in 1924, part of the Roaring Twenties undoubtedly, when Carolina, then called the White Phantoms, won the old Southern Conference tournament in Atlanta, long before the Omni days, and in concluding a 26-0 season they were proclaimed national champions by the Helms Foundation. They were the sole proclaimer of national college basketball kings in those days. The party after a ticker-tape report on the final game's proceedings, and then the students marched from Chapel Hill to Durham, partied all night and rode the jitney back to the Hill.

But it has always taken a college community to generate the celebration. When the Hanes Hosiery women returned to Winston-Salem with the National AAU championship three times, starting in 1951, they waited until they got to work the next day to get plaudits.

In the past decade, especially in Raleigh, normal practice sessions on the home floor before embarking on tournament trips have become the "in thing" for team followers. Nobody can match the turnouts for the 1974 N.C. State Wolfpack workouts, but it must be remembered they played every single tournament within the state.

Carolina came home from New Orleans in 1982 and held its team party in Kenan Stadium, no place else was large enough, because 20,000 walked down through the pines and celebrated. The 1983 Wolfpack told jokes for 14,000 in jam-packed Reynolds Coliseum on campus when they returned East from Albuquerque.

But there was a gap somewhere in there. In 1939 when Wake Forest was selected to play in the very first NCAA tournament, one of eight teams, not too many people knew about the event, including the newspapers. Coach Murray Greason's Deacons quickly took the train to and from Philadelphia, played and lost, and got on with the baseball season which was already underway, and more important, too.

Maybe it was post-World War II nonchalance, but getting to the national finals in 1946 (losing to Oklahoma State in Madison Square Garden) was still a subdued matter although there were 2,000 requests for the 300 tickets allotted. The Tar Heels rode home on the train with the university president, Dr. Frank Porter Graham, and had a nice chat. Coach Everett Case's fast-moving Wolfpack returned from several early tournaments in the Garden, such as 1947 NIT and 1950 NCAA, and fans greeted the team at the airport and back on campus. The same applied to Coach Vic Bubas' Duke teams in the 60s, and the numerous final four trips for Coach Dean Smith's Tar Heels starting in 1967. Students and fans welcomed them home with joy, if not the national title.

It was not confined to the Big Four, not by any means. The fever is statewide. Western Carolina almost took NAIA honors in Kansas City in 1963, and their air route home to the mountains was somewhat circuitous, Kansas City via Little Rock to Knoxville. Traveling in two station wagons across the mountains to Cullowhee they were greeted at Clingman's Dome atop the Great Smokies, and wildly-cheering students formed a mile-long caravan down the North Carolina side of the mountain. From Cherokee on, roadside residents cheered and finally a state highway patrolman, siren blaring, led the team through Sylva and on to Cullowhee for a big pep rally.

Winston-Salem State's victory in the NCAA College Division tournament at Evansville, Indiana in 1967 came with outstanding play from Earl Monroe and Co. but a lousy job from the airline crew. As the first NCAA title ever won by a black college, in any sport, a big celebration was planned in Winston-Salem when Coach Bighouse Gaines returned with the team. Cheerleaders drove home overnight, the team would fly. But a broken starter delayed the plane's departure seven hours, until 4 p.m. and the home parade didn't materialize as anticipated. However, townspeople and students quickly organized a motorcade from Smith Reynolds Airport to the coliseum. Bighouse recalled, "Must have been 4,000 people there, up on the stage, we all had something to say. It was great. I was a genius then . . . until I lost some games in December the next season."

When Eastern Airlines brought the Guilford College Quakers home from Kansas City, the state's only NAIA championship, it was spring break at the college and the students had gone home. They got back on Sunday afternoon after the team, but several hundred fans were at the Greensboro airport in 1973. Coach Jack Jensen remembered more vividly the happening after the District 26 tournament in High Point: "When we got back to Quaker Square, they had rolled the corner. I don't know if students today would know what that means, but it meant the students had every roll of toilet tissue on campus and they had covered everything on the corner. Looked like a concentrated snow fall. About 500 students celebrated with us."

But let's go back to granddad for a refresher course in the art of celebrating. The old Atlanta Auditorium really began tournament basketball in the South, and North Carolina's dominance focused Tar Heel attention. No television, no radio, what kind of world did they live in? Exist in? Through Western Union, the telegraph company before they became a way to send money, there was reported back to Chapel Hill the scoring plays, but scores like 23-19, that didn't take much reporting. Townspeople and students did gather in the old Pickwick Theatre, listen to the play-by-play as announced from the wire messages, yell to head cheerleader Vic Huggins' encouragement.

In 1924 Carolina went undefeated, climaxed with a 26-18 triumph over Alabama, about 11 p.m. since Atlanta was on CST then. Word spread quickly among the 2,529 students, and a bonfire came into being at the Old Well in midcampus, some 800 students had a snake dance through the campus, with an impromptu 25-piece marching band. Well after midnight when they gathered at President Chase's home, he joined in. It was 3 a.m. when somebody yelled, "Let's go to Durham," and off they went, walking the 12 miles of the old highway. They paraded the downtown street, went to the homes of star players Cart Carmichael and Jack Cobb. By dawn they slept on the sidewalks or in hotel lobbies, and it was reported "they started returning to campus by jitneys" the next morning. Classrooms were empty. The team, on a slow train to Greensboro before transferring to Durham, got home in a day or two.

National champions bring out the best in North Carolinians. Carolina 1957 also brought a new dimension to the college game — live TV, in exciting black-and-white, came from the national finals in Kansas City where the late C. D. Chesley inaugurated his contribution to the sport in North Carolina. Triple overtime games kept the state awake for two nights, each well after midnight North Carolina time.

Chapel Hill went wild in the backyards, and the late Pat McGuire, the coach's wife, kept a lot of stories about new friends she had never seen before, and at midnight in her backyard. Several thousand students left dormitories and fraternity houses to block Franklin Street, the main thoroughfare in the village. Police blocked the street until 3 a.m. Police compared the celebration to V-J Day 12 years before. Unwound rolls of toilet paper were fed to a huge bonfire, along with $20 hats and an eight-foot step ladder. They marched to the home of Chancellor Robert House who for the second straight night exchanged cheers and small talk. Duke University students came over to participate.

The Carolina team met thousands more at Raleigh-Durham Airport the next afternoon, but two of the key people were missing. Lennie Rosenbluth flew to New York for a national TV program, and Coach Frank McGuire stayed in Kansas City where he would coach the NABC East-West All-Star game on Monday. McGuire remembered recently, as I jogged his recollections: "What a letdown. I had to stay in Kansas City, there with Harry Gotkin and Jack Larocha, my closest friends. Just us, what a lonesome town and we had just won a national championship. I missed probably the greatest celebration in a lifetime, back in Chapel Hill. It was great. Four Irish Catholics and one Jewish boy, all from New York City, and being accepted by all the people at home. And the letters I got, unbelievable what some people did because they were superstitious. One guy went for a cup of coffee, we went ahead, they kept him out of the room. One guy wouldn't even go to the bathroom."

Next came 1974, and since the N.C. State's venue kept them in the state the whole tournament time, there was probably more firsthand, person-touching participation by students and fans. It peaked

with the Final Four in Greensboro, the first time the NCAAs had come South. Not having tickets for this, fans flocked to the Wolfpack's final workout in Reynolds Coliseum, some 5,000 students and fans. Mothers with 3-4 kids tagging along. Five charter busses from Eastern North Carolina, a populace that Everett Case cultivated, natives from tobacco lands to help the coach create Tobacco Road in the fears of visiting college basketball teams. They came to see if David Thompson was ready, having that terrible fall on his head in the Eastern Region five days before. Coach Norman Sloan closed drills with a 3-on-2 fast break, and when Thompson, dribbling downcourt, saw the coach walk to center court, signal for end of drills, he went to the air and fired a 35-footer. Which went in. The 5,000 cheered. The team showered and dressed, went out to board the charter bus at 6:07 p.m. . . . and there were 2,500 fans waiting. Coach spoke, so did Thompson and Burleson. When Monte Towe tried, nobody could see him, so DT and Tom hoisted him to their shoulders.

NCAA practice in Friday afternoon at the Final Four site had been open to the public for years, few responded except the coaches in convention. In the Greensboro Coliseum at 3 p.m. when the Wolfpack had its turn, there were 9,000 fans. It was a record finally bettered in Albuquerque in 1983.

For many State's win over UCLA on Saturday afternoon was the title, but there was still a final game. Some 6,000 students staged the usual march from campus to the Capitol, about 20 blocks up Hillsborough Street which had been blocked off by city police prearrangements. It was a cacophony of loud auto horns and constant yells until 8 p.m. A busload from St. Augustine's College joined in, so did the streakers. Monday night was the finale, and despite 30-degree weather, thousands again marched to the Capitol.

The team bussed home late Tuesday morning, a pep rally had been set up for Reynolds Coliseum, the home court, at 12 noon, and 7,000 turned out, including fans from Rocky Mount, Greenville and all over Eastern Carolina. The Wolfpack ran on the stage, led by the midget Towe, everybody said something, Sloan got the key to the city, and 7,000 cheered the whole time.

In 1982 freshman Dan Timberlake, in the midst of another Chapel Hill party, said to a reporter, "They did it in '57 when my father was here, and they did it now when I'm here." Chapel Hill police Major Coy Durham compared, since he was at both: "We had so much property damage in 1957 you wouldn't believe it. This was a lot better." For many Tar Heels the fun began in New Orleans, an excellent place to win a championship because the fun is built in. They had a 72-hour party there.

For those still in the village Mardi Gras in North Carolina began 30 seconds after the Houston semifinal game. Downtown bars, with wide screen TV, emptied, the dorms and frats emptied. Franklin Street was blocked off, as usual in postgame. Beer flowed, deliveries up 450 percent for the weekend. Blue paint sprayed, Huggins Hardware almost sold out.

But Monday night was something else, 30,000 from everywhere, it seemed, and they stayed until 4 a.m. "This is the best party on the East Coast," said Bill Wilson, a senior at East Carolina University who drove the 80 miles up. He watched the game perched in a tree looking over several heads at a 12-inch black-and-white portable. Two guys danced nude on the roof of the Foster Building. Traffic was totally blocked, except for a slow-moving ambulance. A pregnant woman had gone into labor on the sidewalk. Whatever cars had been left on the street, for whatever reason, were damaged and windows broken. TV camera crews from all over the state worked hard, in living color, light blue. They did not need to solicit any zany acts, they came naturally with blue-faced, blue-haired, blue-clothed people of the Aquarius Age.

The team flew home Tuesday, although Coach Dean Smith and his wife returned commercially, got routed via Miami and missed the celebration. This final party came in Kenan Stadium, and the north stands were filled, 20,000. Capt. Jimmy Black was the first speaker on team arrival about 3 p.m., and when the ovation died down 30 minutes later, TV helicopters still hovered for position in all four corners of Blue Heaven.

To repeat and thus remind, Raleigh and Eastern Carolina have a way of celebrating championships while they're happening. It did in 1974, remember, and it certainly carried over in 1983. After so many ACC titles, it was surprising, actually, the Wolfpack fans' reaction to the latest march through Georgia, Valvano instead of Sherman. Said Willis Casey, State athletic director for longer than anybody else in the ACC: "Reaction of our N. C. State fans has not been a surprise, but that they reacted as stongly as they did in the conference win indicated what would happen if we kept winning. The conference championship still means so much, and anybody who has ever been to the conference championship feels that. I was ecstatic at winning the conference title, we needed it. We needed a big win or two, but I never dreamed it would be this big (national)."

The "first" Virginia win in Atlanta came on a Sunday afternoon, so students celebrated on Hillsborough Street adjacent to the campus into the evening. Monday there was a pep rally on the Brickyard, on-campus meeting site, and 5,000 turned out to yell for the team. The Wolfpack headed West for all its NCAA play, and after each game, there was a party, joined by students from North Carolina and Duke because, after all, it was a team from North Carolina they were yelling for, and it was party-time. Between Utah and New Mexico, there was a

Monday practice in Reynolds with 2,000 fans. Coach Jim Valvano got on the PA: "We didn't really have a practice planned today, just shoot around a little, but we'll have a little scrimmage so you can see the next NCAA champions play." Among the fans — Ethel Holt of Whitsett, age 83, and Jessica Jackson of Raleigh, age 7.

The final Four brought out the people. Saturday afternoon, after the semifinal, the crowd was only 2,000 with the usual beer coolers and a new supply of red paint, but it was Easter weekend and the students had gone home. Monday night, after Houston at the buzzer, the Brickyard really came alive, from 11 p.m. until well after 4 a.m., and the crowd swelled to 25,000 or more with Eastern Carolina well represented. There were arrests for vandalism, like paint-spraying the buildings, color—red. Furniture was tossed on bonfires. By the end, city and university officials said the celebrations cost $100,000 in security overtime and property damage. The Wolfpack had a long run of it, of course—Sunday after the ACC plus six nights more.

Monday brought the team home from the West where it proved the fastest draw on the desert. Several thousand fans ignored announced warnings to stay away from the airport, please. It was about 5 p.m. when the Wolfpack arrived, and along the interstate and on the overpasses others cheered as the caravan slowly moved to the campus. Waiting in Reynolds Coliseum were 14,000 in a frenzy by the time Valvano stepped on stage with Chancellor Bruce Poulton, followed by the players who each said something. The Ides of March had been total fun, and Thurl Bailey, the tall senior, added a pensive observation after Sidney Lowe and Dereck Whittenburg cut the jokes: "It's a family with us." It had been a big, big, red-blooded big family.

In the aftermath of consecutive national titles, for a party-going state, there were a few souvenirs and commemorative items put together for the 1982 Blues and the 1983 Reds. It would cost a couple thousand dollars to purchase the full supply, in either color, and some did. They will celebrate every time they walk in the den or office or bedroom. Just a reminder is needed. The North Carolina way.

GEORGE GLAMACK

All-America

Carolina

CARTWRIGHT CARMICHAEL 1923, 1924
Court leader in low-scoring days. All-Southern three years. Senior on team that won national championship 1924. Baseball outfielder as well. 6'-1", 185 lbs, Durham, North Carolina.

JACK COBB 1924, 1925, 1926
Nicknamed Spratt. Top scorer on Carolina team that won three straight conference tournaments in Atlanta. All-Southern three years. Helms Foundation national player of the year. 6'-2", 175 lbs, Durham, North Carolina.

GEORGE GLAMACK 1940, 1941
All-conference two years. Scored 458 points as senior, 20.6 average. Set school record career points 918. Helms Foundation national player of year as junior and senior. 6'-6", 220 lbs, Johnstown, Pennsylvania.

JIM JORDAN 1945
All-conference. 6'-2", 175 lbs.

JOHN DILLON 1946
Nicknamed Hook. All-conference. All-finals NCAA. 6'-1", 170 lbs, Atlanta, Georgia.

LENNIE ROSENBLUTH, 1956, 1957
Helms Foundation national player of year. ACC athlete of year and player of year 1957. All-conference three years. All-finals NCAA. Led team scoring 25.5 points as sophomore, 26.7 as junior, 27.9 as senior. Led ACC scoring as junior. Second school record career 2,045 points. 6'-5", 195 lbs, New York City.

PETE BRENNAN 1958
All-conference two years. All-finals NCAA. ACC player of the year. Dixie Classic outstanding player. Led ACC rebounding as junior 14.7. 6'-6", 205 lbs, Brooklyn, New York.

LEE SHAFFER 1960
All-conference two years. Led ACC scoring as senior 18.2 points. 6'-7", 220 lbs, Pittsburgh, Pennsylvania.

LENNIE ROSENBLUTH

SAM PERKINS

JOHN DILLON

DOUG MOE 1961

All-conference two years. Dixie Classic outstanding player. 6'-6", 215 lbs, Brooklyn, New York.

BILLY CUNNINGHAM 1964, 1965

All-conference three years. ACC player of year as senior. Led ACC scoring two years, led ACC rebounding three years. School record career rebounds with 1,062. 6'-6", 218 lbs, Brooklyn, New York.

BOB LEWIS 1966, 1967

All-conference three years. All-region NCAA. Led ACC scoring as junior 27.4 points. 6'-3", 180 lbs, Washington, D.C.

LARRY MILLER 1967, 1968

All-conference three years. ACC athlete of the year 1968. ACC player of the year twice. Tournament outstanding player two years. 6'-3", 210 lbs, Catasauqua, Pennsylvania.

CHARLIE SCOTT 1969, 1970

All-conference three years. All-finals NCAA. ACC Athlete of the year. Outstanding player tournament. All-region 1969. Led ACC scoring as senior 27.1 points. Fourth school record scoring with 2,007 points. 6'-6", 178 lbs, New York City.

DENNIS WUYCIK 1972

All-conference two years. All-region NCAA. 6'-6", 215 lbs, Ambridge, Pennsylvania.

BILL CHAMBERLAIN 1972

All-NIT. 6'-6", 175 lbs, New York City.

ROBERT McADOO 1972

All-conference. All-finals NCAA. ACC tournament outstanding player award 1972. 6'-9", 215 lbs, Greensboro, North Carolina.

BOBBY JONES 1974

All-conference two years. Led ACC shooting percentages three years. School record career field goal shooting 60.7 percent. USA Olympic team 1972. 6'-9", 215 lbs, Charlotte, North Carolina.

MITCH KUPCHAK 1975, 1976

All-conference two years. ACC player of the year as senior. Led conference rebounds as senior. Second school career rebounding 1,006. USA Olympic team 1976. 6'-4", 230 lbs, Brentwood, New York.

TOMMY LaGARDE 1977

All-conference. USA Olympic team 1976. 6'-10", 230 lbs, Detroit Michigan.

PHIL FORD 1976, 1977, 1978

All-conference three years. Player of year as senior, ACC athlete of the year two years. Tournament outstanding player as freshman 1975. School record career scoring 2,290 points. School record career assists 753. USA Olypic team 1976. 6'-2", 170 lbs, Rocky Mount, North Carolina.

249

BILL WERBER

MIKE O'KOREN 1978, 1979, 1980
All-conference three years. All-finals NCAA. 6'-8", 210 lbs, Jersey City, New Jersey.

AL WOOD 1980, 1981
All-conference three years. Set NCAA scoring record in semifinals 1981. Third school career scoring 2,015 points. 6'-1", 192 lbs, Charlotte, North Carolina.

JAMES WORTHY 1982
All-conference two years. All-finals NCAA. Helms Foundation national co-player of year 1982. ACC athlete of year. Tournament outstanding player. 6'-9", 224 lbs, Gastonia, North Carolina.

SAM PERKINS 1982, 1983
All-conference two years. ACC tournament outstanding player as freshman 1981. 6'9", 220 lbs, Latham, New York.

MICHAEL JORDAN 1983
All-conference. All-finals NCAA 1982. 6'-5", 189 lbs, Wilmington, North Carolina.

Duke

BILL WERBER 1930
All-Southern two years, directed Duke attack to Southern Conference tournament finals two years. All-American in baseball also, signed with New York Yankees. 5'-10", 170 lbs, Berwyn, Maryland.

BILL MOCK 1940
All-conference as senior.

ED KOFFENBERGER 1946, 1947
All-conference two years. Led team scoring with 15.4 as senior, 11.7 as junior.

DICK GROAT 1951, 1952
All-conference two years. National top scorer as junior, holding school record single season 831 points, also second at 780 as senior. Averaged 26 points as senior. School record 48 points on North Carolina. All-American in baseball two years. 6'-0", 175 lbs, Swissvale, Pennsylvania.

ART HEYMAN 1961, 1962, 1963
National player of year as senior. ACC player of year. All-conference three years. All-finals NCAA. School career leading scorer, three-year play, 25.1 average and 1,984 total points. 6'-5", 205 lbs, Rockville Center, New York.

DICK GROAT

JEFF MULLINS

GENE BANKS

JEFF MULLINS 1964
Conference player of year as senior. All-conference three years. All-finals NCAA. School record single game scoring NCAA playoffs, 43 vs Villanova. Third school season scoring 750. 6'-4", 185 lbs, Lexington, Kentucky.

JACK MARIN 1966
All-conference two years. All-finals NCAA. Led team scoring as senior with 18.9 points. 6'-6", 200 lbs, Farrell, Pennsylvania.

BOB VERGA 1966, 1967
All-confererence three years, all-tournament three years. Led ACC and team scoring senior year 26.1 points. School record scoring average for season, senior year. 6'-0", 180 lbs, Sea Girt, New Jersey.

MIKE LEWIS 1968
All-conference. Led team rebounding as junior and senior, also ACC as senior with 14.4 per game. Top team scorer as senior 21.6 points. 6'-7", 225 lbs, Missoula, Montana.

RANDY DENTON 1971
All-conference. Third school career rebounds with 1,067. Led team scoring as senior 20.4 points, also rebounds 14.8. 6'-10, 240 lbs, Raleigh, North Carolina.

JIM SPANARKEL 1978, 1979
All-conference two years. All-finals NCAA. Led team scoring as junior 19.2 and as senior 20.8 points. School career scoring, third with 2,012 points. 6'-5", 190 lbs, Jersey City, New Jersey.

MIKE GMINSKI 1978, 1979, 1980
ACC player of year. All-conference three years. All-finals NCAA. Led team rebounding four years, led team scoring as junior and senior. School career record in scoring 2,323 points and in rebounding 1,242 rebounds. 6'-11", 245 lbs, Monroe, Connecticut.

GENE BANKS 1981
All-conference. All-tournament as sophomore and senior. All-NCAA regional. Led team scoring as senior 18.1 points. School career scoring ranks second with 2,079 points. 6'-7", 205 lbs, Philadelphia, Pennsylvania.

N. C. STATE

MORRIS JOHNSON 1930
All-Southern two years. All-tournament 1929 when N.C. State won conference championship. Captain 1930.

DICK DICKEY

SAMMY RANZINO

DAVID THOMPSON

DICK DICKEY 1948, 1949, 1950
Everett Case's first recruiting class. All-conference four years. Dixie Classic's first outstanding player 1949. Led scoring 12.1 as freshman, 15.5 sophomore and 11.8 junior. 6'-2", 195 lbs, Alexandria, Indiana.

SAMMY RANZINO 1949, 1950, 1951
Conference player of year 1950, Dixie Classic outstanding player 1950. All-conference three years. led conference scoring two years, led team scoring 18.9 as junior, 20.8 as senior. Second Wolfpack career scoring, 1,967 points in 132 games. 6'-1", 188 lbs, Gary, Indiana.

BOBBY SPEIGHT 1952, 1953
All-conference two years. Led team scoring 15.9 as junior, 16.9 as senior. Third school career rebounding. 6'-8", 188 lbs, Raleigh, North Carolina/Akron, Ohio.

RON SHAVLIK 1955, 1956
Conference player of the year 1956, Dixie Classic outstanding player as junior and senior. All-conference twice. Led team scoring 22.1 as junior, 18.2 as senior. School record in career rebounding, career free throws. Second high school single game scoring: 55 vs William & Mary. 6'-9", 195 lbs, Denver, Colorado.

VIC MOLODET 1956
All-conference two years, all-Dixie Classic two years. Led team scoring two years, 13.8 as sophomore, 18.2 as senior. Hit 16 consecutive free throws vs Wake Forest 1955. 6'-0", 165 lbs, East Chicago, Indiana.

LOU PUCILLO 1959
Conference player of year 1959. All-conference two years. Led team scoring 15.7 as junior. Held school career assist record for almost decade. 5'-9", 157 lbs, Philadelphia, Pennsylvania.

DAVID THOMPSON 1973, 1974, 1975
National player of year 1974 and 1975. ACC player of year three seasons, all-conference three times. Scoring averages: 24.7 sophomore, 26.0 junior, 29.9 senior. School record career 2,309 points in 86 games. School most points seasons: 838 and 805. Single game high: 57 vs Buffalo State, 6'-4", 195 lbs, Shelby, North Carolina.

MONTE TOWE 1974
All-conference as junior. NCAA all-district team, NCAA all-final team 1974. 5'-6", 145 lbs, Converse, Indiana.

KENNY CARR 1976
All-conference two years. Third in school record points season 798 as junior. Fourth school career points, 1,772 in 86 games. 6'-7", 225 lbs, Hyattsville, Maryland.

CHARLES WHITNEY 1980
Nicknamed Hawkeye. All-conference two years. Third in school career scoring, 1,964 points in 117 games. 6'-5" 219 lbs, Washington, D.C.

Wake Forest

DICKIE HEMRIC 1954, 1955
Leading scorer (2,587) and rebounder (1,802) in Wake Forest history. All-Southern Conference 1952-53, all-ACC 1954-55. ACC Player of the year 1954-55. Scoring per year: 538 points, 22.4 average; 623 and 24.9; 680 and 24.3; 746 and 27.6. Career average 24.88. Highest scoring career NCAA until 1960. 6'-6", 227 lbs, Jonesville, North Carolina.

JACK MURDOCK 1957
All-ACC 1975. Led ACC field goal shooting 1956. Led NCAA and ACC in free throw shooting 1956. Held school record for 37 consecutive free throws made. 5'-10", 156 lbs, Raleigh, North Carolina.

LEN CHAPPELL 1961, 1962
All-ACC 1960-61-62. ACC player of the year 1961-62. Only ACC player to average 30 points a game for full season. Member prestigious club of 2,000 points and 1,000 rebounds. Scoring per year: 488 points, 17.4 average; 745 and 26.6; 932 and 30.1. Career 1,213 rebounds, 13.9 average. 6'-8", 240 lbs, Portage, Pennsylvania.

CHARLIE DAVIS 1971
All-ACC 1969-70-71. ACC player of the year 1971. School record 51 points one game (vs American University). Led ACC in free throw shooting, career 87.3. School record career scoring average 24.9, with 1,970 points. Scoring per year: 616 points, 22.8 average; 664 and 25.5; 690 and 26.5. 6'-1", 180 lbs, New York City.

SKIP BROWN 1975, 1977
All-ACC 1975 and 1977. Third year leading scorer at Wake Forest, 2,034 points. Holds school records with 43 consecutive free throws made. Scoring by years: 344 points, 13.2 average; 589 and 22.7; 543 and 20.9; 558 and 18.6. 6'-1", 165 lbs, Kingsport, Tennessee.

ROD GRIFFIN 1977, 1978
All-ACC 1977-78. ACC player of year 1977. School record field goal shooting, 62.1 percent. Career scoring 1,985 points, 947 rebounds. Scoring by years: 348 points, 13.9 average; 482 and 17.9; 532 and 20.5; 623 and 21.5. 6'-6", 225 lbs, Fairmont, North Carolina.

FRANK JOHNSON 1981
All-ACC 1981. Played in more games than any Wake Forest player, 120. School game record with 13 assists. Hardship season 1980 due to injury. 6'-2", 185 lbs, Weirsdale, Florida.

DICKIE HEMRIC

LEN CHAPPELL

CHARLIE DAVIS

Davidson

BUDDY CHEEK 1949
   Leading scorer Southern Conference. All-conference and all-tournament as junior. All-conference as senior. 6'-3", 170 lbs, Selma, Alabama.
FRED HETZEL 1964, 1965
   Leading scorer in school history (three seasons). Southern Conference player of the year three times, all-conference three times. As sophomore 23.5 points, 13.3 rebounds; as junior 22.3 and 13.5; as senior 22.5 and 14.8. Eighth in nation in scoring as senior. SC athlete of the year. 6'-8", 215 lbs, Washington, D.C.
DICK SNYDER 1966
   Southern Conference player of year as senior. All-conference two years. Third in school career scoring. As senior, averaged 26.9 points. SC athlete of the year. 6'5", 210 lbs, North Canton, Ohio.
MIKE MALOY 1969, 1970
   Southern Conference player of the year as junior and senior. All-conference three years. Fourth in school career scoring. As junior averaged 24.6 points, 14.3 rebounds. 6'-7", 200 lbs, New York City.
JOHN GERDY 1979
   Southern Conference athlete of year. All-conference three years. School career scoring record, four years, with 2,483 points. As senior, sixth nationally with 26.7 points average. 6'-5", 190 lbs, Little Falls, New Jersey.

FRED HETZEL

DICK SNYDER

Season/Coaching Records

Carolina Records

Season	Conference Championship	Won-Lost	Coach	Captains
1911		7-4	Nat Cartmell	Marvin Ritch
1912		4-5	Nat Cartmell	Junius Smith
1913		5-6	Nat Cartmell	Ben Edwards
1914		10-8	Nat Cartmell	Meb Long
1915		6-10	Chick Doak	Meb Long
1916		12-6	Chick Doak	John G. Johnson
1917		5-4	Howell Peacock	George Tennent
1918		9-3	Howell Peacock	George Tennent
1919		9-7	Howell Peacock	Reynolds Cuthberson
1920		7-9	Fred Boye	Billy Carmichael
1921		11-8	Fred Boye	Carlyle Shepard
1922	(SC)	14-3		Cart Carmichael
1923		15-1		Monk McDonald
1924	(SC)	26-0	Norman Shepard	Winton Green
1925	(SC)	18-5	Monk McDonald	Jack Cobb
1926	(SC)	20-5	Harlan Sanborn	Bill Dodderer
1927		17-7	James Ashmore	Bunn Hackney
1928		16-2	James Ashmore	Billy Morris
1929		17-8	James Ashmore	Rufus Hackney
1930		14-11	James Ashmore	Puny Harper
1931		15-9	James Ashmore	Artie Marpet
1932		16-5	Bo Shepard	Tom Alexander
1933		12-5	Bo Shepard	Wilmer Hines
1934		18-4	Bo Shepard	Dave McCachren
1935	(SC)	23-2	Bo Shepard	Stuart Aiken
1936	(SC)	21-4	Walter Skidmore	Jim McCachren
1937		18-5	Walter Skidmore	Earl Ruth
1938		16-5	Walter Skidmore	Earl Ruth
1939		10-11	Walter Skidmore	Bill McCachren
1940	(SC)	23-3	Bill Lange	Ben Dilworth

Season	Conference Championship	Won-Lost	Coach	Captains
1941		19-9	Bill Lange	George Glamack-Jimmy Howard
1942		15-8	Bill Lange	Bob Rose
1943		12-10	Bill Lange	George Payne-George McCachren
1944		17-10	Bill Lange	game captains
1945	(SC)	22-6	Ben Carnevale	game captains
1946		30-5	Ben Carnevale	Lew Hayworth
1947		19-8	Tom Scott	Jim Hamilton-Jim White
1948		20-7	Tom Scott	Bob Paxton
1949		20-8	Tom Scott	Dan Nymicz
1950		17-12	Tom Scott	Nemo Nearman
1951		12-15	Tom Scott	Charlie Thorn-Hugo Kappler
1952		12-15	Tom Scott	Howard Deasy
1953		17-10	Frank McGuire	Vince Grimaldi-Jack Wallace.
1954		11-10	Frank McGuire	game captains
1955		10-11	Frank McGuire	Paul Likens-Al Lifson
1956		18-5	Frank McGuire	Jerry Vayda
1957	(SC)	32-0	Frank McGuire	Lennie Rosenbluth
1958		19-7	Frank McGuire	Pete Brennan
1959		20-5	Frank McGuire	Danny Lotz
1960		18-6	Frank McGuire	Harvey Salz
1961		19-4	Frank McGuire	Doug Moe-York Larese
1962		8-9	Dean Smith	Jim Hudock
1963		15-6	Dean Smith	Larry Brown-Yogi Poteet
1964		12-12	Dean Smith	Charlie Shaffer-Mike Cooke
1965		15-9	Dean Smith	Billy Cunningham
1966		16-11	Dean Smith	Bob Bennett-John Yokley
1967	(ACC)	26-6	Dean Smith	Bob Lewis-Tom Gauntlett
1968	(ACC)	28-4	Dean Smith	Larry Miller
1969	(ACC)	27-5	Dean Smith	Bill Bunting-Rusty Clark-Joe Brown-Dick Grubar-Gerald Tuttle
1970		18-9	Dean Smith	Charlie Scott-Ed Fogler-Jim Delany
1971		26-6	Dean Smith	Lee Dedmon-Dale Gipple
1972	(ACC)	26-5	Dean Smith	Dennis Wuycik-Steve Previs
1973		25-8	Dean Smith	George Karl-Donn Johnston
1974		22-6	Dean Smith	Bobby Jones-Darrell Elston
1975	(ACC)	23-8	Dean Smith	Ed Stahl-Brad Hoffman-Mickey Bell

Season	Conference Championship	Won-Lost	Coach	Captains
1976		25-4	Dean Smith	Bill Chambers-Dave Hanners-Mitch Kupchak
1977	(ACC)	28-5	Dean Smith	Bruce Buckley-Woody Coley-Walter Davis-John' Kuester-Tommy LaGarde
1978		23-8	Dean Smith	Phil Ford-Tom Zaliagiris
1979	(ACC)	23-6	Dean Smith	Dudley Bradley-Ged Doughton-Randy Wiel
1980		21-8	Dean Smith	Dave Colescott-Mike O'Koren-John Virgil-Jeff Wolf-Rich Yonaker
1981	(ACC)	29-8	Dean Smith	Pete Budko-Eric Kenny-Mike Pepper-Al Wood
1982	(ACC)	32-2	Dean Smith	Jeb Barlow-Jimmy Black-Chris Brust
1983		28-8	Dean Smith	Jim Braddock

Coaching Records: Carolina

No.	Coach	Seasons	No Years	Won	Lost
1	Nat Cartmell	1911-1914	4	26	23
2	Chick Doak	1915-1916	2	18	23
3	Howell Peacock	1917-1919	3	23	14
4	Fred Boye	1920-1921	2	18	17
	No coach	1922-1923	2	29	4
5	Norman Shepard	1924	1	26	0
6	Monk McDonald	1925	1	18	5
7	Harlan Sanborn	1926	1	20	5
8	James Ashmore	1927-1931	5	79	37
9	Bo Shepard	1932-1935	4	69	16
10	Walter Skidmore	1936-1939	4	65	25
11	Bill Lange	1940-1944	5	86	40
12	Ben Carnevale	1945-1946	2	52	11
13	Tom Scott	1947-1952	6	100	65
14	Frank McGuire	1953-1961	9	164	58
15	Dean Smith	1962-	22	496	153
			73	1289	489

Total Games 1778

Winning Percentage 72.5

Duke Records

Season	Conference Championship	Won-Lost	Coach	Captains
1906		2-3	W. W. Card	T. G. Stem
1907		4-2	W. W. Card	T. G. Stem
1908		2-3	W. W. Card	Billy Lilly
1909		8-1	W. W. Card	
1910		4-4	W. W. Card	P. J. Kiker
1911		4-3	W. W. Card	H. G. Hedrick
1912		6-1	W. W. Card	C. B. Brinn
1913		11-8	J. E. Brinn	
1914		11-9	Noble L. Clay	
1915		11-9	Noble L. Clay	
1916		9-11	Bob Doak	
1917		20-4	Chick Doak	
1918		10-5	Chick Doak	
1919		6-5	H. P. Cole	
1920		10-4	W. J. Rosenthies	
1921		9-6	F. J. Egan	
1922		6-12	James Baldwin	
1923		14-7	J. S. Burbage	
1924		19-6	J. S. Burbage	
1925		4-9	G. C. Buckheit	
1926		8-12	G. C. Buckheit	Pete Moss
1927		4-9	G. C. Burkheit	M. W. Butler
1928		9-5	G. C. Buckheit	D. L. Kelly
1929		12-8	Eddie Cameron	Coke Candler
1930		18-2	Eddie Cameron	Bo Farley
1931		14-7	Eddie Cameron	
1932		14-11	Eddie Cameron	
1933		17-5	Eddie Cameron	
1934		18-6	Eddie Cameron	Phil Weaver-Herb Thompson
1935		18-8	Eddie Cameron	Sam Bell
1936		20-6	Eddie Cameron	Charles Kunkle
1937		15-8	Eddie Cameron	Ken Podger
1938	(SC)	15-9	Eddie Cameron	Fred Edwards-John Hoffman
1939		10-12	Eddie Cameron	Ed Swindell-Bob O'Mara
1940		19-7	Eddie Cameron	Bill Parsons
1941		14-8	Eddie Cameron	Glenn Price-Tom Connelly
1942	(SC)	22-2	Eddie Cameron	Ray Spuhler
1943	(SC)	20-6	Gerry Gerard	

Season	Conference Championship	Won-Lost	Coach	Captain
1944	(SC)	13-3	Gerry Gerard	
1945		13-9	Gerry Gerard	
1946		21-6	Gerry Gerard	Ed Koffenberger
1947		19-8	Gerry Gerard	Ed Koffenberger-John Seward
1948		17-12	Gerry Gerard	Doug Ausbon
1949		13-9	Gerry Gerard	Ben Collins
1950		15-15	Gerry Gerard	Ceep Youmans-Tom Hughes
1951		20-13	Harold Bradley	Scotty York
1952		24-6	Harold Bradley	Dick Groat
1953		18-8	Harold Bradley	Bernie Janicki-Rudy D'Emilio-Rudy Lacy
1954		22-6	Harold Bradley	Bernie Janicki-Rudy D'Emilio
1955		20-8	Harold Bradley	Joe Belmont-Ronnie Mayer
1956		19-7	Harold Bradley	Joe Belmont
1957		13-11	Harold Bradley	
1958		18-7	Harold Bradley	Bobby Joe Harris-Jim Newcome
1959		13-12	Harold Bradley	Marty Joyce-Jerry Robertson
1960	(ACC)	17-11	Vic Bubas	Howard Hurt
1961		22-6	Vic Bubas	Howard Hurt
1962		20-5	Vic Bubas	Art Heyman-Buzz Mewhort
1963	(ACC)	27-3	Vic Bubas	Art Heyman
1964	(ACC)	26-5	Vic Bubas	Jeff Mullins
1965		20-5	Vic Bubas	Denny Ferguson
1966	(ACC)	26-4	Vic Bubas	Steve Vacendak
1967		18-9	Vic Bubas	Bob Verga
1968		22-6	Vic Bubas	Mike Lewis
1969		15-13	Vic Bubas	Dave Golden-Steve Vandenberg
1970		17-9	Bucky Waters	Larry Saunders
1971		20-10	Bucky Waters	Larry Saunders
1972		14-12	Bucky Waters	Pat Doughty-Alan Shaw-Gary Melchionni
1973		12-14	Bucky Waters	Alan Shaw-Gary Melchionni
1974		10-16	Neill McGeachy	Kevin Billerman
1975		13-13	Bill Foster	Bob Fleischer-Kevin Billerman
1976		13-14	Bill Foster	Willie Hodge-Terry Chili
1977		14-13	Bill Foster	Tate Armstrong-Mark Crow

Season	Conference Championship	Won-Lost	Coach	Captains
1978	(ACC)	27-7	Bill Foster	Jim Sparnarkel
1979		22-8	Bill Foster	Jim Spanarkel-Mike Gminski
1980	(ACC)	24-9	Bill Foster	Mike Gminski-Bob Bender
1981		17-13	Mike Krzyzewski	Gene Banks-Kenny Dennard
1982		10-17	Mike Krzyzewski	Vince Taylor-Tom Emma
1983		11-17	Mike Krzyzewski	Tom Emma

Coaching Records: Duke:

No.	Coach	Seasons	No. Years	Won	Lost
1	W. W. (Cap) Card	1906-1912	7	30	17
2	J. C. Brinn	1913	1	11	8
3	Noble Clay	1914-1915	2	22	18
4	Bob Doak	1916	1	9	11
5	Chick Doak	1917-1918	2	30	9
6	H. P. Cole	1919	1	6	5
7	W. J. Rothensies	1920	1	10	4
8	F. J. Egan	1921	1	9	6
9	James Baldwin	1922	1	6	12
10	J. S. Burbage	1923-1924	2	33	13
11	G. C. Buckheit	1925-1928	4	25	35
12	Eddie Cameron	1929-1942	14	226	99
13	Gerry Gerard	1943-1950	8	131	78
14	Harold Bradley	1951-1959	9	167	78
15	Vic Bubas	1960-1969	10	213	67
16	Bucky Waters	1970-1973	4	63	45
17	Neill McGeachy	1974	1	10	16
18	Bill Foster	1975-1980	6	113	64
19	Mike Krzyzewski	1981-	3	38	47
			78	1152	632

Total Games 1729

Win Percentage 66.6

N.C. State Records

Season	Conference Championship	Won-Lost	Coach	Captains
1911		1-1		
1912		0-6	W. C. Hopkins	
1913		4-7	E. D. Sandborn	E. J. Phillips
1914		6-7	John Hegarty	E. J. Phillips
1915		5-5	H. S. Tucker	J. H. Mason
1916		2-5	E. D. Sandborn	J. H. Mason
1917		10-8	Harry Hartsell	Ben Temple
1918		12-3	Harry Hartsell	Elbert F. Lewis
1919		11-3	Tal Stafford	F. D. Cline
1920		11-5	Richard Crozier	F. D. Cline
1921		6-14	Richard Crozier	J. H. Ripple
1922		6-13	Harry Hartsell	T. N. Park
1923		5-8	Harry Hartsell	Thomas Leeper
1924		7-16	Richard Crozier	Red Johnson
1925		11-7	Gus Tebell	Red Johnson
1926		19-3	Gus Tebell	F. P. Pickens
1927		12-5	Gus Tebell	Gordon Greshman
1928		10-8	Gus Tebell	Jack McDowall
1929	(SC)	15-6	Gus Tebell	Henry Young
1930		11-6	Gus Tebell	John Johnson
1931		8-8	R. R. Sermon	game captains
1932		10-6	R. R. Sermon	Bud Rose
1933		11-8	R. R. Sermon	George Nelms
1934		11-6	R. R. Sermon	Bob McQuage
1935		10-9	R. R. Sermon	Ray Rex
1936		15-4	R. R. Sermon	Charles Aycock
1937		15-9	R. R. Sermon	Neil Dalrymple
1938		13-6	R. R. Sermon	Connie Mac Berry
1939		10-7	R. R. Sermon	P. G. Hill-Bill Mann
1940		8-11	R. R. Sermon	James Sevier
1941		6-9	Bob Warren	Ray Smith
1942		15-7	Bob Warren	G. V. Strayhorne- J. C. Tabscott
1943		7-9	Leroy Jay	Bernie Mock
1944		5-13	Leroy Jay	game captains
1945		10-11	Leroy Jay	game captains
1946		6-12	Leroy Jay	game captains
1947	(SC)	26-5	Everett Case	Leo Katkaveck

Season	Conference Championship	Won-Lost	Coach	Captains
1948	(SC)	29-3	Everett Case	Leo Katkaveck
1949	(SC)	25-8	Everett Case	Vic Bubas-Warren Cartier
1950	(SC)	27-6	Everett Case	Dick Dickey
1951	(SC)	30-7	Everett Case	Sammy Ranzino
1952	(SC)	24-10	Everett Case	Lee Terrill
1953		26-6		Bob Speight
1954	(ACC)	26-7	Everett Case	Mel Thompson
1955	(ACC)	28-4	Everett Case	Dave Gotkin
1956	(ACC)	24-4	Everett Case	Phil DiNardo
1957		15-11	Everett Case	John Maglio-Cliff Hafer-Nick Pond-Bob Seitz
1958		18-6	Everett Case	Whitey Bell
1959	(ACC)	22-4	Everett Case	Lou Pucillo
1960		11-15	Everett Case	Dan Englehardt
1961		16-9	Everett Case	Stan Niewierowski
1962		11-6	Everett Case	Russ Marvel
1963		10-11	Everett Case	John Speaks-Ken Rohloff
1964		8-11	Everett Case	Pete Auksel
1965	(ACC)	21-5	*Everett Case-Press Maravich	Larry Lakins-Pete Coker-Tommy Mattocks
1966		18-9	Press Maravich	Tommy Mattocks-Pete Coker
1967		7-19	Norman Sloan	game captains
1968		16-10	Norman Sloan	Eddie Beidenbach-Bill Kretzer
1969		15-10	Norman Sloan	Dick Braucher-Joe Serdich
1970	(ACC)	23-7	Norman Sloan	Vann Williford-Rick Anheuser
1971		13-14	Norman Sloan	Al Heartley
1972		16-10	Norman Sloan	Paul Coder
1973	(ACC)	27-0	Norman Sloan	game captains
1974	(ACC)	30-1	Norman Sloan	game captains
1975		22-6	Norman Sloan	game captains
1976		21-9	Norman Sloan	Kenny Carr
1977		17-10	Norman Sloan	Kenny Carr
1978		21-10	Norman Sloan	game captains
1979		18-12	Norman Sloan	game captains
1980		20-8	Norman Sloan	Hawkeye Whitney-Clyde Austin
1981		14-13	Jim Valvano	game captains
1982		22-10	Jim Valvano	game captains
1983	(ACC)	26-10	Jim Valvano	Sidney Lowe-Dereck Whittenberg-Thurl Bailey

*Everett Case retired after two games (1-1)

273

ROBERT McADOO

Coaching Records: N.C. State

No.	Coach	Seasons	No. Years	Won	Lost
1	Coach unknown	1911	1	1	1
2	W. L. Hopkins	1912	1	0	6
3	E. D. Sandborn	1913, 1916	2	6	12
4	John Hegarty	1914	1	6	7
5	H. S. Tucker	1915	1	5	5
6	Harry Hartsell	1917-1918 1922-1923	4	33	31
7	Tal Stafford	1919	1	11	3
8	Richard Crozier	1920-1921 1924	3	24	35
9	Gus Tebell	1925-1930	6	78	35
10	R. R. (Doc) Sermon	1931-1940	10	111	74
11	Bob Warren	1941-1942	2	21	16
12	Leroy Jay	1943-1946	4	28	45
13	Everett Case	1947-1964*	19*	377	134
14	Press Maravich	1965-1966	2*	38	13
15	Norman Sloan	1967-1980	14	266	127
16	Jim Valvano	1981-	3	62	33
			73	1067	577

Total Games 1644

Winning Percentage 64.9

*Case retired after 2nd game 1965, record 1-1.

Wake Forest Records

Season	Conference Championship	Won-Lost	Coach	Captains
1906		3-3	J. R. Crozier	Vanderbilt Couch
1907		4-0	J. R. Crozier	Vanderbilt Couch
1908		8-3	J. R. Crozier	Vanderbilt Couch
1909		6-1	J. R. Crozier	Vanderbilt Couch
1910		1-0	J. R. Crozier	W. C. Allen
1911		8-7	J. R. Crozier	Robert Holding
1912		9-6	J. R. Crozier	Hugh Beam
1913		9-7	J. R. Crozier	Bruce Holding

Season	Conference Championship	Won-Lost	Coach	Captains
1914		10-7	J. R. Crozier	G. M. Billings
1915		12-4	J. R. Crozier	Alex Hall
1916		16-2	J. R. Crozier	Ham Davis
1917		9-6	J. R. Crozier	Howard Handy
1918		4-12	E. T. MacDonnell	Howard Handy
1919		6-9	Irving Carlyle	Howard Handy
1920		9-4	Bill Holding	F. C. Feezor
1921		7-10	J. L. White Jr.	George Heckman
1922		11-6	Bill Holding	J. B. Carlyle
1923		12-5	Phil Utley	George Heckman
1924		18-7	Hank Garrity	Murray Greason
1925		15-7	Hank Garrity	Fred Emmerson
1926		13-6	R. S. Hayes	Monk Ober
1927		22-3	James Baldwin	Monk Ober
1928		6-14	James Baldwin	Ralph James
1929		5-8	Pat Miller	Al Dowtin
1930		2-11	Pat Miller	Ty Jones
1931		8-10	R. S. Hayes	Eustis Mills
1932		4-8	Fred Emmerson	Spider Webb
1933		4-5	Fred Emmerson	Charles Owen
1934		5-9	Murray Greason	Ernest Swing
1935		6-10	Murray Greason	Bill Clark
1936		9-12	Murray Greason	Clyde Hatcher
1937		15-6	Murray Greason	Doyt Morris
1938		7-12	Murray Greason	Stanley Apple
1939		18-6	Murray Greason	Jim Waller
1940		13-9	Murray Greason	Bill Sweel
1941		9-9	Murray Greason	Vince Convery
1942		16-7	Murray Greason	Jim Bond-Herb Cline
1943		1-10	Murray Greason	Everett Berger
1944	No Team			
1945		3-14	Murray Greason	Milton Marney
1946		12-6	Murray Greason	Henry Lougee
1947		11-13	Murray Greason	Deran Walters
1948		18-11	Murray Greason	Jack Gentry-Deran Walters
1949		11-13	Murray Greason	Willard Kaylor-Jim Patton
1950		14-16	Murray Greason	Jim Patton
1951		16-14	Murray Greason	Jack Mueller
1952		10-19	Murray Greason	Tunney Brooks
1953	(SC)	22-7	Murray Greason	Billy Lyles-Al DePorter
1954		17-12	Murray Greason	Al DePorter
1955		17-12	Murray Greason	Dickie Hemric
1956		19-9	Murray Greason	Lowell Davis

Season	Conference Championship	Won-Lost	Coach	Captains
1957		19-9	Murray Greason	Jack Williams-Jim Gilley-Ernie Wiggins-Jack Murdock
1958		6-17	Bones McKinney	Wendell Carr
1959		10-14	Bones McKinney	Olin Broadway
1960		21-7	Bones McKinney	Dave Budd
1961	(ACC)	19-11	Bones McKinney	Alley Hart-Jerry Steele
1962	(ACC)	22-9	Bones McKinney	Len Chappell-Billy Packer
1963		16-10	Bones McKinney	Dave Wiedeman
1964		16-11	Bones McKinney	Frank Christie
1965		12-15	Bones McKinney	Ronny Watts
1966		8-18	Jack Murdock	Bob Leonard
1967		9-18	Jack McCloskey	Paul Long
1968		5-21	Jack McCloskey	David Stroupe
1969		18-9	Jack McCloskey	Jerry Montgomery
1970		14-13	Jack McCloskey	Charlie Davis-Dickie Walker
1971		16-10	Jack McCloskey	Charlie Davis-Neil Pastushok
1972		8-18	Jack McCloskey	Rich Habegger-John Lewkowicz
1973		12-15	Carl Tacy	Willie Griffin-Eddie Payne
1974		13-13	Carl Tacy	Tony Byers-Bobby Dwyer-Mike Parrish
1975		13-13	Carl Tacy	Cal Stamp-Mike Parrish-Skip Brown-Jerry Schellenberg
1976		17-10	Carl Tacy	Henry Hicks-Skip Brown-Rod Griffin
1977		22-8	Carl Tacy	Jerry Schellenberg
1978		19-10	Carl Tacy	Rod Griffin
1979		12-15	Carl Tacy	Frank Johnson
1980		13-14	Carl Tacy	Frank Johnson
1981		22-7	Carl Tacy	Frank Johnson
1982		21-9	Carl Tacy	Jim Johnstone-Guy Morgan-Mike Helms
1983		20-12	Carl Tacy	Alvis Rogers

Coaching Records: Wake Forest

No.	Coach	Seasons	No. Years	Won	Lost
1	Richard Crozier	1906-1917	12	95	46
2	E. T. MacDonnell	1918	1	4	12
3	Irving Carlyle	1919	1	6	9
4	Bill Holding	1920, 1922	2	20	10
5	J. L. White	1921	1	7	10
6	Phil Utley	1923	1	12	5
7	Hank Garrity	1924-1925	2	33	14
8	R. S. Hayes	1926-1931	2	21	16
9	James Baldwin	1927-1928	2	28	17
10	Pat Miller	1929-1930	2	7	19
11	Fred Emmerson	1932-1933	2	9	16
12	Murray Greason	1934-1943 1945-1957	23*	288	245
13	Bones McKinney	1958-1965	8	122	94
14	Jack Murdock	1966	1	8	18
15	Jack McCloskey	1967-1972	6	70	89
16	Carl Tacy	1973-	11	184	126
			77	914	746

Total Games 1660

Winning Percentage 55.1

*No team 1944

Davidson Records

Season	Conference Championship	Won-Lost	Coach	Captain
1909		1-2	J. W. Rhea	J. L. Fairly
1910		2-3		J. L. McClintock
1911		0-2		R. W. Miles
1912		4-2		Lewis McDuffie
1913		0-1	W. T. Cook	Locke White

Season	Conference Championship Won-Lost	Coach	Captain
1914	0-0		Jim Gibbon
1915	3-3		Tom Somerville
1916	11-8		
1917	11-6	Bill Fetzer	Dutch Hengeveld
1918	7-5	Bill Fetzler	T. W. Hawkins
1919	3-6		
1920	3-10	Fred Hengeveld	D. M. Chalmers
1921	7-7	Fred Hengeveld	Lewis Schenck
1922	10-3	Fred Hengeveld	Pat Crawford
1923	9-9	H. M. Grey	G. W. Mauze
1924	10-9	Monk Younger	C. M. Davis
1925	18-6	Monk Younger	Ralph Boggs
1926	8-9	Monk Younger	Flake Laird
1927	10-8	Monk Younger	T. F. Anderson
1928	9-7	Monk Younger	B. A. Wilson
1929	10-8	Monk Younger	Carl Pritchett
1930	12-7	Monk Younger	Frontis Johnston
1931	8-8	Monk Younger	Bill Goodson
1932	3-12	Flake Laird	Doc Mathis
1933	4-12	Flake Laird	Bruce Peabody
1934	6-13	Flake Laird	Charlie Harris
1935	13-10	Flake Laird	Jim Morgan
1936	4-15	Flake Laird	Maurice Peabody-Jim Quick
1937	13-10	Flake Laird	Bill Quick
1938	10-12	Norman Shepard	Bill Kiesewetter
1939	19-10	Norman Shepard	Ned Iverson
1940	8-13	Norman Shepard	Footsie Cowan
1941	11-12	Norman Shepard	Jimmy Hogg
1942	12-13	Norman Shepard	Tommy Yarborough-Dave Spencer
1943	18-6	Norman Shepard	Jack Wayman-John Belk
1944	16-7	Norman Shepard	Jim Lowry
1945	9-10	Norman Shepard	Jim Lowry
1946	13-12	Norman Shepard	Ed White
1947	17-8	Norman Shepard	George Peters-Ed White
1948	19-9	Norman Shepard	Mike Williams-Buddy Cheek
1949	18-7	Norman Shepard	Mike Williams-Buddy Cheek
1950	10-16	Boyd Baird	Whit Cobb
1951	7-19	Boyd Baird	Fred Hengeveld-Tommy Haller
1952	7-18	Boyd Baird	Bill Brooks

279

Season	Conference Championship	Won-Lost	Coach	Captain
1953		4-17	Danny Miller	Joe Dudley
1954		7-16	Danny Miller	John Bennett
1955		8-14	Danny Miller	Hobby Cobb
1956		11-15	Danny Miller-Tom Scott	Hobby Cobb
1957		7-20	Tom Scott	Dick Weeks
1958		9-15	Tom Scott	
1959		9-15	Tom Scott	Dave Hollingsworth-Semi Mintz
1960		5-19	Tom Scott	John Huie
1961		9-14	Lefty Driesell	Jim Nuckels-Joe Markee
1962		14-11	Lefty Driesell	D. G. Martin
1963		20-7	Lefty Driesell	Bill Jarman
1964		22-4	Lefty Driesell	Terry Holland
1965		24-2	Lefty Driesell	Fred Hetzel
1966	(SC)	21-7	Lefty Driesell	Dick Snyder
1967		15-12	Lefty Driesell	Rod Knowles-Tom Young-Tom Youngdale-Dave Moser
1968	(SC)	24-5	Lefty Driesell	Rod Knowles-Wayne Huckel
1969	(SC)	27-3	Lefty Driesell	Dave Moser
1970	(SC)	22-5	Terry Holland	Doug Cook-Jerry Kroll-Mike Maloy
1971		15-11	Terry Holland	Steve Kirley
1972		19-9	Terry Holland	Eric Mankin
1973		18-9	Terry Holland	Jack Pecorak
1974		18-9	Terry Holland	game captains
1975		7-19	Bo Brickels	Greg Dunn-Larry Horowitz
1976		5-21	Bo Brickels	Eppa Rixey-Jay Powell
1977		5-22	Dave Pritchett	Marvin Lively-Jerry Stallworth
1978		9-18	Dave Pritchett	Mark Sumwalt-Kevin Doughtry-Brian Coffey
1979		8-19	Eddie Biedenbach	John Gerdy
1980		8-18	Eddie Biedenbach	Ernie Reigel-Rich Perkey
1981		13-14	Eddie Biedenbach	Todd Hayes
1982		14-15	Bobby Hussey	Jamie Hall-Tommy McConnell
1983		13-15	Bobby Hussey	

Coaching Records: Davidson

No.	Coach	Seasons	No. Years	Won	Lost
1	J. W. Rhea	1909	1	1	2
	No coach	1910-1912 1914-1916 1919	7	23	24
2	W. T. Cook	1913	1	0	1
3	Bill Fetzer	1917-1918	2	18	11
4	Fred Hengeveld	1920-1922	3	20	20
5	H. M. Grey	1923	1	9	9
6	Monk Younger	1924-1931	8	85	62
7	Flake Laird	1932-1937	6	43	74
8	Norman Shepard	1938-1949	12	170	119
9	Boyd Baird	1950-1952	3	24	53
10	Danny Miller	1953-1956	4	30	62
11	Tom Scott	1957-1960	4	30	69
12	Lefty Driesell	1961-1969	9	176	65
13	Terry Holland	1970-1974	5	92	43
14	Bo Brickels	1975-1976	2	12	40
15	Dave Pritchett	1977-1978	2	14	40
16	Eddie Biedenbach	1979-1981	3	29	51
17	Bobby Hussey	1982-	2	27	30
			75	803	775

Total Games 1578

Winning Percentage 50.9

Conference Records

Southern Conference

Beginning of basketball tournament in Atlanta as an open event in 1921, becoming Southern Conference championship in 1924, through 1932.

1921

Tournament

(Southern Conference held open tournament for Southern teams.)
(15 teams, Alabama bye, Friday-Wednesday, February 25-26-28, March 1-2, Atlanta Auditorium, Atlanta, Georgia.)

First Round—Mercer 50, South Carolina 22; Kentucky 50, Tulane 28; Mississippi State 41, Furman 7; Millsaps 46, Tennessee 29; Georgia 47, Newberry 23; Auburn 45, Clemson 25; Georgia Tech 53, Birmingham Southern 11.

Quarterfinals—Kentucky 49, Mercer 25; Miss. State 28, Millsaps 11; Georgia 32, Auburn 24; Georgia Tech 31, Alabama 22.

Semifinals—Kentucky 28, Miss. State 13; Georgia 26, Georgia Tech 21.

Championship—Kentucky 20, Georgia 19.

1922

Tournament

(Southern Conference held open tournament for Southern teams.)
(25 teams, Friday-Wednesday, February 24-25-27, March 1-2, Atlanta Auditorium, Atlanta, Georgia.)

First Round—North Carolina 35, Howard 22; Auburn 32, Newberry 21; Vanderbilt 37, The Citadel 22; Georgia 43, Oglethorpe 12; Chattanooga 57, Furman 30; Tulane 31, Clemson 20; Georgetown 42, Kentucky 21; Mercer 32, Centre 17.

Second Round—North Carolina 32, Auburn 27; Georgia 27, Vanderbilt 26; Alabama over Washington & Lee by default; Tennessee 19, Mississippi College 18; Georgia Tech 34, Miss. State 30; South Carolina 34, Wofford 18; Chattanooga 25, Tulane 21; Mercer 35, Georgetown 22.

First two of the four outstanding Charlotte brothers at Carolina, Dave McCachren, left, and Jim McCachren, both All-Southern.

Quarterfinals—North Carolina 33, Georgia 25; Alabama 29, Tennessee 25; Georgia Tech 34, South Carolina 23; Mercer 35, Chattanooga 22.

Semifinals—North Carolina 20, Alabama 11; Mercer 29, Georgia Tech 14.

Championship—North Carolina 29, Mercer 14.

1923

Tournament

(Southern Conference held open tournament for Southern teams.)
(24 teams, Tuesday-Saturday, February 27-28, March 1-2-3, Atlanta Auditorium, Atlanta, Georgia.)

First Round—Furman 44, Millsaps 21; North Carolina 28, Mississippi College 21; Centre 27, Clemson 23, Georgia 33, Tennessee 19; Vanderbilt 36, LSU 10; Chattanooga 43, Georgetown 27; Alabama 44, Wofford 25; Mercer 45, Auburn 24.

Second Round—Mississippi State 47, Furman 21; Mississippi 34, North Carolina 32; Georgia Tech 34, Centre 26; Georgia over Tulane by default; Virginia Tech 26, Vanderbilt 23; Chattanooga over Sewanee by default; Alabama 49, South Carolina 24; Mercer 34, Newberry 22.

Quarterfinals—Mississippi State 33, Mississippi 24; Georgia Tech 27, Georgia 23; Chattanooga 38, Virginia Tech 23; Mercer 28, Alabama 23.

Semifinals—Mississippi State 25, Georgia Tech 17; Chattanooga 24, Mercer 19.

Championship—Mississippi State 31, Chattanooga 21.

1924

Standings

	All Games			All Games	
*North Carolina	26	0	Miss. State	13	8
Tulane	15	3	South Carolina	11	9
Kentucky	13	3	VMI	8	6
Virginia	12	3	Tennessee	10	8
Alabama	12	4	Georgia Tech	9	10

Georgia	16	5	Vanderbilt	7	15
Mississippi	16	6	N.C. State	7	16
Washington & Lee	9	5	LSU	8	12
			Maryland	4	6
			Florida	5	10
			Sewanee	2	7
			Clemson	2	12
			Auburn		--

*Won championship in tournament.

Tournament

Southern Conference held tournament for conference members only.)

(17 teams, Thursday-Tuesday, February 28-29, March 1-3-4. Atlanta Auditorium, Atlanta, Georgia.)

First Round—Clemson 17, Florida 15.

Second Round—North Carolina 41, Kentucky 20; Vanderbilt 42, Clemson 13, Tulane 60, South Carolina 23; Mississippi State 35, Tennessee 18; Auburn 35, Georgia Tech 29; Alabama 44, Mississippi 42; Georgia 36, Washington & Lee 24; Maryland 34, VMI 19.

Quarterfinals—North Carolina 37, Vanderbilt 20; Mississippi State. 38, Tulane 30; Alabama 40, Auburn 19; Georgia 29, Maryland 25.

Semifinals—North Carolina 33, Mississippi State 23; Alabama 37, Georgia 20.

Championship—North Carolina 26, Alabama 18.

1925

Standings

	All Games			All Games	
Tulane	18	3	LSU	10	7
Virginia	12	2	South Carolina	10	7
*North Carolina	18	5	VMI	6	5
Alabama	15	4	Vanderbilt	12	13
Maryland	11	4	Georgia	9	11
Mississippi	17	8	Tennessee	6	8
Miss. State	14	9	Clemson	4	14
Kentucky	13	8	Florida	2	7
Washington & Lee	8	5	Sewanee	2	7
N.C. State	11	7	Georgia Tech	3	11
			Auburn		--

* Won championship in tournament. **285**

Tournament

(19 teams, Tuesday-Thursday, February 27-28, March 1-3-4, Atlanta Auditorium, Atlanta, Georgia.)

First Round—Maryland 27, Alabama 21; Virginia 31, South Carolina 25; North Carolina 42, Virginia Tech 13.

Second Round—N.C. State 30, Maryland 18; Tulane 37, Washington & Lee 20; Mississippi 27, VMI 20; Virginia 29, Auburn 27; Georgia over Clemson default; Kentucky 31, Mississippi State 26; Georgia Tech 31, Sewanee 14; North Carolina 35, LSU 21.

Quarterfinals—Tulane 41, N.C. State 24; Mississippi 32, Virginia 24; Georgia 32, Kentucky 31; North Carolina 34, Georgia Tech 26.

Semifinals—Tulane 44, Mississippi 23; North Carolina 39, Georgia 14.

Championship—North Carolina 36, Tulane 28.

1926

Standings

	All Games			All Games	
N.C. State	19	3	LSU	9	9
Mississippi	16	2	Florida	7	7
Maryland	14	2	Alabama	10	11
Kentucky	15	3	Vanderbilt	8	18
*North Carolina	20	5	Sewanee	4	6
Georgia	18	6	Georgia Tech	5	10
Miss. State	14	8	Virginia Tech	3	10
South Carolina	8	5	Clemson	4	17
Virginia	8	6	Auburn		---
VMI	8	6			
Washington & Lee	9	7			
Tennessee	9	8			

*Won championship in tournament.

Tournament

(16 teams, even bracket in all remaining Atlanta events; February 26-27, March 1-2, Atlanta Auditorium, Atlanta, Georgia.)

First Round—North Carolina 52, Clemson 21; Virginia 29, Tulane 25; Georgia Tech 30, Alabama 27; Mississippi 50, Sewanee 16; Kentucky 32, VMI 25; Georgia 48, Tennessee 25; N.C. State 32, Auburn 26; Miss. State 22, Maryland 19.

Quarterfinals—North Carolina 25, Virginia 23; Mississippi 36, Georgia Tech 24; Kentucky 39, Georgia 34; Miss. State 32, N.C. State 29 (OT).

Semifinals—North Carolina 37, Mississippi 24; Miss. State 31, Kentucky 26.

Championship—North Carolina 38, Miss State 23.

All-Tournament

(Selected for *Atlanta Journal* by Media Panel)

First Team—Jack Cobb (North Carolina); Artie Newcomb (North Carolina); Stone (Miss. State); E. Johnson (Miss. State); Jenkins (Kentucky).

Second Team—Bill Dodderer (North Carolina); Bunn Hackney (North Carolina); Billy Devin (North Carolina); Mohney (Kentucky); Nolan Richardson (Georgia).

1927

Standings

	All Games			All Games	
*Vanderbilt	20	4	Maryland	10	9
South Carolina	14	4	Virginia	9	10
North Carolina	17	7	LSU	7	9
Miss. State	17	7	Alabama	3	8
Georgia Tech	17	10	Tennessee	7	12
Mississippi	13	5	Florida	6	20
N.C. State	12	5	VMI	4	11
Georgia	14	8	Sewanee	3	11
Washington & Lee	10	6	Kentucky	3	13
			Clemson	2	13
			Auburn	---	

* Won championship in tournament

Tournament

(February 25-26-27, March 1, Atlanta Auditorium, Atlanta, Georgia.)

First Round—South Carolina 32, N.C. State 26; Georgia Tech 40, Mississippi State 24; Vanderbilt 44, W&L 32; North Carolina 32, Tennessee 17; Auburn 38, Virginia Tech 33; Georgia 36, VMI 14.

Quarterfinals—South Carolina 32, Georgia Tech 18; Vanderbilt 32, Mississippi 20; North Carolina 28, Auburn 15; Georgia 27, Maryland 22.

Semifinals—Vanderbilt 31, South Carolina 25; Georgia 23, North Carolina 20.

Championship—Vanderbilt 46, Georgia 44.

1928

Standings

	All Games			All Games	
North Carolina	16	2	*Mississippi	10	9
Maryland	14	4	Alabama	10	10
LSU	14	4	Clemson	8	9
Virginia	20	6	Vanderbilt	5	7
Kentucky	12	6	South Carolina	7	12
Miss. State	13	7	Florida	5	16
Georgia Tech	9	6	Washington & Lee	5	12
Georgia	13	10	Sewanee	2	7
N.C. State	10	8	Tulane	2	14
VMI	7	6	Tennessee	0	12

*Won championship in tournament.

Tournament

(February 24-25-27-28, Atlanta Auditorium, Atlanta, Georgia.)

First Round—Mississippi, 40, N.C. State 36; LSU 44, North Carolina 38; Georgia 47, VMI 36; Kentucky 56, South Carolina 40; Auburn 27, Clemson 26; Georgia Tech 50, Florida 25; Virginia 42, Alabama 18; Mississippi State 44, Washington & Lee 24.

Quarterfinals—Mississippi 55, LSU 28; Kentucky 33, Georgia 15; Auburn 30, Georgia Tech 29; Mississippi State 44, Virginia 28.

Semifinals—Mississippi 41, Kentucky 28; Auburn 42, Mississippi State 34.

Championship—Mississippi 32, Auburn 31.

1929

Standings

	Conference		All Games	
Washington & Lee	7	1	16	2
North Carolina	12	2	17	8
Georgia Tech	10	2	15	6
Georgia	13	4	17	7
Tulane	9	4	9	5
Kentucky	7	4	12	5
Alabama	10	6	16	10
Clemson	6	4	15	12
Tennessee	6	4	11	5

Duke	5	4	12	8
*N.C. State	6	5	15	6
Mississippi	7	8	9	9
Virginia	5	7	9	10
Miss. State	5	7	7	16
LSU	5	9	8	13
Virginia Tech	3	6	4	13
Vanderbilt	2	5	4	12
South Carolina	4	9	8	13
Florida	4	10	7	13
Auburn	3	9		---
Maryland	2	8	7	9
VMI	1	7	6	7
Sewanee	0	7	3	8

(Duke joined conference.)
* Won championship in tournament.

Tournament

(March 1-2-4-5, Atlanta Auditorium, Atlanta, Georgia.)

First Round—Mississippi 37, Maryland 35; Washington & Lee 32, LSU 22; N.C. State 48, Tennessee 32; Clemson 30, Georgia Tech 26; Georgia 42, Auburn 24; Kentucky 27, Tulane 15; Duke 37, Alabama 32; North Carolina 42, Mississippi State 18.

Quarterfinals—Mississippi 50, Washington & Lee 28; N.C. State 31, Clemson 28; Georgia 28, Kentucky 26; Duke 24, North Carolina 17.

Semifinals—N.C. State 34, Mississippi 32; Duke 43, Georgia 37.

Championship—N.C. State 44, Duke 35.

1930

Standings

	Conference		All Games	
*Alabama	10	0	20	0
Duke	9	1	18	2
Kentucky	9	1	16	3
Washington & Lee	9	2	16	4
Tennessee	7	2	13	4
Georgia	7	3	17	6
Tulane	7	3	16	7
Clemson	8	4	16	9
Sewanee	5	3	6	5

Maryland	8	5	16	5
N.C. State	7	5	11	6
Mississippi	6	6	6	7
LSU	6	7	10	11
Florida	2	3	10	4
Georgia Tech	5	8	9	15
North Carolina	4	7	14	11
VMI	2	6	4	10
Miss. State	2	7	5	8
Virginia	2	8	3	12
Virginia Tech	2	10	5	14
Vanderbilt	1	9	6	16
Auburn	1	9	---	
South Carolina	0	10	6	10

* Won championship in tournament.

Tournament

(February 28, March 1-3-4, Atlanta Auditorium, Atlanta, Georgia.)

First Round—Washington & Lee 33, Mississippi 29; Tennessee 28, VMI 20; Alabama 31, Clemson 22; Georgia 27, North Carolina 17; Sewanee 25, N.C. State 19; Kentucky 26, Maryland 21; Georgia Tech 53, Tulane 31; Duke 43, LSU 34.

Quarterfinals—Tennessee 38, Washington & Lee 29; Alabama 29, Georgia 26; Kentucky 26, Sewanee 22; Duke 44, Georgia Tech 35.

Semifinals—Alabama 32, Tennessee 22; Duke 37, Kentucky 32.

Championship—Alabama 31, Duke 24.

All-Tournament

First Team—Harry Councilor (Duke); Corbett (Tennessee); Lindy Hood (Alabama); Paul McBrayer (Kentucky); Bill Werber (Duke).

Second Team—Sandy Sanford (Georgia); Earl Smith (Alabama); Joe Croson (Duke); Bobby Dodd (Tennessee); W. Laney (Alabama).

1931

Standings

	Conference		All Games	
Georgia	15	1	23	2
*Maryland	8	1	14	4
Alabama	11	2	14	6
Kentucky	8	3	15	3

Auburn	7	4		---
Washington & Lee	4	3	11	7
Duke	5	4	14	7
North Carolina	7	6	15	9
Vanderbilt	7	6	16	8
Georgia Tech	8	7	9	8
N.C. State	5	5	8	8
LSU	4	4	7	8
Virginia	3	4	11	9
Clemson	3	5	6	7
Sewanee	3	6	5	9
Tennessee	4	8	11	10
Mississippi	2	4	6	9
Virginia Tech	3	7	5	10
VMI	2	9	4	12
Tulane	2	11	6	14
South Carolina	1	12	1	15

(Auburn, no team)

* Won championship in tournament.

Tournament

(February 27-28, March 2-3, Atlanta Auditorium, Atlanta, Georgia).

First Round—Auburn 33, Virginia 26; Georgia 32, Washington & Lee 31; North Carolina 23, Vanderbilt 21; Maryland 37, LSU 33; Florida 53, Georgia Tech 48; Tennessee 26, Alabama 20; Duke 31, Clemson 27; Kentucky 33, N.C. State 28.

Quarterfinals—Georgia 31, Auburn 27; Maryland 19, North Carolina 17; Florida 35, Tennessee 30; Kentucky 35, Duke 30.

Semifinals—Maryland 26, Georgia 25; Kentucky 56, Florida 35.

Championship—Maryland 29, Kentucky 27.

1932

Standings

	Conference		All Games	
Kentucky	9	1	15	2
Maryland	9	1	16	4
Auburn	9	2		--
Alabama	11	3	16	4
North Carolina	6	3	16	5
Virginia	6	3	10	8

Georgia Tech	6	3	7	5
*Georgia	7	4	14	7
Mississippi	8	5	8	7
N.C. State	6	4	10	6
Duke	6	5	14	11
LSU	8	8	11	9
Tennessee	5	5	8	6
South Carolina	2	2	9	7
Vanderbilt	5	7	8	11
Miss. State	4	7	5	10
Tulane	5	9	6	9
Florida	4	10	8	12
Washington & Lee	3	8	9	10
Virginia Tech	2	8	8	9
Clemson	2	9	7	13
Sewanee	1	8	5	9
VMI	0	9	0	14

* Won championship in tournament.

Tournament

(February 26-27-29, March 1, Atlanta Auditorium, Atlanta, Georgia.)

First Round—North Carolina 35, Tennessee 25; Kentucky 50, Tulane 30; LSU 36, Georgia Tech 33; Auburn 34, N.C. State 33; Florida 39; Maryland 24; Duke 44, Vanderbilt 32; Virginia 20, Alabama 16; Georgia 48, Miss. State 26.

Quarterfinals—North Carolina 43, Kentucky 42; Auburn 30, LSU 22; Duke 33, Florida 22; Georgia 40, Virginia 19.

Semifinals—North Carolina 52, Auburn 31; Georgia 43, Duke 32.

Championship—Georgia 26, North Carolina 24.

All-Tournament

(Selected for AP by Tournament Coaches)

First Team—Virgil Weathers (North Carolina); T. W. Lumpkin (Auburn); Bill Strickland (Georgia), Tom Alexander (North Carolina), Leroy Young (Georgia).

Second Team—Jim Thompson (Duke); Wilmer Hines (North Carolina); Forest Sale (Kentucky); Lou Berger (Maryland); Vernon Smith (Georgia).

Southern Conference

The basketball tournament moved to Raleigh in 1933 with the withdrawal of 13 members who formed the Southeastern Conference. It moved to Durham in 1947, returned to Raleigh in 1951 until the Atlantic Coast Conference was formed in 1954.

1933

Standings

	Conference		All Games	
*South Carolina	4	0	18	2
Duke	7	3	17	5
Maryland	7	3	11	9
North Carolina	6	3	12	5
Virginia	5	3	12	6
N.C. State	6	4	11	8
Virginia Tech	3	7	5	10
VMI	2	8	5	10
Washington & Lee	1	8	6	10
Clemson	0	2	10	9

(13 schools withdrew to form Southeastern Conference.)
* Won championship in tournament.

Tournament

(February 24-25-27, Friday-Saturday-Monday, Memorial Auditorium, Raleigh, North Carolina.)

First Round—North Carolina 32, Virginia Tech 27; Washington & Lee 35, N.C. State 34; South Carolina 65, Maryland 28; Duke 38, Virginia 24.

   Semifinals—South Carolina 34, North Carolina 32; Duke 41, Washington & Lee 32.

Championship—South Carolina 33, Duke 21.

All-Tournament

(Selected for AP by Tournament Coaches through 1947.)

First Team—Fred Tompkins (South Carolina); Bus Hall (Virginia Tech); Jim Thompson (Duke); Ben Tompkins (South Carolina); Gilbert Clark (N.C. State).

Second Team—Wilmer Hines (North Carolina); Rufus Vincent (Maryland); Dana Henderson (South Carolina); Virgil Weathers (North Carolina); Herb Thompson (Duke).

1934

Standings

	Conference		All Games	
South Carolina	6	0	17	1
North Carolina	12	2	18	4
Maryland	6	1	11	8
Duke	9	4	18	6
N.C. State	6	5	11	6
*Washington & Lee	4	5	10	6
VMI	3	6	4	10
Virginia	1	9	5	10
Virginia Tech	1	10	1	15
Clemson	0	6	7	12

* Won championship in tournament.

Tournament

(March 1-2-3, Memorial Auditorium, Raleigh, North Carolina.)
First Round—Washington & Lee 45, Maryland 37; N.C. State 43, South Carolina 24; Duke 35, VMI 14; North Carolina 27, Virginia 18.
Semifinals—Washington & Lee 32, N.C. State 28; Duke 21, North Carolina 18.
Championship—Washington & Lee 30, Duke 29.

All-Tournament

First Team—Jimmy Thompson (Duke); Joe Sawyers (W&L); Charlie Smith (W&L); Jim McCachren (North Carolina); Herb Thompson (Duke).
Second Team—Stuart Aiken (North Carolina); Virgil Weathers (North Carolina); Jason Glace (North Carolina); Ray Rex (N.C. State); Bill Downey (VMI).

1935

Standings

	Conference		All Games	
*North Carolina	12	1	23	2
Clemson	3	1	15	2
Duke	10	4	18	8
Maryland	4	3	8	10

N.C. State	6	5	10	9
Virginia	6	5	13	9
South Carolina	5	7	15	9
Washington & Lee	4	7	10	10
VMI	2	9	3	14
Virginia Tech	1	11	3	16

* Won championship in tournament.

Tournament

(February 28, March 1-2, Memorial Auditorium, Raleigh, North Carolina.)

First Round—North Carolina 46, South Carolina 25; N.C. State 42, VMI 30; Duke 39, Virginia 32; Washington & Lee 29, Clemson 25.

Semifinals—North Carolina 30, N.C. State 28; Washington & Lee 31, Duke 27.

Championship—North Carolina 35, Washington & Lee 27.

All-Tournament

First Team—Joe Pette (W&L); Stuart Aiken (North Carolina); Jason Glace (North Carolina); Jim McCachren (North Carolina); Norman Iler (W&L).

Second Team—Melvin Nelson (North Carolina), Dana Henderson (South Carolina); Alex Swails (Clemson) and Charlie Smith (W&L) tied at center; Ray Rex (N.C. State); Bob Field (W&L)

1936

Standings

	Conference		All Games	
Washington & Lee	10	0	19	2
*North Carolina	13	3	21	4
N.C. State	10	3	15	4
Maryland	4	3	13	5
Clemson	5	5	15	7
Duke	4	5	20	6
Virginia	4	8	11	13
South Carolina	1	6	10	9
Virginia Tech	1	9	5	16
VMI	0	10	3	14

* Won championship in tournament

Tournament

(March 5-6-7, Memorial Auditorium, Raleigh, North Carolina.)

First Round—Maryland 47, Duke 35; Washington & Lee 36, Virginia Tech 20; North Carolina 39, Virginia 21; N.C. State 32, Clemson 31.

Semifinals—Washington & Lee 38, Maryland 32; North Carolina 31, N.C. State 28.

Championship—North Carolina 50, Washington & Lee 45.

All-Tournament

First Team—Bernie Buscher (Maryland); Joe Pette (W&L); Bob Spessard (W&L); Jim McCachren (North Carolina); Norman Iler (W&L).

Second Team—Andy Bershak (North Carolina); Kit Carson (W&L); Vic Willis (Maryland); Earl Ruth (North Carolina); Tom Brown (Clemson).

1937

Standings

	Conference		All Games	
*Washington & Lee	11	2	17	4
North Carolina	14	3	18	5
N.C. State	14	7	15	9
Wake Forest	8	4	15	6
Duke	11	6	15	8
South Carolina	7	4	13	7
Richmond	6	4	13	7
Maryland	5	8	9	11
Furman	3	4	8	7
Virginia	5	7	9	10
Davidson	5	8	13	10
VMI	4	8	6	11
Virginia Tech	3	9	6	11
Clemson	2	7	6	15
The Citadel	0	5	7	12
William & Mary	0	12	0	18

(Wake Forest, Davidson, Furman, The Citadel, William & Mary and Richmond joined conference.)
* Won championship in tournament.

Russ Bergman, guard, captained Coach Eddie Cameron's first conference champions in 1938.

Tournament

(March 4-5-6, Memorial Auditorium, Raleigh, North Carolina.)

First Round—North Carolina 34, Duke 30; Wake Forest 33, Richmond 24; N.C. State 42, Maryland 35; Washington & Lee 42, South Carolina 22.

Semifinals—North Carolina 37, Wake Forest 35; Washington & Lee 27, N.C. State 23.

Championship—Washington & Lee 44, North Carolina 33.

All-Tournament

First Team—Jim Waller (Wake Forest); Kit Carson (W&L); Spessard (W&L); Norman Iler (W&L); Earl Ruth (North Carolina).

Second Team—Bill Mann (N.C. State); Andy Bershak (North Carolina); Connie Mac Berry (N.C. State); Ken Podger (Duke); Ramsey Potts (North Carolina).

1938

Standings

	Conference		All Games	
North Carolina	13	2	16	5
N.C. State	10	3	13	6
Clemson	9	4	16	7
The Citadel	7	4	13	5
*Duke	9	5	15	9
Richmond	6	4	15	5
Maryland	6	4	15	9
Washington & Lee	5	4	12	9
Wake Forest	7	8	7	12
Virginia Tech	4	5	6	8
Davidson	4	11	10	12
VMI	2	7	4	11
Furman	1	5	6	13
South Carolina	1	11	3	20
William & Mary	0	7	2	10

(Virginia withdrew from conference.)
* Won championship in tournament.

Tournament

(March 3-4-5, Memorial Auditorium, Raleigh, North Carolina.)

First Round—Clemson 35, Richmond 32; Washington & Lee 48, North Carolina 33; Maryland 45, The Citadel 43; Duke 44, N.C. State 33.

Semifinals—Clemson 38, Washington & Lee 33; Duke 35, Maryland 32.

Championship—Duke 40, Clemson 30.

All-Tournament

First Team—Banks McFadden (Clemson); Kit Carson (W&L); Bob Spessard (W&L); Ed Kitchens (Clemson); George Knepley (Maryland).

Second Team—Waverly Wheeler (Maryland); Fred Edwards (Duke); Connie Mac Berry (N.C. State); Russ Bergman (Duke); Earl Ruth (North Carolina).

1939

Standings

	Conference		All Games	
**Wake Forest	15	3	18	6
Washington & Lee	8	3	13	8
Maryland	8	3	15	9
The Citadel	7	3	13	6
Davidson	9	7	16	8
N.C. State	7	6	10	7
Duke	8	8	10	12
North Carolina	7	7	10	11
*Clemson	6	6	16	8
VMI	6	6	7	10
Richmond	5	5	9	9
William & Mary	4	9	8	13
South Carolina	2	8	5	18
Virginia Tech	2	10	3	14
Furman	0	10	7	17

* Won championship in tournament.
** NCAA 1st round (East) (8 teams invited)

Tournament

(March 1-2-3-4, Memorial Auditorium, Raleigh, North Carolina.)

Preliminary Round (five tied for 7th, plus N.C. State 6th)—Clemson 44, North Carolina 43; Richmond 31, VMI 20; N.C. State 40, Duke 39.

First Round—Davidson 43, Washington & Lee 32; Clemson 30, Wake Forest 28; Maryland 47, Richmond 32; N.C. State 40, The Citadel 38.

Semifinals—Clemson 49, Davidson 33; Maryland 52, N.C. State 29.

Championship—Clemson 39, Maryland 27.

All-Tournament

First Team—George Dewitt (Maryland); Eddie Johnson (Maryland); Banks McFadden (Clemson); George Knepley (Maryland); Ed Swindell (Duke).

Second Team—Jim Waller (Wake Forest); Bill Mann (N.C. State); Jim Rennie (N.C. State); Jack Bryce (Clemson); Russ Bergman (Duke).

1940

Standings

	Conference		All Games	
Duke	13	2	19	7
*North Carolina	11	3	23	3
Washington & Lee	7	3	13	5
Wake Forest	8	4	13	9
Maryland	7	5	14	9
Clemson	9	7	9	12
Richmond	5	4	11	6
The Citadel	6	5	8	9
William & Mary	6	5	12	11
Furman	5	6	11	11
N.C. State	5	10	8	11
Davidson	4	11	8	13
South Carolina	3	10	5	13
VMI	2	8	3	12
Virginia Tech	1	9	3	16

* Won championship in tournament.

Tournament

(February 29, March 1-2, Memorial Auditorium, Raleigh, North Carolina.)

First Round—Wake Forest 40, Richmond 36; North Carolina 50, Clemson 40; Maryland 43, Washington & Lee 30; Duke 40, The Citadel 35.

Semifinals—North Carolina 43, Wake Forest 35; Duke 44, Maryland 32.

Championship—North Carolina 39, Duke 23.

All-Tournament

First Team—Banks McFadden (Clemson); Bill Mock (Duke); George Glamack (North Carolina); George Dewitt (Maryland); Bill Sweet (Wake Forest).

Second Team—Jake Burrows (The Citadel); Glenn Price (Duke); Clyde Allen (Duke); Herb Cline (Wake Forest); Jim Howard (North Carolina).

1941

Standings

	Conference		All Games	
**North Carolina	14	1	19	9
William & Mary	8	3	15	10
South Carolina	8	3	15	9
Washington & Lee	9	4	11	11
*Duke	8	4	14	8
VMI	8	4	10	6
Richmond	7	5	11	10
Wake Forest	7	6	9	9
Clemson	7	8	8	14
Davidson	5	7	10	12
N.C. State	6	9	6	9
Virginia Tech	4	8	7	14
The Citadel	1	8	5	13
Furman	1	10	4	13
Maryland	0	13	1	21

* Won championship in tournament
** 4th NCAA East Regional (8 teams invited)

Tournament

(February 27-28, March 1, Memorial Auditorium, Raleigh, North Carolina.)

First Round—South Carolina 41, Richmond 32; VMI 39, Washington & Lee 32; William & Mary 52, Wake Forest 34; Duke 38, North Carolina 37.

Semifinals—South Carolina 37, VMI 36; Duke 57, William & Mary 42.

Championship—Duke 53, South Carolina 30.

All-Tournament

First Team—Preston Westmoreland (South Carolina); Bob Rose (North Carolina): Chuck Holley (Duke); Cy Valasek (Duke); Emil Sotnyk (VMI).

Second Team—Ed Stumpf (VMI); Ray Spuhler (Duke); George Glamack (North Carolina); Lanny Lofdahl (South Carolina); Bob Foster (VMI).

1942

Standings

	Conference		All Games	
*Duke	12	1	22	2
George Washington	6	2	11	9
Wake Forest	10	5	16	7
South Carolina	7	2	12	9
North Carolina	8	4	15	8
William & Mary	8	4	15	9
N.C. State	7	4	15	7
Washington & Lee	7	7	10	15
Furman	6	7	11	10
Virginia Tech	4	6	10	10
Richmond	4	7	9	9
VMI	4	8	7	11
Davidson	3	7	12	13
Maryland	2	7	7	15
Clemson	1	9	3	14
The Citadel	1	10	2	14

(George Washington joined conference.)
* Won championship in tournament

Tournament

(March 5-6-7, Memorial Auditorium, Raleigh, North Carolina.)
First Round—William & Mary 44, George Washington 43; N.C. State 59, South Carolina 43; Wake Forest 32, North Carolina 26; Duke 59, Washington & Lee 41.
Semifinals—N.C. State 53, William & Mary 52; Duke 54, Wake Forest 45.
Championship—Duke 45, N.C. State 34.

All-Tournament

First Team—Glenn Knox (W&M); Hap Spuhler (Duke); Bones McKinney (N.C. State); Al Vandewegh (W&M); Herb Cline (Wake Forest).
Second Team—Bernie Mock (N.C. State); Pres Westmoreland (South Carolina); Matt Zunic (GW); Jack Tabscott (N.C. State): Cedric Loftis (Duke).

1943

Standings

	Conference		All Games	
Duke	12	1	20	6
*George Washington	8	2	17	6
South Carolina	6	3	15	5
Davidson	7	4	18	6
The Citadel	5	3	9	4
William & Mary	6	4	11	10
N.C. State	7	5	8	11
VMI	7	5	8	8
Maryland	5	5	8	8
Richmond	4	4	11	5
North Carolina	8	9	12	10
Virginia Tech	3	6	7	7
Washington & Lee	2	10	4	12
Wake Forest	1	10	1	12
Clemson	0	10	3	13

* Won championship in tournament

Tournament

(March 4-5-6, Memorial Auditorium, Raleigh, North Carolina.)

First Round—George Washington 49, William & Mary 23; Davidson 33, N.C. State 30; The Citadel 37, South Carolina 23; Duke 57, VMI 41.

Semifinals—George Washington 47, Davidson 40; Duke 56, The Citadel 37.

Championship—George Washington 56, Duke 40.

All-Tournament

First Team—Tommy Peters (Davidson); Bubber Seward (Duke); Bob Gantt (Duke); Cedric Loftis (Duke); John Konizewski (GW).

Second Team—John Shumate (The Citadel); Jim Rausch (GW); Joe Gallagher (GW); Emil Sotnyk (VMI); Gordon Carver (Duke).

1944

Standings

	Conference		All Games	
North Carolina	9	1	17	10
Virginia Tech	3	1	11	4
*Duke	4	2	13	3
Maryland	1	1	4	13
South Carolina	1	1	13	2
William & Mary	1	1	10	11
Richmond	1	2	7	6
Davidson	1	3	16	7
N.C. State	1	4	5	13
The Citadel	0	1	4	3
Clemson	0	1	1	10
VMI	0	4	0	14

(Wake Forest did not have team.)
* Won championship in tournament.

Tournament

(February 24-25-26, Memorial Auditorium, Raleigh, North Carolina.)

First Round—North Carolina 62, Richmond 41; Virginia Tech 38, Davidson 34; Duke 68, William & Mary 25; N.C. State 42, Maryland 23.

Semifinals—North Carolina 39, Virginia Tech 24; Duke 40, N.C. State 32.

Championship—Duke 44, North Carolina 27.

All-Tournament

(Listed two forwards, one center, two guards in order)

First Team—Bernie Mock (North Carolina); Boyce Box (North Carolina); Danny Frederick (Virginia Tech); Gordon Carver (Duke); Bill Wright (Duke).

Second Team—John Dewell (North Carolina); Harry Bushkar (Virginia Tech); Jim Lowry (Duke); Harry Harner (Duke); Jack Fitch (North Carolina).

1945

Standings

	Conference		All Games	
South Carolina	9	0	19	3
Richmond	8	0	13	4

Duke	6	1	13	9
*North Carolina	11	3	22	6
The Citadel	8	4	16	7
N.C. State	7	5	10	11
William & Mary	3	4	8	12
Clemson	3	5	8	8
Maryland	2	5	2	14
Virginia Tech	1	3	6	8
Davidson	2	7	9	9
VMI	1	4	2	10
Wake Forest	0	6	3	14
Furman	0	8	2	14

* Won championship in tournament

Tournament

(February 22-23-24, Memorial Auditorium, Raleigh, North Carolina.)

First Round—North Carolina 52, N.C. State 28; South Carolina 55, Clemson 24; William & Mary 54, The Citadel 41; Duke 76, Maryland 49.

Semifinals—North Carolina 39, South Carolina 26; Duke 57, William & Mary 22.

Championship—North Carolina 49, Duke 38.

All-Tournament

First Team—Jim Jordan (North Carolina); Gordon Carver (Duke); Charles Sokol (South Carolina); Manny Alvarez (North Carolina); Dan Buckley (Duke).

Second Team—John Dillon (North Carolina); Jack Flynn (Maryland); Ed Koffenberger (Duke); Jim Paxton (North Carolina); Stan Magdziak (W&M).

1946

Standings

	Conference		All Games	
**North Carolina	13	1	29	5
*Duke	12	1	21	6
Virginia Tech	7	3	11	8
Furman	7	4	16	4
Wake Forest	8	5	9	6
Maryland	5	4	10	11

William & Mary	5	5	10	10
George Washington	4	5	5	9
N.C. State	5	7	6	12
Clemson	5	7	9	11
South Carolina	4	7	9	11
Davidson	5	11	13	12
Richmond	3	7	8	12
VMI	1	6	1	10
The Citadel	1	7	7	12
Washington & Lee	0	5	2	11

* Won championship in tournament.
**NCAA national 2nd place

Tournament

(February 28, March 1-2, Memorial Auditorium, Raleigh, North Carolina.)

First Round—Virginia Tech 39, George Washington 33; Duke 44, N.C. State 38 (OT); North Carolina 54, Maryland 27; Wake Forest 42, William & Mary 31.

Semifinals—Duke 44, Virginia Tech 38; Wake Forest 31, North Carolina 29.

Championship—Duke 49, Wake Forest 30.

All-Tournament

First Team—Bubber Seward (Duke); Ab Williams (Wake Forest); Ed Koffenberger (Duke); Dick Whiting (Duke); Harry Bushkar (Virginia Tech).

Second Team—Bones McKinney (North Carolina); John Dillon (North Carolina); Jim Jordan (North Carolina); Deran Walters (Wake Forest); Joe Hinerman (Wake Forest).

1947

Standings

	Conference		All Games	
*N.C. State	11	2	26	5
North Carolina	10	2	19	8
Duke	10	4	19	8
George Washington	9	4	21	7
Maryland	9	5	14	10
Richmond	8	5	17	9

South Carolina	7	5	16	9
Washington & Lee	7	6	16	7
Davidson	7	7	17	8
William & Mary	6	6	14	12
Wake Forest	8	9	11	13
Furman	5	7	9	9
Virginia Tech	4	9	13	13
Clemson	2	12	7	16
The Citadel	1	11	5	11
VMI	1	11	3	16

* Won championship in tournament

Tournament

(March 6-7-8, Duke Indoor Stadium, Durham, North Carolina.)

First Round—N.C. State 55, Maryland 43; George Washington 70, Washington & Lee 55; South Carolina 56, Duke 54; North Carolina 55, Richmond 43.

Semifinals—N.C. State 70, George Washington 47; North Carolina 58, South Carolina 33.

Championship—N.C. State 50, North Carolina 48.

All-Tournament

(Selected for AP by Tournament Coaches)

First Team—Bob Paxton (North Carolina); Dick Dickey (N.C. State); Al Adams (South Carolina); James White (North Carolina); Bob Negley (N.C. State).

Second Team—Bill Cantwell (GW); Jim Hamilton (North Carolina); Barry Kreisberg (GW); Leo Katkaveck (N.C. State); Ed Bartels (N.C. State).

Coach of the Year—Everett Case (N.C. State).

1948

Standings

	Conference		All Games	
*N.C. State	12	0	29	3
George Washington	13	3	19	7
North Carolina	11	4	20	7
Maryland	9	6	11	14
Davidson	10	7	19	9
Virginia Tech	7	5	14	8

Duke	8	6	17	12
Wake Forest	8	7	18	11
William & Mary	8	7	13	10
South Carolina	8	7	12	11
Washington & Lee	5	9	7	16
The Cidatel	4	8	8	9
Richmond	4	9	8	14
Furman	3	10	12	15
Clemson	3	14	6	17
VMI	1	12	3	16

** Won championship in tournament.

All-Conference

(Selected by Southern Conference Coaches Association.)

First Team—Dick Dickey (N.C. State); Bob Paxton (North Carolina); Ed Bartels (N.C. State); Buddy Cheek (Davidson); Bill Cantwell (GW).

Second Team—Jack McComas (N.C. State); Ben Collins (Duke); Chet Giermak (W&M); Leo Katkaveck (N.C. State); Norman Kohler (North Carolina).

Coach of the Year—Gerry Gerard (Duke).

Tournament

(March 4-5-6, Duke Indoor Stadium, Durham, North Carolina.)

Preliminary Round (four bottom teams for two spots)—William & Mary 61, Wake Forest 56; Duke 63, South Carolina 48.

First Round—N.C. State 73, William & Mary 52; North Carolina 61, Virginia Tech 40; Duke 54, George Washington 51; Davidson 58, Maryland 51.

Semifinals—N.C. State 55, North Carolina 50; Duke 53, Davidson 37.

Championship—N.C. State 58, Duke 50.

All-Tournament

(Selected by Southern Conference Sports Writers Association through 1953.)

First Team—Jere Bunting (W&M); Ceep Youmans (Duke); Ed Bartels (N.C. State); Leo Katkaveck (N.C. State); Bob Paxton (North Carolina).

Second Team—Paul Horvath (N.C. State); Warren Cartier (N.C. State); Tommy Hughes (Duke); Buddy Cheek (Davidson); Dick Dickey (N.C. State).

Outstanding Player—Bunting.

1949

Standings

	Conference		All Games	
N.C. State	14	1	25	8
William & Mary	10	3	24	10
North Carolina	13	5	20	8
George Washington	10	4	18	8
Davidson	11	6	18	8
Maryland	8	7	9	18
South Carolina	7	6	10	12
Wake Forest	7	7	11	13
Virginia Tech	6	8	10	13
Duke	5	7	13	9
Clemson	6	9	10	11
Washington & Lee	5	9	10	12
Richmond	5	10	8	15
Furman	4	11	9	14
VMI	3	10	3	16
The Citadel	0	11	1	17

* Won championship in tournament.

All-Conference

(Selected by Southern Conference Sports Writers Association through 1953.)

First Team—Chet Giermak (W&M); Coy Carson (North Carolina); Dick Dickey (N.C. State); Sam Ranzino (N.C. State); Ceep Youmans (Duke).

Second Team—Vic Bubas (N.C. State); Buddy Cheek (Davidson); Stan Najeway (Wake Forest); Tommy Hughes (Duke); Maynard Haithcock (GW).

Coach of the Year—Everett Case (N.C. State).

Tournament

(March 3-4-5, Duke Indoor Stadium, Durham, North Carolina.)

First Round—N.C. State 64, Wake Forest 42; North Carolina 79, Maryland 61; George Washington 62, South Carolina 45; William & Mary 54, Davidson 50.

Semifinals—N.C. State 43, North Carolina 40; George Washington 78, William & Mary 74.

Championship—N.C. State 55, George Washington 39.

BUDDY CHEEK, Davidson

All-Tourmament

First Team—Dick Dickey (N.C. State); Chet Giermak (W&M); Vic Bubas (N.C. State); Maynard Haithcock (GW), Hugo Kappler (North Carolina).

Second Team—Bill Cantwell (GW); Paul Horvath (N.C. State); Gene Witkin (GW); Ed McMillan (W&M); Coy Carson (North Carolina).

Outstanding Player—Giermak.

1950

Standings

	Conference		All Games	
*/**N.C. State	12	2	27	6
William & Mary	12	4	23	9
George Washington	12	4	16	9
South Carolina	12	5	13	9
North Carolina	13	6	17	12
Virginia Tech	9	5	15	9
Wake Forest	11	8	14	16
Duke	9	7	15	15
Clemson	8	8	10	10
Davidson	6	12	10	16
Furman	4	8	8	13
Washington & Lee	4	9	8	12
Maryland	5	13	7	18
Richmond	4	13	8	16
The Citadel	2	10	4	16
VMI	2	11	4	17

* Won championship in tournament.
** NCAA national 3rd place

All-Conference

First Team—Sam Ranzino (N.C. State); Dick Dickey (N.C. State); Chet Giermak (W&M); Vic Bubas (N.C. State); Jim Slaughter (South Carolina).

Second Team—Hugo Kappler (North Carolina); Nemo Nearman (North Carolina); John Moffatt (GW); Dick Groat (Duke); Stan Najeway (Wake Forest).

Coach of the Year—Gerry Gerard (Duke).

Tournament

(March 2-3-4, Duke Indoor Stadium, Durham, North Carolina.)

First Round—N.C. State 67, Virginia Tech 42; Wake Forest 65, George Washington 61; Duke 53, South Carolina 41; William & Mary 50, North Carolina 43.

Semifinals—N.C. State 59, Wake Forest 53; Duke 60, William & Mary 50.

Championship—N.C. State 67, Duke 47.

All-Tournament

First Team—Sam Ranzino (N.C. State); Stan Najeway (Wake Forest); Ed McMillan (W&M); Dick Dickey (N.C. State); Ceep Youmans (Duke).

Second Team—Paul Horvath (N.C. State); Dayton Allen (Duke); Jack Mueller (Wake Forest); Vic Bubas (N.C. State); Bill Fleming (Duke).

Outstanding Player—Ranzino.

1951

Standings

	Conference		All Games	
*/**N.C. State	13	1	30	7
West Virginia	9	3	18	9
Clemson	9	4	11	7
William & Mary	13	6	20	11
Duke	13	6	20	13
Virginia Tech	9	5	19	10
South Carolina	12	7	13	12
Maryland	11	8	16	11
North Carolina	9	8	12	15
George Washington	8	9	12	12
Wake Forest	8	9	16	14
Richmond	5	10	7	14
Washington & Lee	5	13	8	17
Davidson	5	15	7	19
The Citadel	2	7	6	11
VMI	3	11	3	18
Furman	1	13	3	20

(West Virginia joined conference.)
* Won championship in tournament.
** 4th NCAA East Regional.

All-Conference

First Team—Dick Groat (Duke); Sam Ranzino (N.C. State); Jim Slaughter (South Carolina); Jay Handlan (W&L); Mark Workman (West Virginia).

Second Team—Paul Horvath (N.C. State); Ed McMillan (W&M); Vic Bubas (N.C. State); Tex Tilson (Virginia Tech); Perry Lewis (W&M).

Coach of the Year—Everett Case (N.C. State).

Tournament

(March 1-2-3, Reynolds Coliseum, Raleigh, North Carolina.)

First Round—N.C. State 83, South Carolina 53; Maryland 50, Clemson 48; Duke 64, Virginia Tech 61; William & Mary 88, West Virginia 67.

Semifinals—N.C. State 54, Maryland 45; Duke 71, William & Mary 69.

Championship—N.C. State 67, Duke 63.

All-Tournament

First Team—Dick Groat (Duke); Ed McMillan (W&M); Paul Horvath (N.C. State); Sam Ranzino (N.C. State); Bill Chambers (W&M).

Second Team—Tex Tilson (Virginia Tech); Dick Koffenberger (Maryland); Bobby Speight (N.C. State); Vic Bubas (N.C. State); Lee Terrill (N.C. State).

Outstanding Player—Groat.

1952

Standings

	Conference		All Games	
West Virginia	15	1	23	4
*/**N.C. State	12	2	24	10
Duke	13	3	24	6
Clemson	11	4	17	7
George Washington	12	6	15	9
Furman	9	5	18	6
Maryland	9	5	13	9
William & Mary	10	6	15	13
South Carolina	8	7	14	10
Wake Forest	7	9	10	19
North Carolina	8	11	12	15
Virginia Tech	3	10	4	16
Richmond	3	11	7	15

Washington & Lee	3	11	6	21
Davidson	4	15	7	18
VMI	2	13	3	21
The Citadel	1	11	8	20

** Won championship in tournament.
** 3rd NCAA East Regional

All-Conference

First Team—Dick Groat (Duke); Mark Workman (West Virginia); Lee Terrill (N.C. State); Dickie Hemric (Wake Forest); Frank Selvy (Furman).

Second Team—Dwane Morrison (South Carolina); Bobby Speight (N.C. State); Jay Handlan (W&L); Bill Chambers (W&M); Johnny Snee (Clemson).

Coach of the Year—Robert (Red) Brown (West Virginia).

Tournament

(March 6-7-8, Reynolds Coliseum, Raleigh, North Carolina.)

First Round—Duke 51, Maryland 48; N.C. State 73, Furman 68; West Virginia 77, William & Mary 64; George Washington 78, Clemson 65.

Semifinals—N.C. State 76, George Washington 64; Duke 90, West Virginia 88.

Championship—N.C. State 77, Duke 68.

All-Tournament

First Team—Dick Groat (Duke); Bobby Speight (N.C. State); Eddie Becker (West Virginia); Frank Selvy (Furman); Mark Workman (West Virginia).

Second Team—Bernie Janicki (Duke); Lee Terrill (N.C. State); Nield Gordon (Furman); Bill Chambers (W&M); Johnny Snee (Clemson).

Outstanding Player—Groat.

1953

Standings

	Conference		All Games	
N.C. State	13	3	23	6
*/**Wake Forest	12	3	22	7
Maryland	12	3	15	8
West Virginia	11	3	19	7
Furman	10	3	21	6
Duke	12	4	18	8

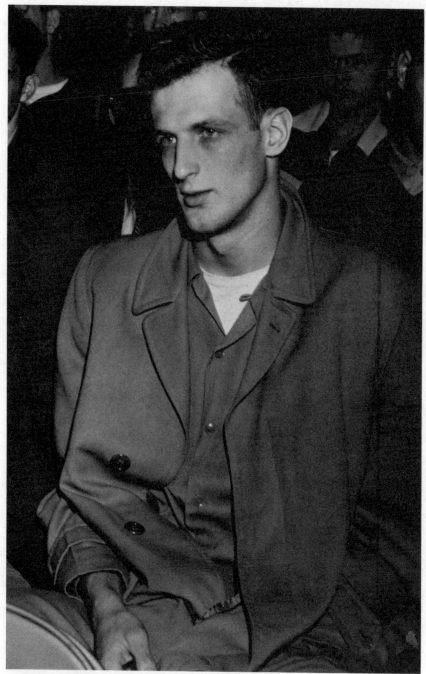

BOBBY SPEIGHT, N.C. State

Richmond	13	5	20	7
North Carolina	15	6	17	10
George Washington	12	6	15	7
Clemson	6	8	8	10
South Carolina	7	12	11	13
William & Mary	6	13	9	13
Virginia Tech	4	13	4	19
Davidson	3	14	4	16
VMI	1	14	5	19
Washington & Lee	1	17	2	20
The Citadel	0	11	4	14

* Won championship in tournament.
** 3rd NCAA East Regional.

All-Conference

First Team—Frank Selvy (Furman); Dickie Hemric (Wake Forest); Bobby Speight (N.C. State); Jim Sottille (West Virginia); Joe Holup (George Washington).

Second Team—Gene Shue (Maryland); Nield Gordon (Furman); Jack Williams (Wake Forest); Mel Thompson (N.C. State); Bill Chambers (William & Mary).

Coach of the Year—Murray Greason (Wake Forest).

Tournament

(March 5-6-7, Reynolds Coliseum, Raleigh, North Carolina.)

First Round—N.C. State 86, North Carolina 54; West Virginia 91, Furman 87; Wake Forest 85, Richmond 70; Maryland 74, Duke 65.

Semifinals—N.C. State 85, West Virginia 80; Wake Forest 61, Maryland 59.

Championship—Wake Forest 71, N.C. State 70.

All-Tournmament

First Team—Gene Shue (Maryland); Dickie Hemric (Wake Forest); Mel Thompson (N.C. State); Frank Selvy (Furman); Nield Gordon (Furman).

Second Team—Jack Williams (Wake Forest); Jim Sottille (West Virginia); Bobby Speight (N.C. State); Billy Lyles (Wake Forest); Eddie Becker (West Virginia).

Outstanding Player—Shue.

Atlantic Coast Conference

Formed in May 1953, first ACC basketball tournament in 1954 in Raleigh, moved to Greensboro 1967, moved throughout conference area since then.

1954

Standings

	Conference		All Games	
Duke	9	1	22	6
Maryland	7	2	23	7
Wake Forest	8	4	17	12
*/**N.C. State	5	3	26	7
North Carolina	5	6	11	10
South Carolina	2	8	10	16
Virginia	1	4	16	11
Clemson	0	9	5	18

(Atlantic Coast Conference formed, 7 members from Southern Conference plus Virginia.)
* Won championship in tournament
** 3rd NCAA East Regional

All-Conference

(Selected by Atlantic Coast Sports Writers Association through present year.)

First Team—Dickie Hemric (Wake Forest); Gene Shue (Maryland); Mel Thompson (N.C. State); Rudy D'Emilio (Duke); Buzz Wilkinson (Virginia).

Second Team—Vic Molodet (N.C. State); Lowell Davis (Wake Forest); Joe Belmont (Duke); Jerry Vayda (North Carolina); Ronnie Mayer (Duke).

Player of the Year—Hemric.

Coach of the Year—Everett Case (N.C. State).

Tournament

(March 4-5-6, Reynolds Coliseum, Raleigh, North Carolina.)

First Round—Wake Forest 58, South Carolina 57 (OT); Maryland 75, Clemson 59; Duke 96, Virginia 68; N.C. State 52, North Carolina 51.

Semifinals—N.C. State 79, Duke 75; Wake Forest 64, Maryland 56 (OT).

Championships—N.C. State 82, Wake Forest 80 (OT).

317

All-Tournament

First Team—Dickie Hemric (Wake Forest); Gene Shue (Maryland); Mel Thompson (N.C. State); Ronnie Shavlik (N.C. State); Skippy Winstead (North Carolina).

Second Team—Buzz Wilkinson (Virginia); Bernie Janicki (Duke); Rudy D'Emilio (Duke); Herb Applebaum (N.C. State); Lowell Davis (Wake Forest).

Outstanding Player—Hemric.

1955

Standings

	Conference		All Games	
*N.C. State	12	2	28	4
**Duke	11	3	20	8
Maryland	10	4	17	7
Wake Forest	8	6	17	10
North Carolina	8	6	10	11
Virginia	5	9	14	15
South Carolina	2	12	10	17
Clemson	0	14	2	21

* Won championship in tournament
** NCAA 1st round

All-Conference

First Team—Dickie Hemric (Wake Forest); Ronnie Shavlik (N.C. State); Buzz Wilkinson (Virginia); Lennie Rosenbluth (North Carolina); Ronnie Mayer (Duke).

Second Team—Bob Kessler (Maryland); Bill Yarborough (Clemson); Joe Belmont (Duke); Vic Molodet (N.C. State); Lowell Davis (Wake Forest).

Player of the Year—Hemric.

Coach of the Year—Everett Case (N.C. State).

Tournament

(March 3-4-5, Reynolds Coliseum, Raleigh, North Carolina.)

First Round—Virginia 68, Maryland 67 (OT); Duke 83, South Carolina 67; N.C. State 101, Clemson 76; Wake Forest 95, North Carolina 82.

Semifinals—N.C. State 85, Wake Forest 70; Duke 90, Virginia 77 (OT).

Championship—N.C. State 87, Duke 77.

RON SHAVLIK, N.C. State

All-Tournament

First Team—Buzz Wilkinson (Virginia); Ronnie Shavlik (N.C. State); Ronnie Mayer (Duke); Dickie Hemric (Wake Forest); Lowell Davis (Wake Forest).

Second Team—Bill Miller (Virginia); Bill Yarborough (Clemson); Vic Molodet (N.C. State); Joe Belmont (Duke); Phil DiNardo (N.C. State).

Outstanding Player—Shavlik.

1956

Standings

	Conference		All Games	
*/**N.C. State	11	3	24	4
North Carolina	11	3	18	5
Wake Forest	10	4	19	9
Duke	10	4	19	7
Maryland	7	7	14	10
Virginia	3	11	10	17
South Carolina	3	11	9	14
Clemson	1	13	9	17

* Won championship in tournament
** NCAA 1st round

All-Conference

First Team—Ronnie Shavlik (N.C. State); Lennie Rosenbluth (North Carolina); Vic Molodet (N.C. State); Lowell Davis (Wake Forest); Joe Belmont (Duke).

Second Team—Ronnie Mayer (Duke); Bob Kessler (Maryland): Bill Yarborough (Clemson); Grady Wallace (South Carolina); Jack Murdock (Wake Forest).

Player of the Year—Shavlik.

Coach of the Year—Murray Greason (Wake Forest).

Tournament

(March 1-2-3, Reynolds Coliseum, Raleigh, North Carolina.)

First Round—Wake Forest 79, South Carolina 64; North Carolina 81, Virginia 77; N.C. State 88, Clemson 84; Duke 94, Maryland 69.

Semifinals—N.C. State 91, Duke 79; Wake Forest 77, North Carolina 56.

Championship—N.C. State 76, Wake Forest 64.

All-Tournament

First Team—Vic Molodet (N.C. State); Lennie Rosenbluth (North Carolina); Jack Murdock (Wake Forest); Jack Williams (Wake Forest); John Maglio (N.C. State).

Second Team—Ronnie Shavlik (N.C. State); Ronnie Mayer (Duke); Bob Kessler (Maryland); Bill Miller (Virginia); Bob McCarty (Virginia).

Outstanding Player—Molodet.

1957

Standings

	Conference		All Games	
*/**North Carolina	14	0	32	0
Maryland	9	5	16	10
Duke	8	6	13	11
Wake Forest	7	7	19	9
N.C. State	7	7	15	11
South Carolina	5	9	17	12
Virginia	3	11	6	19
Clemson	3	11	7	17

* Won championship in tournament
** NCAA national champions

All-Conference

First Team—Lennie Rosenbluth (North Carolina); Grady Wallace (South Carolina); Jack Murdock (Wake Forest); Tommy Kearns (North Carolina); Jack Williams (Wake Forest).

Second Team—Bob O'Brien (Maryland); Pete Brennan (North Carolina); Jim Newcome (Duke); John Richter (N.C. State); Ernie Wiggins (Wake Forest).

Player of the Year—Rosenbluth

Coach of the Year—Frank McGuire (North Carolina).

Tournament

(March 7-8-9, Reynolds Coliseum, Raleigh, North Carolina.)

First Round—South Carolina 84, Duke 81; Maryland 71, Virginia 68; North Carolina 81, Clemson 61; Wake Forest 66, N.C. State 57.

Semifinals—North Carolina 61, Wake Forest 59; South Carolina 74, Maryland 64.

Championship—North Carolina 95, South Carolina 75.

All-Tournament

First Team—Lennie Rosenbluth (North Carolina); Grady Wallace (South Carolina); Jack Williams (Wake Forest); Pete Brennan (North Carolina); Jack Murdock (Wake Forest).

Second Team—Tommy Kearns (North Carolina); John Nacincik (Maryland); Ray Pericola (South Carolina); Joe Quigg (North Carolina); Bob Cunningham (North Carolina).

Outstanding Player—Rosenbluth.

1958

Standings

	Conference		All Games	
Duke	11	3	18	7
N.C. State	10	4	18	6
North Carolina	10	4	19	7
*/**Maryland	9	5	22	7
Virginia	6	8	10	13
Clemson	4	10	8	16
South Carolina	3	11	5	19
Wake Forest	3	11	6	17

* Won championship in tournament.
** 3rd NCAA East Regional

All-Conference

First Team—Pete Brennan (North Carolina); Lou Pucillo (N.C. State); Tommy Kearns (North Carolina); Jim Newcome (Duke); Herb Busch (Virginia).

Second Team—David Budd (Wake Forest); John Richter (N.C. State); Paul Schmidt (Duke); John Nacincik (Maryland); Nick Davis (Maryland) and Bucky Allen (Duke) tied.

Player of the Year—Brennan.

Coach of the Year—Everett Case (N.C. State).

Tournament

(March 6-7-8, Reynolds Coliseum, Raleigh, North Carolina.)

First Round—North Carolina 62, Clemson 51; N.C. State 66, South Carolina 61; Duke 51, Wake Forest 44; Maryland 70, Virginia 66.

Semifinals—Maryland 71, Duke 65 (OT); North Carolina 64, N.C. State 58.

Championship—Maryland 86, North Carolina 74.

All-Tournament

First Team—Pete Brennan (North Carolina); Nick Davis (Maryland); Lou Pucillo (N.C. State); Charles McNeil (Maryland); Tommy Kearns (North Carolina).

Second team—Bucky Allen (Duke); Bob Vernon (Duke); Ray Stanley (North Carolina); Al Bunge (Maryland); Bobby Joe Harris (Duke).

Outstanding Player—Davis.

1959

Standings

	Conference		All Games	
*N.C. State	12	2	22	4
**North Carolina	12	2	20	5
Duke	7	7	13	12
Maryland	7	7	10	13
Virginia	6	8	11	14
Wake Forest	5	9	19	14
Clemson	5	9	8	16
South Carolina	2	12	4	20

* Won championship in tournament
** NCAA 1st round

All-Conference

First Team—Lou Pucillo (N.C. State); York Larese (North Carolina); John Richter (N.C. State); Doug Moe (North Carolina); Carroll Youngkin (Duke).

Second Team—Lee Shaffer (North Carolina); George Stepanovich (N.C. State); Howard Hurt (Duke); Paul Adkins (Virginia); Charles McNeil (Maryland).

Player of the Year—Pucillo.

Coach of the Year—Harold Bradley (Duke).

Tournament

(March 5-6-7, Reynolds Coliseum, Raleigh, North Carolina.)

First Round—Duke 78, Wake Forest 71; North Carolina 93, Clemson 69; N.C. State 75, South Carolina 72 (OT); Virginia 66, Maryland 65.

Semifinals—N.C. State 66, Virginia 63; North Carolina 74, Duke 71.

Championship—N.C. State 80, North Carolina 56.

All-Tournament

First Team—Lou Pucillo (N.C. State); John Richter (N.C. State); Lee Shaffer (North Carolina); Paul Adkins (Virginia); George Stepanovich (N.C. State).

Second Team—Bob MacGillivray (N.C. State), Doug Moe (North Carolina), York Larese (North Carolina); Howard Hurt (Duke); Carroll Youngkin (Duke).

Outstanding Player—Pucillo.

1960

Standings

	Conference		All Games	
North Carolina	12	2	18	6
Wake Forest	12	2	21	7
Maryland	9	5	15	8
*/**Duke	7	7	17	11
South Carolina	6	8	10	16
N.C. State	5	9	11	15
Clemson	4	10	10	16
Virginia	1	13	6	18

* Won championship in tournament
** 2nd NCAA East Regional

All-Conference

First Team—Len Chappell (Wake Forest); Lee Shaffer (North Carolina); Al Bunge (Maryland); York Larese (North Carolina); Choppy Patterson (Clemson).

Second Team—Art Whisnant (South Carolina); Dave Budd (Wake Forest); Paul Adkins (Virginia); Billy Packer (Wake Forest); Bob DiStefano (N.C. State) and Howard Hurt (Duke) tied.

Player of the Year—Shaffer.

Coach of the Year—Horace McKinney (Wake Forest).

Tournament

(March 3-4-5, Reynolds Coliseum, Raleigh, North Carolina.)

First Round—N.C. State 74, Maryland 58; Wake Forest 74, Clemson 59; North Carolina 84, Virginia 63; Duke 82, South Carolina 69.

Semifinals—Duke 71, North Carolina 69; Wake Forest 71, N.C. State 66.

Championship—Duke 63, Wake Forest 59.

All-Tournament

First Team—Len Chappell (Wake Forest); Doug Kistler (Duke); Howard Hurt (Duke); Lee Shaffer (North Carolina); York Larese (North Carolina).

Second Team—Carroll Youngkin (Duke); Dave Budd (Wake Forest); John Frye (Duke); Bob DiStefano (N.C. State); Paul Adkins (Virginia).

Outstanding Player—Kistler.

1961

Standings

	Conference		All Games	
North Carolina	12	2	19	4
*/**Wake Forest	11	3	19	11
Duke	10	4	22	6
N.C. State	8	6	16	9
Maryland	6	8	14	12
Clemson	5	9	10	16
South Carolina	2	12	9	17
Virginia	2	12	3	23

* Won championship in tournament.
** 2nd NCAA East Regional

All-Conference

First Team—Len Chappell (Wake Forest); Art Heyman (Duke); York Larese (North Carolina); Doug Moe (North Carolina); Billy Packer (Wake Forest).

Second Team—Art Whisnant (South Carolina); Tony Laquintano (Virginia); Ken Rohloff (N.C. State); Choppy Patterson (Clemson); Howard Hurt (Duke) and Bob McDonald (Maryland) tied.

Player of the Year—Chappell.

Coach of the Year—Horace McKinney (Wake Forest).

Tournament

(March 2-3-4, Reynolds Coliseum, Raleigh, North Carolina.)
(North Carolina did not play.)

First Round—Wake Forest bye; Maryland 91, Clemson 75; South Carolina 80, N.C. State 78; Duke 89, Virginia 54.

Semifinals—Wake Forest 98, Maryland 76; Duke 92, South Carolina 75.

Championship—Wake Forest 96, Duke 81.

All-Tournament

First Team—Len Chappell (Wake Forest); Art Heyman (Duke); Billy Packer (Wake Forest); John Frye (Duke); Art Whisnant (South Carolina).

Second Team—Bill Stasiulatis (Maryland); Scotti Ward (South Carolina); Dave Wiedeman (Wake Forest); Carroll Youngkin (Duke); Choppy Patterson (Clemson).
Outstanding Player—Chappell.

1962

Standings

	Conference		All Games	
**/*Wake Forest	12	2	22	9
Duke	11	3	20	5
N.C. State	10	4	11	6
North Carolina	7	7	8	9
South Carolina	7	7	15	12
Clemson	4	10	12	15
Maryland	3	11	8	17
Virginia	2	12	5	18

* Won championship in tournament.
** NCAA national 3rd place.

All-Conference

First Team—Len Chappell (Wake Forest); Art Heyman (Duke); Jeff Mullins (Duke); Art Whisnant (South Carolina); Jon Speaks (N.C. State).
Second Team—Larry Brown (North Carolina); Dave Wiedeman (Wake Forest); John Punger (N.C. State); Tony Laquintano (Virginia); Jim Hudock (North Carolina).
Player of the Year—Chappell.
Coach of the Year—Bob Stevens (South Carolina).

Tournament

(March 1-2-3, Reynolds Coliseum, Raleigh, North Carolina.)
First Round—Clemson 67, N.C. State 46; Duke 71, Maryland 58; Wake Forest 81, Virginia 58; South Carolina 57, North Carolina 55.
Semifinals—Wake Forest 88, South Carolina 75; Clemson 77, Duke 72.
Championship—Wake Forest 77, Clemson 66.

All-Tournament

First Team—Len Chappell (Wake Forest); Jim Brennan (Clemson); Art Heyman (Duke); Jeff Mullins (Duke); Billy Packer (Wake Forest).

Second Team—Dave Wiedeman (Wake Forest); Jerry Greenspan (Maryland); Bob Robinson (South Carolina); Ronnie Collins (South Carolina); Art Whisnant (South Carolina).
Outstanding Player—Chappell.

1963

Standings

	Conference		All Games	
*/**Duke	14	0	27	3
Wake Forest	11	3	16	10
North Carolina	10	4	15	6
Clemson	5	9	12	13
N.C. State	5	9	10	11
South Carolina	4	10	9	15
Maryland	4	10	8	13
Virginia	3	11	5	20

* Won championship in tournament.
** NCAA national 3rd place.

All-Conference

First Team—Art Heyman (Duke); Billy Cunningham (North Carolina); Jeff Mullins (Duke); Dave Wiedeman (Wake Forest); Larry Brown (North Carolina).
Second Team—Scotti Ward (South Carolina); Gene Engel (Virginia); Jim Brennan (Clemson); Jerry Greenspan (Maryland); Ken Rohloff (N.C. State).
Player of the Year—Heyman.
Coach of the Year—Vic Bubas (Duke).

Tournament

(February 28, March 1-2, Reynolds Coliseum, Raleigh, North Carolina.)
First Round—North Carolina 93, South Carolina 76; Wake Forest 80, Maryland 41; Duke 89, Virginia 70; N.C. State 79, Clemson 78.
Semifinals—Duke 82, N.C. State 65; Wake Forest 56, North Carolina 55.
Championship—Duke 88, Wake Forest 57.

All-Tournament

First Team—Art Heyman (Duke); Jeff Mullins (Duke); Dave Wiedeman (Wake Forest); Billy Cunningham (North Carolina); Ken Rohloff (N.C. State).

Second Team—Jay Buckley (Duke); Larry Brown (North Carolina); Bob Woollard (Wake Forest); Frank Christie (Wake Forest); Buzzy Harrison (Duke).
Outstanding Player—Heyman.

1964

Standings

	Conference		All Games	
**/*Duke	13	1	26	5
Wake Forest	9	5	16	11
Clemson	8	6	13	12
South Carolina	7	7	10	14
North Carolina	6	8	12	12
Maryland	5	9	9	17
Virginia	4	10	8	16
N.C. State	4	10	8	11

* Won championship in tournament.
** NCAA national 2nd place

All-Conference

First Team—Billy Cunningham (North Carolina); Jeff Mullins (Duke); Ronnie Collins (South Carolina); Chip Conner (Virginia); Frank Christie (Wake Forest).
Second Team—Jim Brennan (Clemson); Hack Tison (Duke); Jay Buckley (Duke); Butch Hassell (Wake Forest); Buzzy Harrison (Duke).
Player of the Year—Mullins.
Coach of the Year—Vic Bubas (Duke).

Tournament

(March 5-6-7, Reynolds Coliseum, Raleigh, North Carolina.)
First Round—Clemson 81, Maryland 67; Wake Forest 79, Virginia 60; Duke 75, N.C. State 44; North Carolina 80, South Carolina 63.
Semifinals—Duke 65, North Carolina 49; Wake Forest 86, Clemson 64.
Championship—Duke 80, Wake Forest 59.

All-Tournament

First Team—Jeff Mullins (Duke); Jay Buckley (Duke); Billy Cunningham (North Carolina); Frank Christie (Wake Forest); Bob Leonard (Wake Forest).

Billy Cunningham became the "Kangaroo Kid" when he was All-American at Carolina, and in 1983 he coached the Philadelphia 76ers to the NBA championship over Los Angeles, in a sweep.

Second Team—Hack Tison (Duke); Butch Hassell (Wake Forest); Ronny Watts (Wake Forest); Denny Ferguson (Duke); Nick Milasnovich (Clemson).
Outstanding Player—Mullins.

1965

Standings

	Conference		All Games	
*/**N.C. State	11	3	20	5
Maryland	10	4	18	8
North Carolina	10	4	15	9
Wake Forest	6	8	12	15
Clemson	4	10	8	15
Virginia	3	11	7	18
South Carolina	2	12	6	17

* Won championship in tournament.
** 3rd NCAA East Regional

All-Conference

First Team—Billy Cunningham (North Carolina); Larry Lakins (N.C. State); Jack Martin (Duke); Bob Leonard (Wake Forest); Bob Verga (Duke).
Second Team—Jay McMillen (Maryland); Bob Lewis (North Carolina); Randy Mahaffey (Clemson); Steve Vacendak (Duke); Ronny Watts (Wake Forest).
Player of the Year—Cunningham.
Coach of the Year—Press Maravich (N.C. State).

Tournament

(March 4-5-6, Reynolds Coliseum, Raleigh, North Carolina.)
First Round—Maryland 61, Clemson 50; N.C. State 106, Virginia 69; Duke 62, South Carolina 60; Wake Forest 92, North Carolina 76.
Semifinals—Duke 101, Wake Forest 81; N.C. State 76, Maryland 67.
Championship—N.C. State 91, Duke 85.

All-Tournament

First Team—Bob Leonard (Wake Forest); Larry Worsley (N.C. State); Bob Verga (Duke); Steve Vacendak (Duke); Larry Lakins (N.C. State).
Second Team—Tommy Mattocks (N.C. State); Gary Ward (Maryland); Ronny Watts (Wake Forest); Jay McMillen (Maryland); Jack Marin (Duke).

Everett Case Award (outstanding player selected by coaches)—Worsley.

1966

Standings

	Conference		All Games	
*/**Duke	12	2	26	4
N.C. State	9	5	18	9
Clemson	8	6	15	10
North Carolina	8	6	16	11
Maryland	7	7	14	11
South Carolina	4	10	11	13
Virginia	4	10	7	15
Wake Forest	4	10	8	18

* Won championship in tournament.
** NCAA national 3rd place.

All-Conference

First Team—Bob Lewis (North Carolina); Jack Marin (Duke); Bob Verga (Duke); Eddie Biedenbach (N.C. State); Bob Leonard (Wake Forest).
Second Team—Larry Miller (North Carolina); Pete Coker (N.C. State); Steve Vacendak (Duke); Paul Long (Wake Forest); Gary Ward (Maryland).
Player of the Year—Vacendak.
Coach of the Year—Vic Bubas (Duke)

Tournament

(March 3-4-5, Reynolds Coliseum, Raleigh, North Carolina.)
First Round—South Carolina 60, Clemson 52; N.C. State 86, Virginia 77; Duke 103, Wake Forest 73; North Carolina 77, Maryland 70.
Semifinals—Duke 21, North Carolina 20; N.C. State 75, South Carolina 62.
Championship—Duke 71, N.C. State 66.

All-Tournament

First Team—Eddie Biedenbach (N.C. State); Steve Vacendak (Duke); Tommy Mattocks (N.C. State); Bob Verga (Duke); Mike Lewis (Duke).
Second Team—Skip Harlicka (South Carolina); Larry Miller (North Carolina); Jack Marin (Duke); Bob Riedy (Duke); Bob Lewis (North Carolina).
Everett Case Award (outstanding player)—Vacendak.

1967

Standings

	Conference		All Games	
*/** North Carolina	12	2	26	6
Duke	9	3	18	9
South Carolina	9	5	17	8
Clemson	9	5	17	8
Wake Forest	5	9	9	18
Maryland	5	9	11	14
Virginia	4	10	9	17
N.C. State	2	12	7	19

* Won championship in tournament.
** NCAA national 4th place

All-Conference

First Team—Larry Miller (North Carolina); Bob Verga (Duke); Bob Lewis (North Carolina); Paul Long (Wake Forest); Randy Mahaffey (Clemson).

Second Team—Jim Connelly (Virginia); Mike Lewis (Duke); Jim Sutherland (Clemson); Jack Thompson (South Carolina); Gary Gregor (South Carolina).

Player of the Year—Miller.

Coach of the Year—Dean Smith (North Carolina).

Tournament

(March 9-10-11, Greensboro Coliseum, Greensboro, North Carolina.)

First Round—South Carolina 57, Maryland 54; Duke 99, Virginia 78; North Carolina 56, N.C. State 53; Wake Forest 63, Clemson 61 (2 OT).

Semifinals—North Carolina 89, Wake Forest 79; Duke 69, South Carolina 66.

Championship—North Carolina 82, Duke 73.

All-Tournament

First Team—Larry Miller (North Carolina); Bob Verga (Duke); Al Salvadori (South Carolina); Bob Lewis (North Carolina); Paul Long (Wake Forest).

Second Team—Mike Lewis (Duke); Rusty Clark (North Carolina); Jack Thompson (South Carolina); Jerry Montgomery (Wake Forest); Randy Mahaffey (Clemson) and Dick Grubar (North Carolina) tied.

Everett Case Award (outstanding player)—Miller.

1968

Standings

	Conference		All Games	
*/**North Carolina	12	2	28	4
Duke	11	3	22	6
N.C. State	9	5	16	10
South Carolina	9	5	15	7
Virginia	5	9	9	16
Maryland	4	10	8	16
Clemson	3	11	4	20
Wake Forest	3	11	5	21

* Won championship in tournament.
** NCAA national 2nd place.

All-Conference

First Team—Larry Miller (North Carolina); Mike Lewis (Duke); Charlie Scott (North Carolina); Skip Harlicka (South Carolina); Eddie Biedenbach (N.C. State).

Second Team—Rusty Clark (North Carolina); Gary Gregor (South Carolina); George Zatezalo (Clemson); Mike Katos (Virginia); Frank Standard (South Carolina).

Player of the Year—Miller.

Coach of the Year—Dean Smith (North Carolina).

Tournament

(March 7-8-9, Charlotte Coliseum, Charlotte, North Carolina.)

First Round—N.C. State 63, Maryland 54; Duke 43, Clemson 40; North Carolina 83, Wake Forest 70; South Carolina 101, Virginia 78.

Semifinals—North Carolina 82, South Carolina 79 (OT); N.C. State 12, Duke 10.

Championship—North Carolina 87, N.C. State 50.

All-Tournament

First Team—Larry Miller (North Carolina); Gary Gregor (South Carolina); Dick Grubar (North Carolina); Jack Thompson (South Carolina); Skip Harlicka (South Carolina).

Second Team—Charlie Scott (North Carolina); Rusty Clark (North Carolina); Eddie Biedenbach (N.C. State); Vann Williford (N.C. State); Mike Lewis (Duke).

Everett Case Award (outstanding player)—Miller.

1969

Standings

	Conference		All Games	
*/**North Carolina	12		2	275
South Carolina	11	3	21	7
Duke	8	6	15	13
N.C. State	8	6	15	10
Wake Forest	8	6	18	9
Virginia	5	9	10	15
Maryland	2	12	8	18
Clemson	2	12	6	19

* Won championship in tournament.
** NCAA national 4th place.

All-Conference

First Team—John Roche (South Carolina); Charlie Davis (Wake Forest); Bill Bunting (North Carolina); Charlie Scott (North Carolina); Vann Williford (N.C. State).

Second Team—Butch Zatezalo (Clemson); Dick Grubar (North Carolina); Tom Owens (South Carolina); Will Hetzel (Maryland); Randy Denton (Duke).

Player of the Year—Roche.

Coach of the Year—Frank McGuire (South Carolina).

Tournament

(March 6-7-8, Charlotte Coliseum, Charlotte, North Carolina.)

First Round—Duke 99, Virginia 86; South Carolina 92, Maryland 71; North Carolina 94, Clemson 70; Wake Forest 81, N.C. State 73.

Semifinals—North Carolina 80, Wake Forest 72; Duke 68, South Carolina 59.

Championship—North Carolina 85, Duke 74.

All-Tournament

First Team—Charlie Scott (North Carolina); Charlie Davis (Wake Forest); Dick DeVenzio (Duke); Steve Vandenberg (Duke); John Roche (South Carolina).

Second Team—Jerry Montgomery (Wake Forest); Bill Bunting (North Carolina); Dave Golden (Duke); Dick Grubar (North Carolina); Vann Williford (N.C. State).

Everett Case Award (outstanding player)—Scott.

1970

Standings

	Conference		All Games	
South Carolina	14	0	25	3
North Carolina	9	5	18	9
**/*N.C. State	9	5	23	7
Duke	8	6	17	9
Wake Forest	6	8	14	13
Maryland	5	9	13	13
Virginia	3	11	10	15
Clemson	2	12	7	19

* Won championship in tournament.
** 3rd NCAA East Regional

All-Conference

First Team—John Roche (South Carolina); Charlie Scott (North Carolina); Vann Williford (N.C. State); Charlie Davis (Wake Forest); Tom Owens (South Carolina).

Second Team—Randy Denton (Duke); Will Hetzel (Maryland); Butch Zatezalo (Clemson); Paul Coder (N.C. State), Ed Leftwich (N.C. State).

Player of the Year—Roche.

Coach of the Year—Norman Sloan (N.C. State).

Tournament

(March 5-6-7, Charlotte Coliseum, Charlotte, North Carolina.)

First Round—South Carolina 34, Clemson 33; Virginia 95, North Carolina 93; N.C. State 67, Maryland 57; Wake Forest 81, Duke 73.

Semifinals—South Carolina 79, Wake Forest 63; N.C. State 67, Virginia 66.

Championship—N.C. State 42, South Carolina 39 (2 OT).

All-Tournament

First Team—Vann Williford (N.C. State); Charlie Davis (Wake Forest); Tom Owens (South Carolina); Chip Case (Virginia); Tom Riker (South Carolina).

Second Team—Charlie Scott (North Carolina); John Roche (South Carolina); Bill Gerry (Virginia); Ed Leftwich (N.C. State); Joe Dunning (N.C. State).

Everett Case Award (outstanding player)—Williford.

1971

Standings

	Conference		All Games	
North Carolina	11	3	26	6
*/**South Carolina	10	4	23	6
Duke	9	5	20	10
Wake Forest	7	7	16	10
Virginia	6	8	15	11
N.C. State	5	9	13	14
Maryland	5	9	14	12
Clemson	3	11	9	17

* Won championship in tournament.
** 4th NCAA East Regional.

All-Conference

First Team—Charlie Davis (Wake Forest); John Roche (South Carolina); Dennis Wuycik (North Carolina); Randy Denton (Duke); Tom Owens (South Carolina).

Second Team—Barry Parkhill (Virginia); George Karl (North Carolina); Bill Gerry (Virginia); Ed Leftwich (N.C. State); Jim O'Brien (Maryland).

Player of the Year—Davis.

Coach of the Year—Dean Smith (North Carolina).

Tournament

(March 11-12-13, Greensboro Coliseum, Greensboro, North Carolina.)

First Round—North Carolina 76, Clemson 41; South Carolina 71, Maryland 63; N.C. State 68, Duke 61; Virginia 85, Wake Forest 84.

Semifinals—North Carolina 78, Virginia 68; South Carolina 69, N.C. State 56.

Championship—South Carolina 52, North Carolina 51.

All-Tournament

First Team—Barry Parkhill (Virginia); Tom Owens (South Carolina); John Roche (South Carolina); Lee Dedmon (North Carolina); Paul Coder (N.C. State).

Second Team—Al Heartley (N.C. State); George Karl (North Carolina); Bill Chamberlain (North Carolina); Tom Riker (South Carolina); Charlie Davis (Wake Forest).

Everett Case Award (outstanding player)—Dedmon and Roche tied.

1972

Standings

	Conference		All Games	
*/**North Carolina	9	3	26	5
Maryland	8	4	27	5
Virginia	8	4	21	7
Duke	6	6	14	12
N.C. State	6	6	16	10
Wake Forest	3	9	8	18
Clemson	2	10	10	16

(South Carolina withdrew from conference.)
* Won championship in tournament.
** NCAA national 3rd place.

All-Conference

First Team—Barry Parkhill (Virginia); Robert McAdoo (North Carolina); Tom McMillen (Maryland); Dennis Wuycik (North Carolina); Tom Burleson (N.C. State).

Second Team—Bill Chamberlain (North Carolina); Gary Melchionni (Duke); Alan Shaw (Duke); George Karl (North Carolina); Len Elmore (Maryland).

Player of the Year—Parkhill.

Coach of the Year—Bill Gibson (Virginia).

Tournament

(March 9-10-11, Greensboro Coliseum, Greensboro, North Carolina.)

First Round—North Carolina bye; Maryland 54, Clemson 52; Virginia 74, Wake Forest 65; Duke 73, N.C. State 60.

Semifinals—North Carolina 63, Duke 48; Maryland 62, Virginia 57.

Championship—North Carolina 73, Maryland 64.

All-Tournament

First Team—Barry Parkhill (Virginia); Dennis Wuycik (North Carolina); Robert McAdoo (North Carolina); George Karl (North Carolina); Tom McMillen (Maryland).

Second Team—Jim O'Brien (Maryland); Scott McCandlish (Virginia); Gary Melchionni (Duke); Len Elmore (Maryland); Steve Previs (North Carolina).

Everett Case Award (outstanding player)—McAdoo.

1973

Standings

	Conference		All Games	
*N.C. State	12	0	27	0
North Carolina	8	4	25	8
**Maryland	7	5	23	7
Duke	4	8	12	14
Virginia	4	8	13	12
Clemson	4	8	12	14
Wake Forest	3	9	12	15

** Won championship in tournament.
** 2nd NCAA East Regional.

All-Conference

First Team—David Thompson (N.C. State); Tom Burleson (N.C. State); Tom McMillen (Maryland); George Karl (North Carolina); Gary Melchionni (Duke).

Second Team—Bobby Jones (North Carolina); Len Elmore Maryland); Chris Redding (Duke); Barry Parkhill (Virginia); Tony Byers (Wake Forest).

Player of the Year—Thompson.

Coach of the Year—Norman Sloan (N.C. State).

Tournament

(March 8-9-10, Greensboro Coliseum, Greensboro, North Carolina.)

First Round—N.C. State bye; Wake Forest 54, North Carolina 52 (OT); Maryland 77, Clemson 61; Virginia 59, Duke 55.

Semifinals—N.C. State 63, Virginia 51; Maryland 73, Wake Forest 65.

Championship—N.C. State 76, Maryland 74.

All-Tournament

First Team—Tom Burleson (N.C. State); David Thompson (N.C. State); Tom McMillen (Maryland); John Lucas (Maryland); Eddie Payne (Wake Forest).

Second Team—Bobby Jones (North Carolina); Jim O'Brien Maryland); Gus Gerard (Virginia); Barry Parkhill (Virginia); Tony Byers (Wake Forest).

Everett Case Award (outstanding player)—Burleson.

1974

Standings

	Conference		All Games	
*/**N.C. State	12	0	30	1
Maryland	9	3	23	5
North Carolina	9	3	22	6
Virginia	4	8	11	16
Clemson	3	9	14	12
Wake Forest	3	9	13	13
Duke	2	10	10	16

* Won championship in tournament.
** NCAA national champions.

All-Conference

First Team—David Thompson (N.C. State); Bobby Jones (North Carolina); Len Elmore (Maryland); Monte Towe (N.C. State); John Lucas (Maryland).

Second Team—Tom Burleson (N.C. State); Tom McMillen (Maryland); Gus Gerard (Virginia); Darrell Elston (North Carolina); Tony Byers (Wake Forest).

Player of the Year—Thompson.

Coach of the Year—Norman Sloan (N.C. State).

Tournament

(March 7-8-9, Greensboro Coliseum, Greensboro, North Carolina.)

First Round—N.C. State bye; Maryland 85, Duke 65; North Carolina 76, Wake Forest 62; Virginia 68, Clemson 63.

Semifinals—N.C. State 87, Virginia 66; Maryland 105, North Carolina 85.

Championship—N.C. State 103, Maryland 100 (OT).

All-Tournament

First Team—David Thompson (N.C. State); Tom Burleson (N.C. State); Tom McMillen (Maryland); John Lucas (Maryland); Maurice Howard (Maryland).

Second Team—Len Elmore (Maryland); Owen Brown (Maryland); Gus Gerard (Virginia); Monte Towe (N.C. State); Billy Langloh (Virginia).

Everett Case Award (outstanding player)—Burleson.

1975

Standings

	Conference		All Games	
***Maryland	10	2	24	5
*/**North Carolina	8	4	23	8
Clemson	8	4	17	11
N.C. State	8	4	22	6
Virginia	4	8	12	13
Duke	2	10	13	13
Wake Forest	2	10	13	13

* Won championship in tournament.
** 3rd NCAA East Regional.
*** 2nd NCAA Midwest Regional.

All-Conference

First Team—David Thompson (N.C. State); Mitch Kupchak (North Carolina); John Lucas (Maryland); Skip Brown (Wake Forest); Skip Wise (Clemson).

Second Team—Wayne Rollins (Clemson); Bob Fleisher (Duke); Owen Brown (Maryland); Brad Davis (Maryland); Maurice Howard (Maryland).

Player of the Year—Thompson.

Coach of the Year—Lefty Driesell (Maryland).

Tournament

(March 6-7-8, Greensboro Coliseum, Greensboro, North Carolina.)

First Round—Maryland bye; North Carolina 101, Wake Forest 100 (OT); Clemson 78, Duke 76; N.C. State 91, Virginia 85.

Semifinals—N.C. State 87, Maryland 85; North Carolina 76, Clemson 71 (OT).

Championship—North Carolina 70, N.C. State 66.

All-Tournament

First Team—David Thompson (N.C. State); Mitch Kupchak (North Carolina); Kenny Carr (N.C. State); Phil Ford (North Carolina); Skip Wise (Clemson).

Second Team—John Lucas (Maryland); Wally Walker (Virginia); Walter Davis (North Carolina); Skip Brown (Wake Forest); Monte Towe (N.C. State).

Everett Case Award (outstanding player)—Ford.

MITCH KUPCHAK

1976

Standings

	Conference		All Games	
***North Carolina	11	1	25	4
Maryland	7	5	22	6
N.C. State	7	5	21	9
Clemson	5	7	18	10
Wake Forest	5	7	17	10
*/**Virginia	4	8	18	12
Duke	3	9	13	14

* Won championship in tournament.
** NCAA 1st round East.
*** NCAA 1st round Mideast.

All-Conference

First Team—Mitch Kupchak (North Carolina); John Lucas (Maryland); Kenny Carr (N.C. State); Phil Ford (North Carolina); Tate Armstrong (Duke).

Second Team—Wally Walker (Virginia); Walter Davis (North Carolina); Wayne Rollins (Clemson); Rod Griffin (Wake Forest); Skip Brown (Wake Forest).

Player of the Year—Kupchak.

Rookie of the Year—Jim Spanarkel (Duke).

Coach of the Year—Dean Smith (North Carolina).

Tournament

(March 4-5-6, Capitol Centre, Landover, Maryland.)

First Round—North Carolina bye; Maryland 80, Duke 78 (OT); Virginia 75, N.C. State 63; Clemson 76, Wake Forest 63.

Semifinals—North Carolina 82, Clemson 74; Virginia 73, Maryland 65.

Championship—Virginia 67, North Carolina 62.

All-Tournament

First Team—Wally Walker (Virginia); Billy Langloh (Virginia); Marc Iavaroni (Virginia); Mitch Kupchak (North Carolina); Tate Armstrong (Duke) and Phil Ford (North Carolina) tied.

Second Team—Maurice Howard (Maryland); Steve Sheppard (Maryland); Bobby Stokes (Virginia); Stan Rome (Clemson); Walter Davis (North Carolina).

Everett Case Award (outstanding player)—Walker.

1977

Standings

	Conference		All Games	
*/**North Carolina	9	3	28	5
***Wake Forest	8	4	22	8
Clemson	8	4	22	6
Maryland	7	5	19	8
N.C. State	6	6	17	11
Duke	2	10	14	13
Virginia	2	10	12	17

* Won championship in tournament.
** NCAA national 2nd place.
*** 2nd NCAA Midwest Regional.

All-Conference

First Team—Rod Griffin (Wake Forest); Phil Ford (North Carolina); Skip Brown (Wake Forest); Kenny Carr (N.C. State); Walter Davis (North Carolina).

Second Team—Wayne Rollins (Clemson); Jim Spanarkel (Duke); Brad Davis (Maryland); Tommy LaGarde (North Carolina); Stan Rome (Clemson).

Player of the Year—Griffin.

Rookie of the Year—Mike Gminski (Duke) and Charles Whitney (N.C. State) tied.

Coach of the Year—Dean Smith (North Carolina).

Tournament

(March 3-4-5, Greensboro Coliseum, Greensboro, North Carolina.)

First Round—North Carolina bye; Virginia 59, Wake Forest 57; Clemson 82, Duke 74; N.C. State 82, Maryland 72.

Semifinals—North Carolina 70, N.C. State 56; Virginia 72, Clemson 60.

Championship—North Carolina 75, Virginia 69.

All-Tournament

First Team—Phil Ford (North Carolina); Mike O'Koren (North Carolina); Bobby Stokes (Virginia); Marc Iavaroni (Virginia); John Kuester (North Carolina) and Kenny Carr (N.C. State) tied.

Second Team—Steve Castellan (Virginia); Billy Langloh (Virginia); Walter Davis (North Carolina); Jim Spanarkel (Duke); Mike Gminski (Duke).

Everett Case Award (outstanding player)—Kuester.

KENNY CARR

1978

Standings

	Conference		All Games	
***North Carolina	9	3	23	8
*/**Duke	8	4	27	7
N.C. Stae	7	5	21	10
Virginia	6	6	20	8
Wake Forest	6	6	19	10
Maryland	3	9	15	13
Clemson	3	9	15	12

** Won championship tournament.
** NCAA national 2nd place.
** NCAA 1st round West.

All-Conference

First Team—Phil Ford (North Carolina); Rod Griffin (Wake Forest); Jim Spanarkel (Duke); Mike Gminski (Duke); Mike O'Koren (North Carolina).

Second Team—Gene Banks (Duke); Frank Johnson (Wake Forest); Jeff Lamp (Virginia); Clyde Austin (N.C. State); Charles Whitney (N.C. State).

Player of the Year—Ford.
Rookie of the Year—Gene Banks (Duke).
Coach of the Year—Bill Foster (Duke).

Tournament

(March 1-2-4, Wednesday-Thursday-Saturday afternoon, Greensboro Coliseum, Greensboro, North Carolina.)

First Round—North Carolina bye; Duke 83, Clemson 72; Maryland 109, N.C. State 108 (3 OT); Wake Forest 72, Virginia 61.

Semifinals—Duke 81, Maryland 69; Wake Forest 82, North Carolina 77.

Championship—Duke 85, Wake Forest 77.

All-Tournament

First Team—Mike Gminski (Duke); Leroy McDonald (Wake Forest); Rod Griffin (Wake Forest); Jim Spanarkel (Duke); Gene Banks (Duke).

Second Team—Phil Ford (North Carolina); Frank Johnson (Wake Forest); Kenny Dennard (Duke); Lawrence Boston (Maryland); Larry Gibson (Maryland).

Everett Case Award (outstanding player)—Spanarkel.

1979

Standings

	Conference		All Games	
*/**North Carolina	9	3	23	6
***Duke	9	3	22	8
Virginia	7	5	19	10
Maryland	6	6	19	11
Clemson	5	7	19	10
N.C. State	3	9	18	12
Wake Forest	3	9	12	15

* Won championship in tournament.
** NCAA 2nd round East.
*** NCAA 2nd round East.

All-Conference

First Team—Mike Gminski (Duke); Jeff Lamp (Virginia); Jim Spanarkel (Duke); Charles Whitney (N.C. State); Al Wood (North Carolina).

Second Team—Mike O'Koren (North Carolina); Gene Banks (Duke); Lee Raker (Virginia); Frank Johnson (Wake Forest); Larry Gibson (Maryland).

Player of the Year—Gminski.
Rookie of the Year—Buck Williams (Maryland).
Coach of the Year—Dean Smith (North Carolina).

Tournament

(March 1-2-3, Greensboro Coliseum, Greensboro North Carolina.)

First Round—North Carolina bye; Duke 58, Wake Forest 56; N.C. State 82, Virginia 78; Maryland 75, Clemson 67.

Semifinals—North Carolina 102, Maryland 79; Duke 62, N.C. State 59.

Championship—North Carolina 71, Duke 63.

All-Tournament

First Team—Jim Spanarkel (Duke); Mike O'Koren (North Carolina); Dudley Bradley (North Carolina); Mike Gminski (Duke); Dave Colescott (North Carolina).

Second Team—Charles Whitney (N.C. State); Al Wood (North Carolina); Larry Gibson (Maryland); Jeff Lamp (Virginia); Clyde Austin (N.C. State).

Everett Case Award (outstanding player)—Bradley.

1980

Standings

	Conference		All Games	
***Maryland	11	3	24	7
xNorth Carolina	9	5	21	8
yN.C. State	9	5	20	8
zClemson	8	6	23	9
Virginia	7	7	24	10
*/**Duke	7	7	24	9
Wake Forest	4	10	13	14
Georgia Tech	1	13	8	18

(Georgia Tech joined conference.)
* Won championship in tournament.
** 2nd NCAA Mideast Regional.
*** 4th NCAA East Regional.
x NCAA 2nd round Midwest.
y NCAA 2nd round East.
z 2nd NCAA West Regional.

All-Conference

First Team—Charles Whitney (N.C. State); Albert King (Maryland); Mike Gminski (Duke); Mike O'Koren (North Carolina); Billy Williams (Clemson).

Second Team—Jeff Lamp (Virginia); Gene Banks (Duke); Buck Williams (Maryland); Greg Manning (Maryland); Al Wood (North Carolina).

Player of the Year—King.

Rookie of the Year—Ralph Sampson (Virginia).

Coach of the Year—Lefty Driesell (Maryland).

Tournament

(February 28-29, March 1, Greensboro Coliseum, Greensboro, North Carolina.)

First Round—North Carolina 75, Wake Forest 62; Maryland 51, Georgia Tech 49 (OT); Duke 68, N.C. State 62; Clemson 57, Virginia 49.

Semifinals—Maryland 91, Clemson 85; Duke 75, North Carolina 61.

Championship—Duke 73, Maryland 72.

All-Tournament

First Team—Albert King (Maryland); Gene Banks (Duke); Mike Gminski (Duke); Al Wood (North Carolina); Greg Manning (Maryland).

347

Second Team—Vince Taylor (Duke); Billy Williams (Clemson); Brook Steppe (Georgia Tech); Buck Williams (Maryland); Ernest Graham (Maryland).

Everett Case Award (outstanding player)—King.

1981

Standings

	Conference		All Games	
***Virginia	13	1	29	4
*/**North Carolina	10	4	29	8
x Wake Forest	9	5	22	7
y Maryland	8	6	21	10
Duke	6	8	17	13
Clemson	6	8	20	11
N.C. State	4	10	14	13
Georgia Tech	0	14	4	23

* Won championship in tournament.
** NCAA national 2nd place.
*** NCAA national 3rd place.
x NCAA 2nd round Mideast.
y NCAA 2nd round Mideast.

All-Conference

First Team—Ralph Sampson (Virginia); Al Wood (North Carolina); Jeff Lamp (Virginia); Frank Johnson (Wake Forest); Gene Banks (Duke).

Second Team—Buck Williams (Maryland); Albert King (Maryland); James Worthy (North Carolina); Larry Nance (Clemson); Sidney Lowe (N.C. State).

Player of the Year—Sampson.

Rookie of the Year—Sam Perkins (North Carolina).

Coach of the Year—Terry Holland (Virginia).

Tournament

(March 5-6-7, Capitol Centre, Landover, Maryland.)

First Round—Wake Forest 80, Clemson 71; Virginia 76, Georgia Tech 47; North Carolina 69, N.C. State 54; Maryland 56, Duke 53.

Semifinals—Maryland 85, Virginia 62; North Carolina 58, Wake Forest 57.

Championship—North Carolina 61, Maryland 60.